LEARNING FROM LOCAL AUTHORITY BUDGETING

Learning from Local Authority Budgeting

Edited by
HOWARD ELCOCK
Newcastle-upon-Tyne Polytechnic

GRANT JORDAN
University of Aberdeen

Avebury

Aldershot · Brookfield USA · Hong Kong · Singapore · Sydney

Published by
Gower Publishing Company Limited,
Gower House, Croft Road, Aldershot, Hants GU11 3HR, England

Gower Publishing Company,
Old Post Road, Brookfield, Vermont 05036, United States of America.

British Library Cataloguing in Publication Data

Learning from local authority budgeting.
    1. Local budgets —— Great Britain
    I. Elcock, Howard   II. Jordan, Grant
    336.3'9'0941   HJ9423

ISBN 0-566-05384-5 ✓

Printed and bound in Great Britain by
Athanaeum Press Limited, Newcastle-upon-Tyne

Contents

Editors' foreword

This book is the product of a research project carried out under the auspices of the Public Administration Committee of the Joint University Council and funded by a grant from the Leverhulme Trust. We thank the Trust for their generous financial support and the Council for its assistance in many ways. We are also most grateful to our colleagues in seventeen Universities, Polytechnics and Colleges throughout the United Kingdom for carrying out research and preparing their Reports punctually. On their behalf, we would also like to thank the members and officers of the participating local authorities for their co-operation and friendly assistance with our work.

The project has also benefitted from the advice of a Steering Group made up of academics and senior officials from local government. They were:

Mr.Keith Bridge, Formerly Chief Executive Officer, Humberside County Council
Mr.Michael Clarke, Director, Local Government Training Board
Mr.J.L.Davies, Director of Finance, Wrekin Borough Council
Professor Michael Goldsmith, University of Salford
Mr.C.W.Holtham, Director of Finance, Hammersmith and Fulham London Borough Council
Dr.Arthur Midwinter, University of Strathclyde
Dr.John Sewel, University of Aberdeen

We also owe a debt of gratitude to Sir James Swaffield, formerly Controller of the Greater London Council and Frank Stacey Memorial Lecturer 1983, for encouraging the Public Administration Committee to become involved in work of relevance to local government. To all the above we are grateful. We hope they will approve of the results of our labours but we accept the responsibilities for their inadequacies.

HOWARD ELCOCK
GRANT JORDAN

List of contributors

Dr.Dennis Balsom

Lecturer in Politics,
University College of
Wales, Aberystwyth.

Mr.Paul Barberis

Senior Lecturer in
Public Administration,
Manchester Polytechnic

Mr.John Barlow

Lecturer in Public
Administration,
Lancashire Polytechnic

Dr.John Berridge

Senior Lecturer in
Politics, University
of Dundee

Dr.Roger Clements

Senior Lecturer in
Politics, University
of Bristol

Mr.M.Connolly

Head of the Department
of Law and Administration,
University of Ulster

Ms.J.Charlton

Senior Lecturer in
Public Administration,
Glasgow College of
Technology

Mr.Stephen Cope

Postgraduate student,
London School of Economics
and Political Science

Mr.Michael Dyer

Lecturer in Politics,
University of Aberdeen

Professor Howard Elcock

Head, School of
Government, Newcastle-
upon-Tyne Polytechnic

Mr.Chris Game

Institute of Local
Government Studies,
University of Birmingham

Mr.Paul Griffiths

Senior Lecturer in
Public Administration,
Polytechnic of Wales

Mr.R.H.Haigh

Head of the Department
of Public Sector Studies,
Sheffield Polytechnic

Ms.Sylvia Horton

Principal Lecturer in
Public Administration,
Portsmouth Polytechnic

Mr.Grant Jordan

Senior Lecturer in
Politics, University
of Aberdeen

Mr.Clive Martlew

Lecturer in Public
Administration,
Glasgow College of
Technology

Mr.Ray McChesney

Lecturer in Public
Administration,
University of Ulster

Mr.J.McDonagh

Senior Lecturer in
Economics, City of
Birmingham Polytechnic

Mr.David Morris

Principal Lecturer in
Public Sector Studies,
Sheffield Polytechnic

Dr.Michael Parkinson

Director, Centre for
Urban Studies,
University of Liverpool

Mr.Brian Rance

Senior Lecturer in
Planning, City of
Birmingham Polytechnic

Mr.J.Rouse

Principal Lecturer in
Economics, City of
Birmingham Polytechnic

Dr.John Sewel

Director, Regional
Centre for Social
and Economic Policy,
University of Aberdeen

Mr.Arnold Skelton

Lecturer in Public
Administration,
Manchester Polytechnic

Mr.Stephen Williams

Senior Lecturer in
Politics, Bristol
Polytechnic

The authorities

1.   BANFF AND BUCHAN DISTRICT COUNCIL
2.   TAYSIDE REGIONAL COUNCIL
3.   STIRLING DISTRICT COUNCIL
4.   LANCASHIRE COUNTY COUNCIL
5.   LIVERPOOL CITY COUNCIL
6.   OLDHAM METROPOLITAN BOROUGH COUNCIL
7.   SHEFFIELD CITY COUNCIL
8.   BIRMINGHAM CITY COUNCIL
9.   REDDITCH DISTRICT COUNCIL
10   CEREDIGION DISTRICT COUNCIL
11. MID GLAMORGAN COUNTY COUNCIL
12. AVON COUNTY COUNCIL
13. KINGSWOOD DISTRICT COUNCIL
14. PORTSMOUTH CITY COUNCIL
15. HARROW LONDON BOROUGH COUNCIL
16. BELFAST CITY COUNCIL

1. Introduction: budgeting — changing expectations

GRANT JORDAN

This project allows comparisons of the budgetary procedures of 16 local authorities in the financial year 1985-86 as they set their budgets for 1986-87. Each of the studies was conducted by an individual or team from a member institution of the Public Administration Committee of the Joint University Council - usually working on a geographically convenient authority. The use of local teams increased the number of cases we could cover and allowed researchers to exploit (and develop) local relationships and expertise.

Of course comparison would have been much simpler had the same researchers attempted all cases but that would have made the research more expensive, would in practice have demanded a reduction in the number of cases studied and would have neglected the possibility of using the existing local knowledge and background with which our teams started. It would also not have developed the local relationships between administration teachers and practitioners that we think important. Apart from anything else, the utilisation of local knowledge was adopted as means of stimulating research in a cost-effective manner.

The 16 cases were not a sample. The list was principally compiled on the basis of which member institutions of the PAC responded to an inquiry about potential participation. Most researchers had an established relationship with a particular local authority or had access to a local authority of particular interest. However, the range of cases was made greater by some participants offering up different types of authorities and aiding the editors by studying one rather than another to increase the scope of the exercise. One participant was recruited to the project after it had started because there was no case study from London in the original scheme.

This method of selecting authorities makes us careful not to refer to our local authorities as a sample but we are not defensive about the range of the participating authorities. Had we set out in a more structured fashion to find a certain number of (say) county councils or non-metropolitan borough councils, we would still be reluctant to say that the examples were representative of all. It was the variability between councils that interested us.

It (almost) goes without saying that the comparisons could have been more sophisticated had the studies been conducted over a longer time. However, the use of locally based researchers means that they were usually able to put the single year in a context of changing practice. A more serious point about time is that different local authorities were at different stages in their electoral shelf life: it is a reasonable expectation that the emphases in the budgetary year before an election might differ from those when re-election is not so pressing. However, there would have been research design costs in attempting something other than the simple 'common year' adopted; for instance, other factors, such as rate support regime would have changed.

A prime purpose of the research was to provide better, more realistic, teaching material for those conducting (and organising) the research. We hope that the individual studies are of interest to the authorities studied and that they (and other authorities) can 'read across' the other cases to look for practices and ideas that could be of use. From our point of view there is no abstract 'best practice'. Best budgetary practice will mean best for a particular authority in particular conditions. This is not to say, 'what is, is best' but to express scepticism that one or even a few prescriptive packages will work for all authorities. In any case it is clear from the studies reported that 'bought-in' ideas are often adapted as they are adopted - sometimes changing them far from their original form and intention. The case studies then are menus from which those making budgets can draw. We have preferred description to evaluation.

A. The Policy Context: The Grants System

This study is about the response within local authorities to financial restraint. The table below shows that in real terms there has been no dramatic reduction in spending - or at least the major cuts have not been under the controversial Thatcher Governments:

Table 1.1

LOCAL AUTHORITY EXPENDITURE* (England and Wales)

	74/5	75/6	76/7	77/8	78/9	79/80	80/1	81/2	82/3
current prices £m	12599	15345	16360	17050	18823	22425	26613	28024	30176
at 1975 prices £m	15029	14790	13959	13021	12995	13536	13490	12982	12999

* capital and current less debt interest

(Source: Table 4.3 Local Government Trends 1983)

The much publicised local government cuts are more cuts in terms of the central government contribution to local spending than in the spending itself:

Table 1.2

CENTRAL GOVERNMENT SUPPORT (1980/86)

	'Relevant expenditure' £m	Grant percentage contributed by Central Government
1980/1	14806	60.1
1981/2	17338	59.1
1982/3	20463	56.1
1983/4	22307	52.8
1984/5	22883	51.9
1985/6	24161	48.7
1986/7	25329	46.4

(from Jackson and Meadows, 1985, p.36, amended).

It is central to local authorities' defence against the charge of 'over-spending' that the rate increases of recent years have been caused by the need to compensate for falling central government grants rather than increases in spending. Table 8.1 shows very clearly how the governmental share of Sheffield's budget has fallen from well over half to one third during the 1980s.

Conventionally, a distinction is made between current expenditure and capital expenditure. (1) The former is essentially expenditure necessary for the provision of services but which does not create assets (e.g. salaries, heating of public buildings, maintenance) whereas the latter does create assets (e.g. houses, schools, equipment with a long life). Because capital assets have a long life, they can be financed over a longer term. About seven-eighths of local authority spending goes on current expenditure (in England and Wales in 1981/2, capital expenditure was only about 10 per cent of the total).

Current expenditure and the annual costs of financing long term capital expenditure are jointly known as the **revenue** budget. Revenue expenditure is categorised under three sets of accounts:

- the major category is the rate fund account

- where appropriate (depending on the functions administered by the local authority) there will be a housing revenue account. A surplus in this account may be transferred to the rate fund and deficits must be made up from the rate fund.

- trading service accounts - for transport, airports, direct labour organisations, etc.

Much of the budgetary process is taken up with the setting of spending priorities within a local authority. The level of resources available to spend, however, is vitally affected by the attitude of central government in the support it gives.

The Block Grant

The Block Grant is the development under the Conservative Government of the system of central government support for local spending.

The principal purpose of support is to allow different local authorities to provide comparable levels of services. Without some system of balancing, poorer authorities - whose electorates might be most in need of expensive services - would be least able to provide them.

The Government pays grant at the difference between what central government thinks the local authority **needs** to spend and the **resources** it would have if it charged what the government would like to see as the standard rate in the pound to be levied on rate payers.

Table 1.3 below shows that the block grant is the largest flow of money from central to local government but there are also specific grants - e.g. police, transport, capital grants, housing, urban regeneration and a subsidy to give relief on domestic rates - these being politically sensitive.

In 1986/7 the proportion of these types of governmental support were:

Table 1.3

1986/7 EXCHEQUER GRANT TO LOCAL AUTHORITIES (England Only)

	£m	%
Block grant	8,260	70.4
Specific and supplementary grant	2,776	23.6
Domestic rate relief	708	6.0
Aggregate Exchequer Grant	11,764	100.0

One of the main criticisms of the earlier rate support grant system - which the block grant was meant to avoid - was that the level of grant depended on past spending. In effect past high spending was 'rewarded' by higher grant. In introducing the rate support grant settlement for 1980/81 in November 1979, the Secretary of State observed, "high-spending authorities can actually attract to themselves a larger share of the resources grant at the expense of other more prudent authorities." (quoted in Gibson and Travers, p.17). This defect has not been completely eradicated.

Several bits of terminology need to be introduced before the calculation of grant can be described. The most controversial aspect is probably the establishing of Grant Related Expenditures (or GREAs). These are assessments by the Department of the Environment of what each local authority needs to provide an average standard and range of service. Although GREAs are an important step in the rate calculation process, the vital statistic initially used was 'threshold'. This was the GREA for the authority plus ten per cent of the national average GREA for that class of authority. This statistic was used in recognition that the GREA assessment itself could not be fully accurate.

Although the block grant process was introduced by a Government which gave priority to reducing local spending, it was argued that the block grant mechanism, did not mean Government infringement of local discretion over level of rates and services. Thus the Minister, Tom King, argued in committee stage of the Local Government, Planning and Land Bill (1980) that:

"My department will not be in the business of saying how much each authority should spend, where it should make cuts or on what it should spend money. I have tried to make clear that this is a matter for local authorities....I have some influence over the distribution of public funds but the ultimate decision on rates and the volume of expenditure of local authorities is a matter for councillors themselves."

However, even then local government sources saw the change as intolerable - for example the Secretary of the Association of Metropolitan Authorities argued that it meant central government "... prescribing what each local authority in the country should spend with the back up of personal sanctions to enforce that plan." (Municipal Review, April 1980, p.5).

The GREA was used in devising the Grant Related Poundage (GRP). This is the rate in the pound a local authority would charge if it spent at GREA. GRP would be the same for all local authorities if all authorities spent at GREA. If spending is higher than central government feels is necessary, a difference in the formula produces a higher GRP for the local authority and hence a lower percentage of the total paid for by block grant. A differential in the GRP formula is used to discourage high spending. Below 'threshold' the spending of £1 extra per head of population adds 0.69p to the rates in 1985/6. Above the threshold each extra pound cost the local rate payers 0.8625p.

The calculations were made even less predictable by the introduction of multipliers. These were introduced to limit loss of grant by some authorities which would have otherwise occurred because of the change in the methods of calculations. The multipliers reflect political judgements by the central government about the acceptability of the outcomes of the technical calculations. These various changes in the methodology of central assessment can have very real impacts on the local authority. For example the change in the sewerage needs assessment in Scotland in one of our authorities implied a reduction in budget from £2.2 million to £1.4 million.

The block grant system was designed to encourage reductions in local government spending because the rate of grant decreases as the expenditure of an authority increases. This has the effect of reducing the percentage of local authority expenditure provided by the central government. This system did not have the desired effect of reducing spending and in 1981 specific **targets** were set for each authority. These targets were not based on need but were set at a standard based on a level 5.6 per cent below 1978/9 budgets. Partnering the 'targets' was a 'hold back' or penalty. If local government spending in total exceeded the Government's plans, then money would be held back from over-spending authorities.

As targets were related to past spending, there was a risk that low spending authorities would be most at risk of penalty. Many low spending authorities were Conservative and thus - for obvious reasons - it was decided that hold back should not apply to all those spending over target but only those who were over target **and** above GREA.

In each year, amendments were made to the system - the trend being to make 'over-spending' more and more costly for any local authority. Over-spending by 1 per cent above target meant an extra 2p rate; 2 per cent above target a 6p extra rate; escalating to 77p extra rate on an over-spend of 10 per cent. By 1984/5 a 3 per cent over-spend meant 24p rate imposition - and 15 per cent over target meant a rate of 122p in the pound.

Under the Rates Act 1984, a further development was the possibility that Government would intervene to limit the rates of some (or all) local authorities. Because some authorities were ignoring the targets being prepared to pay for above target services wholly from rate income – sometimes agreeing to forfeit their entire Block Grant – Government decided that it had to control rates directly. In 1984 eighteen authorities (including Portsmouth) were **rate capped.** The eighteen breached the (arbitrary) limit of spending 20 per cent above GRE and more than 4 per cent above target, as well as having budgets greater than £10 million. As well as the financial penalty affecting the discretion of the local authority, there is the point strongly made by the Audit Commission (1984) that the changes in the system produced undesirable uncertainty. CIPFA (1984, p.24) said, "... actual arrangements for calculating the (central government) grant are very complicated and certainly confusing."

The terminology, if not the intentions, were further changed in the 1986/7 settlement announced in December 1985. The main feature was the abolition of targets and a return to GREAs as the basic measure of assessing 'satisfactory' spending. A threshold is maintained (10 per cent above GRE) which steeply reduces grant for the 'defaulters'. Municipal Review, (January/February 1986) in its explanation of the new regime concludes, "The Government claims that the 1986/7 Settlement means a simpler and fairer grant system. In reality, local authorities are faced with a bewildering mass of technical complexities, distortions and uncertainties." In the light of these complexities, local authority officers and politicians more than ever require some kind of simplifying 'aids to calculation'. One common way to approach the subject is simply to maximise grant.

On the whole, the process of budget making is internal to the authority. Only in a small number of authorities was there an important aspect of conflict between local and central government. Local authority activity largely accepts the financial hand dealt: only a small amount of effort (however well publicised) goes into confrontation and attempts to secure greater funding. However, a number of other external influences can also be identified, such as local political parties, statutory consultations and electorates, as well as often the decisive but diffuse influence of local political sub-cultures. We can explore the issues raised by our studies by seeing how expectations of budgetary processes have changed in recent years.

B. The Traditional Budget

The literature on budgeting contains a range of expectations about processes and responses that seem to be found as 'normal' in widely different situations. As with any introduction to the study of budgeting this chapter necessarily draws heavily on the work of Aaron Wildavsky – thus it draws upon an approach that has been extended from its original context of US Congressional budgetary behaviour to very different environments (see Wildavsky, 1975). In particular, the approach has also been used by Heclo and Wildavsky in their study of budgeting in British central government (1978, 1981 ed.). Wildavsky (1978, p.501) claims, that "the traditional budget reigns supreme virtually everywhere, in practice if not in theory." After summarising the Wildavsky type analysis, we cover challenges to that approach –

both academic criticisms of the Wildavsky approach and models of 'rational' practice developed to remedy what were seen as defects in the traditional pattern. Finally, we look at some recent works which claim that the sustained financial pressure on the public sector of the past decade has led to changed budgetary behaviour.

The Wildavsky model has been traced by Wildavsky himself (Dempster and Wildavsky 1979, p.379) to Dahl and Lindblom's original concept of incrementalism: "Incrementalism is a method of social action that takes existing reality as one alternative and compares the probable gains and losses of closely related alternatives by making relatively small adjustments in existing reality, or making larger adjustments about whose consequences approximately as much is known as about the consequence of existing reality, or both." (Dahl and Lindblom 1953, p.82). Incrementalism is certainly the key feature but we can develop the components of this type of analysis as follows. Budgeting is (among other things):

- annual

- anticipatory

- allocative

- competitive

- repetitive

- incremental

- political

- social

- simplified

Annual

Budgets tend to be made for one year. This practice can be fixed by statute, or as a consequence of the financial cycles of other bodies (e.g. annual grants from central government) but the annual principle is so 'normal' that it is usually adopted unthinkingly. It is perhaps trivial but nonetheless a clear example of the way in which custom determines practice. Although the budget document will refer to one twelve month period, the process of preparing the document, monitoring expenditure in the budget and auditing how it was spent, will take place in a financial cycle of two to three years. Many financial decisions will have consequences which extend for more than 12 months but financing will be done in annual instalments. It is worth distinguishing the longer term horizon of 'financial planning' from the shorter term budgetary focus. (see Hotham 1984, p.108)

Anticipatory

Budgets are set in advance. This has the consequence that the resources being allocated are often estimated. Precision - in an accounting sense - can be legitimately applied only retrospectively to past performance. However, the assumption that finance is an exact science spills over into budgeting but there is a difference between the 'hard' numbers of audit and the 'softer' numbers of budgeting.

Allocative

Budgeting has the twin purposes of estimating resources and allocating these to specific purposes. Normally there is central allocation but the expenditure will be made by what are often termed **spending departments.** Wildavsky (1975, p.44) terms this distinction between those who spend and those who allocate, **advocates** and **guardians.** In central and local government, it seems almost inevitable that some central body is invented to weigh up bids.

Competitive

In the usual patterns spending departments find that their estimated needs are in excess of the previous year. Their **"bids"** will together (usually) exceed resources available, therefore the job of the central decision makers is to resolve the departmental competition.

Repetitive

The reiterative nature of budgetary cycles is important in that the preceding year's expenditure, usually termed the base, is accepted as demonstrating a reasonable approximation of the distribution pattern for the coming year. Wildavsky (1984, p.13) observes, "The largest determining factor in the size and content of this year's budget is last year's budget." Prior commitment is one important factor circumscribing the freedom to make serious alterations on a one year basis. On the capital side of the budget, projects have to be financed over a number of years: on the revenue side costs such as salaries are on-going unless fundamental change takes place. Moreover, because the pattern of allocations has been arrived at by adjustments over time, it is assumed by most participants to be a reasonably accurate guide to priorities.

Incremental

Because experience suggests that new budgets are similar in shape to their predecessors, this similarity to the past pattern is used as a simplifying principle. Wildavsky, (1984, p.15) claimed, "Budgeting is **incremental** not comprehensive. The beginning of wisdom about an agency budget is that it is almost never actively reviewed as a whole every year in the sense of reconsidering the value of all existing programs".

Using data from Richard Fenno (dating from the 1960s) Wildavsky (1984, p.14) attempts to illustrate the incremental nature of budgetary outcomes by citing the following pattern of increases in allocations made to 37 domestic (US) agencies over 12 years:

Range of Increase

0.5%	6-10%	11-20%	21-30%	31-40%	41-50%	51-100%	101+%
number of cases 149	84	93	52	21	15	24	7

Because experience has taught that adjustments tend to be incremental, the best 'aid to calculation' by those involved is to focus attention on the 'add-ons'. British local authority officers seem entirely familiar with the concept of the 'standstill' budget - which is normally used as the base. The 'standstill' is taken to be the overall figure for each spending department and within that departments may be allowed growth - if they find compensatory cuts in their own sub-budgets.

Political

Both in the sense of setting priorities and the manner in which they are set, budgeting is political. In an ideal world it might be that the value of a further increment of a given size for, say, nursery education would be weighed not just against a similar increment for that of services within the same department but against that for environmental protection or roads, grants for industry and so on. Such capacity to discriminate in a cross-sectional manner between expenditures is at the heart of various budgetary reforms but in practice it is difficult sensibly to compare unlikes. There is simply an intellectual difficulty in choosing between such goals. 'Fair shares for all' for competing spending departments is adopted as a principle of allocation both as a good way to maintain peace in the organisation and because less arbitrary techniques have their own significant disadvantages. Therefore, as well as budgetary complications being reduced by resort to incrementalism and close scrutiny only of the margins, increments are customarily distributed, more or less equally, among the advocate departments.

Social

It is worth labelling the budgetary process as social because the social relations within the organisation control the sorts of bids that are made: a climate is established where it is expected that departments will ask for more but the actual decision, 'how much', will be influenced by the fact that over-bidding - even if all the proposed projects are individually worthwhile - leads to a feeling that the department lacks realism and its credibility suffers. Wildavsky (1984, p.21) says, "The appropriation committee lose(s) confidence in it and automatically cut large chunks before looking at the budget in detail. It becomes much more difficult to justify even the items with highest priority because no one will trust an agency that repeatedly comes in too high." Therefore the 'bid' is not simply a plea for all spending that the Department **could** justify but it is a figure calculated as being achievable - realistic for the budgetary climate while avoiding discrediting the department as a source. Eugene Bardach (1974) and Anthony Downs (1957) have talked about 'alarm systems' and 'sub formal' communications within policy systems. Departments must not be over-ambitious but there is the contradictory notion that the estimates should be 'padded'. There is thus a series of self-fulfilling prophecies (Wildavsky 1984, p.23). Departments pad to protect themselves against automatic cuts: the centre automatically cuts because departments pad.......

Simplified

The incremental approach is put forward as an **aid to calculation** because of the 'cognitive limits' of decision makers. Wildavsky would argue that if one attempts synoptic or comprehensive rationality in decision making, the attempt is bound to fail. What is left then is not ration-ality but pseudo-rationality. The incremental process avoids large

9

scale analysis and comparisons among dissimilar activities accepting previous spending as the 'base' and allowing analysis to be concentrated on 'the margin' (the Stirling case study shows the rapid proliferation of documentation as authorities move towards 'rationality').

Wildavsky's prediction of budgetary maximisation by Departments is certainly simple and possibly pessimistic but it does seem to have relevance. The exceptions to the rule that Departments attempt to protect themselves rather than contribute to overall organisational goals are few - and no more conspicuous in Universities and Polytechnics than in local authorities as they indulge in cutback management.

C. Challenges to Budgetary Incrementalism

Incrementalism is ambiguous. Wildavsky's incrementalism is an application in the budgetary context of the incremental model (set out more fully by Lindblom). Many criticisms have been made of the general incremental model - both of its validity as a description and of its general prescriptive position. In practice we have had two decades of experimentation in budget making in local authorities: the theoretical unease about incrementalism perhaps explains why practitioners have not been content to rest with traditional (incremental) practice.

Three major articles show the sorts of criticism of incrementalism in its budgetary form that have been advanced - Le Loup (1978), Bailey and O'Conner (1975) and Goodin and Waldner (1979). Le Loup begins his article by conceding that, "Of all the subfields of political science, budgeting is most dominated by one theory to the exclusion of competing theories. For over a decade, **incrementalism** has dominated conceptualisation, analysis and description of the budgetary process." Drawing on Bailey and O'Conner's (1975) article on "Operationalizing Incrementalism", he found that the number of budgetary outcomes that can be described as incremental (however that unclear concept is clarified) is fewer than one would suspect from the writings of Wildavsky and others such as Fenno (1966). This is a basic challenge to the data cited by Wildavsky in the previous section. Loup's charge is that the incrementalist assumptions of Wildavsky and Fenno structured their analysis, and conclusions and the presentation of their data (Le Loup 1978, p.67).

Bailey and O'Conner (1975, p.60) pointed out that incrementalism as a method of decision (aid to calculation) was quite separate from incrementalism as a type of output. They further claimed that those in the Wildavsky tradition simply ignored data in their studies which did not fit the incremental pattern. They trace back to Lindblom in 1961 (cited in 1968 ed., p.296) the use of incrementalism both to mean, "small or incremental changes from existing policies" and "a limited set of policy alternatives". In particular they draw attention to Wildavsky's highly 'permissive' (i.e. lax) interpretation of incremental as any change up to 30 per cent from the base.

Goodin and Waldner reiterated the question, 'What counts as incremental change?'. They also point to other difficulties. What for example of 'sleeper effects'? Since adverse effects might take time to appear, incrementalists could slowly - yet still disastrously - pursue policies which produce, for example, long term health damage. The incremental strategy of reinforcing what appears as positive interventions, works only when the limited feedback is not misleading. Goodin and Waldner identified three different propositions in the incrementalist family:

> "Incrementalism 1 suggests we respond to results directly: make small interventions, carry on with more of the same if we like the results or, if we do not, next try a small step along another path.
> Whereas incrementalism 1 tries to get by without theory, incrementalism 2 is frankly justified in terms of testing a theory, ... it advocates small steps because they tend to present more nearly controlled experiments with more readily interpretable results.
> Incrementalism 3 argues for the same small steps, justifying them instead on the grounds that such interventions are more likely to be reversible should we come to regret our choice".

The criticisms drew from Dempster and Wildavsky (1979, p.371) an acceptance of the different senses of incrementalism which had developed. Most relevantly they noted, "If you are interested in budgetary problem-solving, incrementalism as a **method** of calculation is the focus of interest." Incrementalism is then a process of deciding in non-comprehensive, non-synoptic, non-heroic style. They go on, "The key terms are 'existing base', 'small number of items' and 'narrow range of increases or decreases'. One knows whether a method of budgetary problem-solving is or is not incremental, then, by whether or not decision making focuses around the existing base (which may be approximated by last year's amount) and by the number of options considered....". This incremental process was seen as related to, but not identical with, a regular pattern of outputs.

Corporate Management

The application of the incremental philosophy in local government has been described by John Stewart (1983, pp.207-8) as the Traditional Approach. He has listed its key features as:

1. Budgetary information is arranged to indicate **what** resources are being spent on, rather than **why** they are being spent;

2. Budgetary information is concentrated on the immediate **budget year** and does not cover any medium or long term plans;

3. Budgetary presentation focuses attention on **proposals for growth,** rather than any review of existing expenditure;

4. Proposals for capital expenditure are considered separately from proposals for revenue expenditure.

In the 1960s and 1970s a set of processes and institutions were introduced as an attempt to give greater facility for selective choice (perhaps in pursuit of a political philosophy) in local authorities. Stewart (1971, p.30) set out the elements of a prescriptive 'rational' local authority process as follows:

(a) The organisation identifies certain needs, present and foreseen, in its environment.

(b) It sets objectives in relation to those needs, i.e. the extent to which it will plan to meet those needs.

(c) It considers alternative ways of achieving those objectives.

(d) It evaluates those alternatives in terms of their use of resources and their effects.

(e) Decisions are made in the light of that evaluation.

(f) These decisions are translated into managerial action.

(g) The result of the action taken is monitored and fed back to modify the continuing process; by altering the perception of needs, the objectives set, the alternatives considered, the evaluation, the decision made or the action taken.

The 'technology' of corporate management included generation of options, development of selection criteria, comparison of departmental programmes, means to establish and implement priorities. A blunt, even harsh, summary of the corporate management 'new wave' is that it failed. Whereas it is comparatively easy to introduce the forms of corporate management, the working habits and assumptions of departmentally based local government are difficult to erode. The financial plan approach recognises some of the concerns of 'rationality' but is less demanding in its requirements than corporate management; authorities have introduced a variety of value for money analyses and innovations in forecasting and budgeting without adopting full scale corporate management. (See Elcock, 1982).

Zero-Base Budgeting

A specific form of the new rationality that is 'in good currency' in the 1980s is Zero-Base Budgeting which is designed, in particular, to extend the scope of analysis beyond the marginal comparison of an incremental process. It has been described as follows:

> In most organisations, the one type of budget request certain to receive intensive screening and analysis is the one that proposes to establish a new service. It is likely to be reviewed as to desirability and need for the service, beneficiaries of the service, reasonableness of proposed costs, potential future implications and availability of funds - often in terms of relative priority of all proposed new services. Zero-Base Budgeting aims to apply the same type of process, in a more sophisticated manner, to all proposed expenditures.
> Essentially Zero-Base Budgeting seeks to accomplish this through a process which divides all proposed activities (and expenditures) into cohesive units of manageable size, subjects them to detailed scrutiny and ultimately establishes a rank order of those units, which, given unlimited resources, would be funded. A selected level of expenditure is then matched against the final rank ordering and if funds are not sufficient to cover the entire listing, lowest priority items are left unfunded until the cumulative total of the funded priority list matches the level of funding that is available. The final priority list, balanced with available funds,

then becomes the budget.

(from Singleton et al, 1976).

Singleton et al, have sympathetically described one of the early US uses of Zero-Base Budgeting in Wilmington, Delaware but even their description goes on to make the point, "Since the variety, quantity and quality of service to be provided is usually a more realistic question than whether or not a given budget unit will be funded at all, each budget unit is divided into several alternative levels of service. In most cases in Wilmington this began with a level at about half of current..." Therefore the 'zero' notion is attractive as a flag but is so extreme as to be off any realistic agenda.

The most famous Zero-Base Budgeting case was the State of Georgia under Governor Jimmy Carter. A report by R.N.Anthony (1977) claims that the consultant installing the Georgia system believed that it was possible to "prepare and analyse a budget from scratch .... This belief did not last long. Well before the end of the first budget cycle, it was agreed that expenditures equal to approximately 80 per cent of the current level of spending would be given only a cursory examination and that attention could be focused on the increment". Anthony's other main criticism is that large numbers of decision packages are simply unmanageable - in Georgia there were 11,000 of them. He noted that if the Governor set aside four hours every day for two months he could spend about a minute on each decision package... If he delegated the job to others, the whole idea of comparing priorities is compromised. Zero-Base Budgeting is a reaction to the sort of budgetary mentality of Dempster and Wildavsky (1979, p.384) "...the budget being a product of past decisions, like an iceberg, hemmed in by mandatory items and political commitments". Maybe budgets **are** like that.

The incomplete implementation of Zero-Base Budgeting raises two general issues which complicate comparisons. Few authorities exemplify either 'perfect' (ideal type) incrementalism or fully operational corporate management (even where the relevant committees and procedures are in place). If the essence of the 'rational' approaches is the facility to redirect funding to different 'heads' in different years then authorities with strong political leadership could do this as easily as corporate structures - although it must be acknowledged that such leaders seldom seem interested in that sort of control.

Cutback Behaviour

The Wildavsky type of budgetary behaviour sketched so far - and even the corporate management alternatives - were developed in the 1960s and 1970s. It can be argued that these are pictures of behaviour under expansionary conditions. Quite different behaviour might have developed in the era of cutbacks that dates from the mid 1970s. In his 1975 book, *Budgeting*, Wildavsky comments on Whitehall's budgetary system that "the Public Expenditure Survey (PESC) is the most important and impressive budgetary reform of our time." By his second (1981, p.xi), edition to *The Private Government of Public Money*, the question was 'What went wrong?'. Daniel Tarschys (1985) in an article in *Scandinavian Political Studies* uses the phrase **"decremental budgeting"** to make his point that the climate has changed from that of vintage incrementalism.

One departmental strategy to preserve their budget was described in Heclo and Wildavsky (1981 ed., p.91) as "sore thumbs" or "beggars sores". When departments are asked to make savings (perhaps to compensate for increases elsewhere) they propose 'savings' which are politically unacceptable. Thus when the Treasury experimented with costed options which asked departments to list the projects they would cut if they had (say) 3 per cent less cash, the department would respond by putting up suggestions that were politically costly. When the response was that something like cutting free school milk could not be allowed, the department was then in a strong position to fend off other cuts: it was hardly their fault that their best option (free school milk cut) had been ruled out.

In 1981, Howard Glennester developed more systematically the responses of 'advocates' to what he terms "a hostile environment". Glennester's extension to the vocabulary of budgeting is instructive but it is also worth noting that he is offering a time-phased series of responses. Two of this early range of departmental responses are based on an assumption that cuts will be a passing phase. He then goes on to describe different approaches that seem to be more appropriate "when spending cuts are for real". If this argument of changed tactics to meet a changed appreciation of the seriousness of the financial situation holds, then our studies of local authorities' actions in a single year perhaps need to be put in a time context. Are the tactics of our focal year the same as in past years or has this been a development of a new range of responses? Glennester's list of responses is certainly not exhaustive but they are very valuable as a language for the kind of practices practitioners adopt.

One of Glennester's 'opening gambits' in response to a 'passing phase' of cuts is Heclo and Wildavsky's "sore thumbs". Another tactic Glennester calls "fairy gold". This is a neat label for another ploy recorded in Heclo and Wildavsky (1981 ed., p.236). They quote one official claiming that departments "are being tempted to use larger amounts in the first of (PESC's) five years and promise to be good boys later". As an example of the scope provided by promising cuts 'tomorrow', they cite the Heath Government in 1970 which was able to claim it was both increasing and reducing defence allocations. The increases were, of course, short term while the decrease was judged against year five of the previous Labour Government's projection. As a response to temporary pressure, it is therefore possible to attempt to pay in "fairy gold" – not real money paying for hard programmes but merely cuts to projections (which can always be restored later).

Glennester's next type of response has proved to be very accurate as a forecast – "sell your assets". He writes, "These have short term attractions, but 'pawnshop' tactics of this kind may cut off future income flows while only postponing the evil day as regards cuts in current spending. Their 'rationality' in the long run economic sense is therefore highly debatable". The criticism of the strategy by Glennester does not undermine its attractiveness for hard pressed local authorities. The major asset is of course the public housing stock. An extension of the 'asset strip' is to 'sell and lease' back by which the authority raises cash for short term consumption.

Glennester's next type of **defensive** reaction to a demand for cuts at first sight looks out of place. He describes how the imposition of charges for certain services can in fact be a cut for the consumer but at least it preserves the activity from the point of view of the department. Charges are then a defensive response.

In terms of magnitude, the most important 'instant' response to demands for cuts is to cut where the effect is less noticeable

- and thus Glennester predicts that departments will cut capital, not current spending. The Audit Commission's report on <u>The Block Grant Distribution System</u> (1984, p.4) shows that capital spending has indeed been disproportionately cut in recent years. As Glennester says, "Deferred building programmes do save real money now.... They are certainly easiest to make in political terms, since no one need be sacked and few people will notice....".

The last of his opening gambits is the logical extension of the Wildavsky approach mentioned above - "protect the base". One way to cut is to abandon any new programmes or improvements to programmes. The politics of the new is that much more difficult than the politics of the entrenched where objections have been digested, client groups in support have developed, staff have been put in post. As Glennester points out however, this natural enough tendency to conservatism does, as a long term strategy, lead to ossification.

To this list of options we can add, "manipulate the base". Given that attention by the central decision maker tends to ignore the base and focus on what is new, departments can try to avoid cuts and smuggle in additions by rewriting history to have their new projects as part of the 'base'.

Another possible strategy is when a department attempts to preserve its programmes by claiming the political cause of the time as their own. Heclo and Wildavsky (1981 ed., p.91) say that this budgetary opportunism should not be surprising, "unless civil servants are assumed to be deaf-mutes who do not hear the political music". The topical argument is, of course, unemployment. Departments will not be slow to discover and promote the employment consequencies of their policies. Midwinter (1984, p.476) labels this strategy support mobilisation. In this approach, the spending department seeks to create a climate of opinion which makes cuts difficult to implement. He claims that in one (unnamed) authority, a service director issued an instruction that every complaint about his service which appeared in the Press should be sent to every member of his committee, the rationale being that a 'bad' service would not be further cut. Another example was a police chief who published his annual report three months early, just before the budget decisions were to be made, to make members aware of rising crime figures at the right time to inhibit cuts in the police budget.

Real Cuts

When Glennester moves to consider the situation when sustained pressure on budgets leads to real cuts, he believes that the organisation is obliged to attempt to confront the issue of allocating cuts rationally instead of deferring choices and fudging as in the first phase. He thus presents a series of ways to achieve cuts - as an extension of the short term strategies to avoid cuts. The first modes of response are "rough justice" and "equal pain for all" - which is the bad news equivalent to Wildavsky's "fair shares for all". Glennester says (1981, p.185) that "The strategy that causes least political cost to ministers around the Cabinet table or council chamber is to be even-handed and call for a five or ten per cent cut all round".

In fact none of the strategies Glennester considers seem to introduce very much deliberative, central choice of allocation. He says of the **cut bureaucracy** idea that "Naturally, administrative costs will be first on the agenda of any politician faced with the reality of cutting

15

real spending. Yet he soon discovers that they form a disappointingly small percentage of the budget and are difficult to achieve in reality".

His next method of coping is, "cut someone else's budget, not your own". He notes, "Between 1974/5 and 1980/1, local government spending is planned to have fallen by 14 per cent in real terms. Central government, on the other hand, has allowed its own spending to rise by 7.7 per cent". In its small way, however, local government can cut back on voluntary bodies and others which look to councils for assistance.

He next suggests, "Cut by cash limit - or let inflation do the work". The idea here is simply to fail to compensate sufficiently for inflation and therefore the spending department will find it has insufficient funds to complete its programmes. The political advantage of this method of achieving cuts is that the cutting appears almost accidental.

Finally, in this class of responses, Glennester notes the possibility of shifting the public burden to private costs. In other language government (central or local) can 'off load' to the voluntary sector or can perhaps find a quango such as the SDA or the MSC available to perform the task under an employment generation scheme. The activity can be retained while not appearing in the expenditure of local authority - which can then claim a 'cut'. Education budgets, in particular in the 1980s, need to be examined carefully for compensation for employment/training schemes.

A "Retrenchment Dynamic"?

A number of studies have, like Glennester's, proposed that different responses will be seen as the duration of the cut back phase extends. One approach by Jorgensen (1984) (as described in Dunsire, Huby and Hood, 1985) predicts three phases:

Phase	Response
"Incremental"	Percentage budget pruning, limitation of spending by cash not volume, deferral of maintenance and capital expenditures, supression of new programmes and posts.
"Managerial"	Conscious and selective choices - organisational restructuring, 'efficiency experts' introduced, retraining staff, changing, off loading, hiring-off, privatisation, longer waiting times, fewer service outlets, protect base, etc.
"Strategic" or "Quantum" cuts	Major permanent selective excisions from substantive programmes.

Dunsire et al. explain the assumptions of the Jorgensen approach as follows:

> ... the normal progression of cutback, as a squeeze on resources tightens, will be from the incrementalist style to the managerial style to the strategic style. The incrementalist phase comes first, when consciously or unconsciously it is assumed that cutbacks are

16

only a temporary phenomenon ... as a resource squeeze continues, it comes to be recognised as a long haul and that many kinds of piecemeal cuts and postponements have their nemesis (a build up of detrimental effects) within only a few years. They are therefore initially cheap but eventually costly ways of retrenching ... for the long haul ... it would be rational to incur the higher 'search' or 'disruption' costs on the promise of more secure benefits - the 'managerial' phase. But in time ... (the) belief in eventual regrowth quite gone, the expectation that sufficient savings can be achieved by managerial or do-it-better processes comes in turn to be abandoned and effort starts to be expended in finding cuts that will generate increasing reductions in public spending, the strategic or quantum cutting phase, dropping whole functions.

Jorgensen's model does indeed - in the words of Dunsire et al. - have "intuitive appeal". There is an underlying logic of economy of response which suggests that organisations will initially respond in a minimalist way before being eventually driven up the ladder of options to engage in responses which are more costly in terms of effort and political 'noise'. However, one can both debate the rank order of costliness of his proposed hierarchy of responses and readily imagine how the predicted pattern would be upset in particular cases. While he presents quantum cuts as the response of last resort, it could well be, for example, that an authority will take the opportunity of cutbacks to force through a cut it wished to make for its own reasons. The axing of a department in a university, or rural schools in a local authority might **look** like an early resort to quantum cuts but instead reflect an opportunistic catching of a tide. Tarschys (1985, p.255) has discussed the concept of "cuttability". Some areas of the budget have legal and political defences which make them immune to casual cutback but on the other hand it is possible that there are expendable areas which might look rather like Jorgensen's quantum cuts.

Another major discussion of cutback behaviour is Levine, Rubin and Wolohojian's (1981) The Politics of Retrenchment: How Local Governments Manage Fiscal Stress. This was based on a set of case histories of four US local authorities based on two waves of interviews twelve months apart. Levine et al. develop (and test) a sophisticated model of how their authorities would (and did) respond. It is set out in Table 1.4.

Like Jorgensen, Levine et al. predicted a changed set of responses as the financial climate deteriorated from "no revenue growth" to "severe decline". In fact the empirical research (predictably) found that the neat theory imperfectly fitted their cases but there was still a discernible pattern. For example, they conclude that in the early phase of retrenchment, many decision makers judged options in terms of their **reversibility**. Therefore delay and rationing were more appealing than programme elimination while there was hope of revenue recovery. On the other hand their findings (1981, p.195) did not support their hypothesis that the authorities studied would adopt strategies in a fixed sequence - "Only Oakland, which experienced a continuing and accelerating decline in revenues, seemed to follow the sequential pattern, with a very short period of delay, followed by resisting and then followed by cutting and smoothing". While they had predicted that 'severe decline' would be associated with a decline in control at the centre of authority, again this was not borne out.

Wolman (1984) is also led by assumptions about the local authority as a problem solving organisation to produce a list of possible

Table 1.4

CHANGES IN RESOURCE LEVELS, POLITICAL STRUCTURE AND ADMINISTRATIVE STRATEGIES

Changes in Resource Levels	Political Structure	Administrative Strategies
Moderate continuous growth	Moderate central control/fragmented interest groups and pluralistic bargaining	Incremental strategies (small divisible projects and service augmentation)
Windfall revenue growth	Some loss of central power/formation of dominant coalitions to capture new resources	Windfall strategies (new programs, large capital projects)
No revenue growth	Weak central control/interest groups fragmented and quiescent	Denial and delay strategies (no growth in allocations but no cuts either, increased borrowing and budget manipulations)
Moderate decline	Weak central control/interest groups fragmented but active	Stretching and resisting strategies (across-the-board cuts)
Severe decline	(1) Recentralization of formal control, or (2) Re-emergence of an informal dominant coalition	Cutting and smoothing strategies (targeted cuts)

18

responses, although he specifically states (p.248), "This listing does not **necessarily** (his emphasis) imply a chronological sequencing" but he does suggest a "preference hierarchy". The first response that is likely, according to Wolman, is to "buy time". This can be achieved in a variety of ways - which do not require expenditure or service reductions or revenue increases:

- draw on cash reserves. He says that local authorities in England and Wales drew down their balances by more than £125 million (more than 10 per cent) in 1982/3.

- borrowing internally from one local authority budget to another. (He cites Coventry applying interest on capital investments to the revenue budget. He also includes the use of capital funds for operating expenses in this category).

- creative book-keeping. As an example he gives Coventry rescheduling its debts to decrease short term repayments. Sam Brittan (1983, p.149) has quoted Goodhart's Law (called after Dr. Charles Goodhart, a Bank of England economist) which states that, "any monetary indicator becomes distorted as a guide to monetary conditions once it is selected for target". Central government restrictions on local authorities have in similar fashion been an invitation to evasion. (An appendix to chapter 11 gives a good example of the sorts of responses local authorities have devised).

- one time revenue raising devices (i.e. mainly asset sales) are another "buy time" device. Wolman's final short run response is short term borrowing - which is adopted although it is recognised by exponents as not addressing the issue of a revenue shortfall for the budgetary year.

Wolman notes that these buying time strategies satisfy - in the short term - consumers and avoid difficult choices for the local authority but he also notes that transferring operating costs to the capital budget and short term budgeting were integral to promoting the eventual fiscal crises of New York and Cleveland.

His second answer to the question of how to cut the deficit without cutting spending is, he says, not realistically present in the UK. The approach he has in mind here is **increase intergovernmental aid** - or 'grantmanship'. He states that in Britain as the central government's funding is determined by a formula the scope for bilateral negotiations does not exist. This neglects the scope of authorities attempting to change the formula from year to year - and some limited cases of disputes about the 'facts'. Cash from the European Community - an external source - gives an extra facility for grantmanship.

According to Wolman (1983, p.252) if "buying time" is an inadequate response local authorities are faced with the choice of increasing sources of revenue (i.e. rates or charges) or cutting expenditures. Citing material by Greenwood, Wolman suggests that local authorities prefer to protect expenditure levels by substituting a decline in one source of finance by an increase in another. Wolman suggests that proximity to an election leads to expenditure cuts rather than rate rises. He says that the average increase in the London boroughs in 1981 was only 0.9 per cent compared with 25.9 per cent the previous year, while the outer London boroughs in the election year of 1981 increased their rates by only 2.9 per cent compared with 25.9 per cent in the previous year. He says other local authorities - not facing re-election - raised their rates by similar amounts in both years. (This option is of course constrained by "over spending" rules from central government).

The next level of his "preference hierarchy" is where reductions are necessary. He assumes that authorities will minimise impact on services and employees. One is to shift the costs to other bodies (off-loading or function transfer). The next approach is efficiency increase. He recognises that however this is attained there will be a reduction in labour but argues that the organisational equilibrium will be preserved if reductions are made by wastage rather than lay-offs. He sees 'contracting out' as part of that device but observes that its unpopularity is because its anti-union/lower wage dimension would cause discontent within the authority. Wolman points out that some costs are simply uncuttable, for instance debt servicing. Of the remaining costs, cuts which do not involve redundancies are preferred. Because of its political costs (in tems of organisational equilibrium), reducing manpower costs is seen as decidedly to the bottom of the list of options. If it is needed it is done by attrition - a hiring freeze. Authorities seem to prefer pay cuts to staff cuts but the attitude of unions is critical.

Wolman's assumption that organisations look for internal equilibrium leads him to expect pro rata or "equal pain" cuts. Four of the UK authorities he examined - Hounslow, Richmond, Coventry and Knowsley - engaged in pro rata reductions as a first step in their expenditure reduction exercise. Wolman goes on to suggest, following Danziger (1978, p.149, 221-2), that one reason for the prevalence of pro rata cuts in the UK is the "absence of a functional equivalent of the American city manager or strong mayor". This might be to underestimate the strong leadership tradition that is found in Britain.

Wolman recognised the 'shroud-waving' type of **threatened cut** - but observed that they were implemented much less frequently. The actual cuts tended to be 'invisible' - maintenance expenditures being especially vulnerable. He quoted two English officers to support his view that general service trimming was more likely than selective elimination: "Services have been reduced at the margins. Day to day maintenance has declined. But the basic fabric of the services are still there. I can't really think of any activities that have been fully eliminated". A London Chief Executive was quoted ascribing the lack of public outcry at cuts as follows, "... cuts have been made at the margin where they won't be noticed. Reducing the number of teachers through attractive retirement packages means increasing pupil-teacher ratios by a bit but few are likely to notice. Some libraries are open slightly fewer hours, some public lavatories are closed, there has been some cutback of central office staff". (Wolman 1984, p.261).

If we contrast Jorgensen, Levine et al. with Wolman we find that the former assume that financial pressure will drive authorities logically and inexorably into 'rational' or targetted cuts. The sequential dynamic is less strong in Wolman. The assumptions of Jorgensen and Levine have already emerged in the literature on English local government in that Greenwood et al. (1980, p.25) attempted to show that "Under conditions of financial restraint government agencies tend to become less incremental". They developed two hypotheses: Periods of a sustained decline in the supply of resources will be characterised by **wider** parameters of budgetary review. That is (a) the 'base' will be decreasingly treated as sacrosanct; and (b) a greater proportion of total estimates will be analysed and reviewed". Furthermore, they argue that "Periods of sustained decline in the supply of resources will be characterised by an increasing utilisation of rational analysis to facilitate budgetary choice". They argue that the first proposition - about challenging the base - stems from the reasonable assumption that budgetary famine will lead to examination of current commitments in order to release funds for new policies. On the second notion - that contracting resources will produce rational analysis - they say is not based on theory but from their empirical research. They say that, "under conditions of a sustained decline in resources, the form of budgetary analysis is more likely to approach the rational model."

Several reservations can be advanced in connection with the INLOGOV data - reservations which the authors conceded. They noted (1980, p.41) that the "image" of rational analysis had to be separated from the "substance" of changed processes. When they wrote there was still a bull market for corporate management and they seemed to acknowledge that claims of "rationalism" could be the local authorities projecting an image of "efficiency and modernity".

Their own data (1980, p.44) records that the sprint to rationality slowed in later years: "the initial impetus of 1974/5 had been slowed by 1976/7". They speculate that the "panic" of the first cuts produced attempts at "rationality" but behaviour reverted over time. They also suggested that the 'reorganisation effect' which coincided with the first cuts might have produced the early (and unsustained?) managerialism. Greenwood's (1983) data show that in some of the 20 local authorities he studied between 1974 and 1980, there was an increase in "budget review capacity". However, he stresses that this is a relative movement away from an incremental approach: "As fiscal pressure was sustained, central actors in the budgetary process...... began to establish structures and procedures that would facilitate a central review of service expenditures ..... The experience of local authorities from 1974 to 1980, then, indicated that traditional incremental arrangements are inappropriate for the management of sustained fiscal pressures". Our own studies certainly confirm the existence of experiments with various forms of central capability but we also confirm that the experiments do not approach the synoptic, comprehensive activity of fully 'corporate and rational' processes.

D. Conclusion

While these various theories of retrenchment dynamic have some data in support, the appeal is basically that of logic - that the authorities' response should be to make fundamental decisions rather than denial and delay. A counter proposition could be that in a time of restraint and uncertainty, financial planning with its longer time horizons is less and less appealing; that the patterns of responses are not phased but fitful as budget makers attempt to exploit changing directions from central government and new discoveries of creative accounting which can bring sudden temporary relief. Finally, budgeting in this climate might become less discriminatory. At worst, fiscal irresponsibility might be the consequence of financial pressure but at best the need for endless change and improvisation to meet deteriorating financial conditions might drive out the opportunity for long term responses.

The budgetary literature is thus divided into sources which see an endemic incrementalism (and who broadly favour that mode of analysis); those who recognise the power of the incrementalist description but believe that other and better methods of policy making are possible; thirdly, there are those who see the validity of the incrementalist description as being eroded as local authorities budget under pressure. Certainly sustained pressure on local authorities need not have the effect intended by central government. The Audit Commission (1984, p.1) noted that English and Welsh Authorities had been building up reserves at an annual rate of at least £400 million in the early 1980s − 2½ times the rate before 1981/2.

Research on local government is complicated by the fact that some form of "rational" analysis has greater "respectability" than the "muddling through" of incrementalism. Thus it is not unusual to find activity that is unambiguously − and quite appropriately − incremental described in terms of synoptic, rational planning (see Jordan 1984 for an example). It is thus common to find the apparatus and jargon of corporate management without the substance.

Another complication, also noted above, is the imperfect versions in practice of the ideal types of behaviour identified in the literature. Thus one way of describing the increased importance (arguably) given to central scrutiny of budgets in the past decade, is to contrast the demand-led budgets of the past with current 'resource-led' budgets (see Chapter 12) or the difference between the budget as a 'control' or 'policy' tool (see Chapter 16). This is a valid notion but of course even demand-led budgets did not accept all bids and even resource-led bids usually still total up departmental 'needs'.

This chapter shows how the academic literature on budgeting has in recent years increasingly discussed the notion that financial pressure leads to changes in budgetary practice. Our case studies will show that in few local authorities have the moves to rationality been substantial and where such attempts have been made they have had to live uneasily with the traditional "aids to calculation" of incrementalism.

Notes

[1] This section is based on the Guide to Local Authority Finance, published by the Chartered Institute of Public Finance and Accountancy, 1984.

PART I ENGLAND

2. Avon County Council

ROGER CLEMENTS

Making the expenditure budget in Avon during 1985/6 was highly party political. On the resource side central government decisions were fundamental and unpredictable.

A Profile of Avon

Avon dates from 1973/4. Its population is 934,000. There are six districts, the largest being Bristol with 400,000 people. There are 25,000 full time equivalent county staff. There are no major declining industries and economic growth is sustained by office relocations, new high technology industries and local aircraft and defence industries. Unemployment is slightly less than the national average, with pockets of severe unemployment in Bristol, Bath and Weston, especially in inner urban areas with ethnic concentrations and in one or two outlying council estates. These economic changes will not reduce unemployment dramatically, nor help the less skilled.

The Alliance has made modest advances, with important political consequences. There are one Labour and nine Conservative MPs. In 1983 47 per cent voted Conservative, 24 per cent Labour and nearly 28 per cent Alliance. The turnout was 75 per cent; the swing was nearly 5 per cent to the Conservatives. The addition to Bristol of parts of Somerset and Gloucestershire was expected to make Avon safely Conservative, a blow to Labour in Bristol, now resentfully subordinated. The Conservatives established an economy-minded regime. However, the 1981 county election gave Labour a majority with 39 seats, Liberals 4, Conservatives 32, and Independent 1, out of a total of 76.

Bristol-based city politics has predominated within the Labour group, helping the party adjust to the new conditions. Also the trend to democratic leadership by young councillors assisted unity, strengthened by factors like resistance to the Government, the pleasure of being in control, commitment to job protection and to the legitimate claims of trade unionism. The Conservative experience has been less happy. In Avon's infancy the Conservative leader put his mark heavily upon the administration and on the group. Effective in office, in opposition his leadership worked less well. Resentment was assuaged by the election as leader in 1983 of a woman of more emollient demeanour but suppressed weaknesses appeared. For much of 1985/6 the group seemed confused despite its wealth of experience. The Alliance group was, except for the leader, wholly new to the council in May 1985. Their problems were mainly their paucity, their central position, lack of cohesion and of county experience.

Recent budgets under Labour have generally been of a 'continuation' plus small development variety, exceeding targets and losing grant, with a rising rate burden but avoiding severe confrontation with government.

Political and Professional Leadership

There is truth in the Alliance leader's view that 97 per cent of the budget was made by officers, in the limited senses that the expenditure budget was based on past and current policy and decisions and the variations that marked significant political differences were small parts of the total. The mass of figures and commentaries were produced by officials. But political parties set the pace; their decisions directly affected budget quantities and priorities, and they laid down guidelines and policy strategy.

The 'professional' input surpassed either 'bureaucratic' or 'organisational' ones. It was the professional view that appealed most to the Labour administration since it was closest to their 'service' orientation. Professional standards permeated officer activity most clearly in the case of the Treasurer. His 'professional' terms of reference legitimised his advice and the giving of it, which, with his affability, gave his observations peculiar weight. He was the most political - not partisan - figure on the official side. He constantly attended council and committee meetings, was often referred to; his reports on many budget aspects were frequent; he enjoyed explaining budget problems. He occasionally attended party group meetings and advisory meetings and spoke at public consultations.

The ideas and professional standards of other chief officers helped shape the budget; they considered their staffs' interests and views; their departments had their own histories, frustrations, weaknesses, strengths. Change occurs daily; it may be guided but it shapes the projects for spending, saving or switching expressed in budget forecasts and informs priorities amongst new and old proposals accumulated from various sources. Development might be popular in one department but in another a more managerial ideology overlapped the professional commitment of the director and the mix of factors changes.

Originally Avon was dominated by one party but the 1981 election introduced a competitive two-party system. Party primacy was elevated further by the May 1985 election which created a three-party system with no one party in a majority. The budget could best express the ambitions of the three parties and realise their electoral promises and appeals. It could not be merely a subject of bureaucratic decision-making or of the closed decision-making of a party's inner leadership or of a coterie of official and party leaders. It was constantly debated in the open arena of the council, the committees, and the media. Moreover, final, unpredictable decisions were made by vote in council, in public.

The character of the party leadership contributed to this result. The leader and deputy leader of the Labour group were young, trained in economics and accountancy, hard-working, articulate, coherent and forceful, with parliamentary expectations. The Conservative spokesman on finance was also a university lecturer, like the Alliance leader, himself also a parliamentary candidate, sharp, articulate, dynamic. The officers respected them all and even the Treasurer had no better technical grasp on the budget and the financial implications of county policies than they.

The official/councillor relationship was closest to the ideal - according to the CEO, as set out in paragraph 151 of the Maud report - when Labour was in office. Officials' reports would be criticised in committee or council as severely as politicians of the ruling party felt they deserved. Senior officers went over final drafts with relevant councillors but the reports were theirs, composed by departmental officers in the form approved by chief officers. Agenda setting was shared by officers and politicians, who had the last word. Interaction between the Treasurer, the Chief Executive and leaders of the ruling group was an almost daily occurrence and backbenchers had easy access. These relationships stood upon a shared view of proper roles and on mutual respect, generally, for each other and the county council was a highly effective organisation.

During the subsequent period, February/March 1986, of political confusion and fast developments, there was much scope for officer/councillor stress. Official loyalties to the erstwhile ruling group, now losing control and their budget and to a new prospective joint administration, faltered as their views on new budgetary proposals put forward by the Alliance and Conservatives were publicly elicited by relentless Labour questioning as to how far they had costed the amendments and assessed the likely service consequences. They were deeply embarrassed.

The final stage emerged in March. Repudiating participation in a triangular circulation of committee chairmanships between nominated party 'spokespersons', Labour withdrew into opposition. The likely degree of stability in the Conservative/Alliance dyarchy was debatable and debated. Labour argued that the power sharing scheme so confused the lines of responsibility that officials would be forced into decision-making but the traditions bequeathed by Labour are strong. Moreover, delegations of authority to officers are exceptionally limited.

Anyway, the Labour regime was ultimately provisional; some kind of unanticipated denouement in February was certain. Public party politics ruled and many people influenced decision-making in many, unequal ways. The Labour deputy leader said decisions are made in private before entering the public arena but much of a public nature contributes to the party line that becomes a committee decision, itself subject to council vote before a hostile opposition.

Structures

There is a Resources Coordination (RC) committee, with 48 members under Labour, now 41. It is responsible for the efficient organisation of the council and its committees, for supervising the conduct and coordination of its work and for the allocation of resources. Important sub-committees are Finance and Administration, Personnel, and Land and Buildings. It has special responsibilities for general policies like equal opportunities, economic development and the promotion of computer services. It normally meets nine days before the six-weekly council meeting to consider a wide range of business, much of it pre-digested by sub-committees.

Much business centred on reports by the Treasurer on budgetary developments and national decisions affecting Avon's budget. The committee discussed and confirmed recommendations, or made proposals concerning programme area problems. It familiarised members with a mass of facts and arguments before the crucial council meetings. In the recent more fluid party situation it has facilitated adjustments before the council meeting, even over budget items. It is not a Policy committee. Policy is made in and between the party groups and finalised in council. Other main standing committees are Community Leisure; Education; Planning, Highways and Transport; Public Protection; and Social Services.

Departments are more various and numerous. Education, apparently a vast monolith, has many semi-autonomous decision centres, from schools to the Polytechnic. Community Leisure covers Libraries and Youth and Community services, whilst Public Protection covers Trading Standards, Scientific Services, Emergency Planning, Fire Brigade and Waste Disposal. The departments are headed by Chief Officers of varying status, professional commitments, public images and responsibility. The Chief Executive Officer stands at the point where the political and the administrative intersect and he must obviate collisions, whilst he is also the hub of the wheel of which fellow chief officers form the rim - all in direct relations with him and with each other. There are regular weekly meetings of the twelve chief officers, and smaller informal meetings of those concerned with specific business.

A corporate approach came in with Avon and most chief officers now welcome it. Corporate management as practised in Avon does not smother departmentalism in a diverse organisation. Departments are, in a sense, uninterested in each other; they get on with their own jobs. In times of continuation budgets this is sensible. The CEO has no department as such, merely a staff of ten. With him lies responsibility for central policies like equal opportunities, transcending departmental boundaries but translated into departmental terms.

Policy coordination by officials occurs at all levels as new ideas or needs or social, say demographic, changes surface. At top level the exchange of reports and formal and informal inter-action acquaint chief officers with common problems and departmental issues. It is the politicians', not the CEO's, role to adjudicate the rare persisting disagreement. Joint reports are common but otherwise they emerge from this corporate process as the departmental reports they are. Within this overall scheme, the Treasurer, the Financial Planning Senior Assistant County Treasurer and his staff had special responsibility for preparing the budget.

The Strategy Behind the 1986/7 Budget

There had been a continuation budget the previous year and Labour could contemplate no cuts in 1986/7. Committees were to plan to maintain the current levels of service - an anodyne strategy concealing potential radical changes in, say, educational provision where school populations were markedly fluctuating, as well as implicitly ignoring central government penalties and demands for retrenchment. But development proposals would be judged and ordered in the light of levels of grant penalties, the likely level where rate capping would be incurred and the commitment of the party to the proposal and its desirability in official eyes. Alliance strategy stresses efficiency and defence of 'front line' services. Conservative strategy paid closer attention to government requirements, but would spread the total response over a period of years - despite Labour taunts, they never contemplated cuts of £30-40 million that year to reach the anticipated 'target'.

In June 1985 the Treasurer told the RC committee that zero-base budgeting was a merely theoretical concept. A full zero-based budget exercise in Avon would require at least four years and many extra staff. A limited zero-based review might be planned for 1987/8. He also dismissed cash limiting and warned of the consequences of a continuation budget. He preferred the Target budget - the determination of the ultimate level of spending with regard to the government's Target, with guidelines for each committee, since significant reductions could be found only by a reappraisal of services.

Labour argued that talk of 'strategies' was illusory without figures being put to 'targets' or 'cash limits'. Their continuation budgeting was based on targets - the target set by established services and their development needs. The Conservatives attempted to install a cash limit strategy but only secured a commitment of the council to consider target budgeting next year. A continuation strategy was formally adopted, without requirements on committees to match development proposals with planned savings. It was really a 'low-growth' budget, although the continuation element set the tone. A mass of services were perceived as essential and trust was placed in the numerous people responsible to do their jobs in cost effective ways, subject to diverse checking devices.

Committees were enjoined critically to examine expenditure and income against existing policies, to examine the justification for all expenditure items, to take all relevant matters into account and to judge between their duty to the ratepayers, and their statutory duty to provide services. There was no special machinery to deal with 'cuts' since no demands for such could enter the budgetary process till the last few weeks, when Alliance and Conservative cuts were largely in Labour's development proposals rather than in the 'continuation' budget; otherwise decisions were based on departmental costings under Treasury aegis and finalised in the political area by majority vote.

Labour had to accept an Alliance proposal, backed by the Conservatives, for an additional budget review procedure. Each service committee appointed a five-member budget review sub-committee and officers were to prepare reports identifying areas meriting study. Sub-committees were to meet twice and report to their parent committees before the RC meeting in November, meanwhile the main committees proceeded with their normal budget meetings.

Each sub-committee was to consider the expenditure items in the 1985/6 budget, the 1986/7 development proposals, the statistics comparing Avon with four other counties, and relevant comment by the Audit Commission. The core requirement was to "examine the justification and need for all items of expenditure in the proposed 1986/7 Revenue Budget". The sub-committees achieved little but gave grist to Labour attacks on the competence and good faith of the opposition. Proceedings speedily closed with a motion, carried <u>nem.con.</u>, that all expenditure as set out in the 1985/6 Financial Control budget, the 1986/7 provisional commitments and development proposals was "fully justified". This made the Conservative/Alliance initiative absurd and dangerously raised Labour euphoria.

All, according to their lights, wished to screw benefit from government grant policies. The Treasurer warned of potential grant losses at various levels of expenditure and explained the 'multiplier'. Labour blamed central government for previous grant losses; the Conservatives stressed the absurdity of courting rate rises by marginal growth in spending and blamed Labour ineptitude and obstinacy; the Alliance blamed central meanness and Labour inefficiency.

All welcomed efforts by the departments and the Treasury to maximise aid from such sources as the NHS, the MSC, the TVEI and specific grants like Urban Aid but they appraised keenly the strings attached, the desirability of the programmes and future commitments. The economic development sub-committee made small applications to the European Social Fund for aid.

Techniques

Performance indicators in the sense of comparison of quantified service provision with similarly quantified objectives, or with quantified past performance, are rarely used. The Performance Review sub-committee an off-shoot of the RC Committee, confines itself to seeking cheaper ways of providing given levels of service in selected areas. It can require a chief officer to make a report to the committee but there is difficulty in identifying worthwhile topics to review. Also a financial appraisal working group reports via the Finance and Administration sub-committee to the RC committee. There are reports to the standing committees on Annual Staff Reviews. Committees require reports on the efficiency of services under their jurisdiction. No one monitoring device is 100 per cent effective but there are many bits of machinery for investigation, appraisal and review and the overall impact is massive and continuous.

Creative accountancy has been crucial in exploiting grant and in meeting expenditure requirements. By the end of 1985 it became apparent that grant penalties for 1986/7 would be less severe than those of the two previous years. It was agreed to take £6 million from funds to support 1984/5 expenditure, cutting out the top levels of penalty in 1984/5 and saving about £18 million before closing the books. Because of underspending by £1.9 million in the 1985/6 budget, block grant would rise by £6.4 million. Deferment of expenditure of £1.1 million (to be accounted for in 1986/7) would recoup £2.8 million, but to eliminate the £27 million grant penalty totally in 1985/6 required £10.3 million of which £8.45 million was identified by December (£4.45 million in balances like the Fire Hydrant Fund). £1 million could be saved on spending in 1985/6 by capitalisation of certain repair and maintenance work, but this should be a one-off expedient to avoid reduced future capital financing.

Assumptions about the proper level of balances and likely inflation rates were elastic. Departments were allowed to sell assets but only exceptionally were proceeds available for re-use by the department; there was no general policy of asset selling. The contingency funds gave considerable marginal flexibility. The Conservatives and Alliance reduced Labour figures for both inflation and general contingencies.

Ironically, in view of Conservative strictures on Labour's use of the general contingency fund, immediately after their own budget was passed the Conservatives and Alliance were forced by Labour and rebel votes from their own parties to raid the 1986/7 contingency fund on behalf of two protesting colleges of further education.

The Process of Making the 1986/7 Budget

In February 1985, Labour, with a majority of two, passed a 'continuation' budget requiring an increase in the precept of 6.5 per cent over 1984/5, and losing £28 million of grant. Labour claimed that if the Tories won the May county elections they would reduce the 1986/7 budget by £30 million, cutting services by 10 per cent and county jobs by 5000. Conservatives blamed the rate rise on bad management and attacked the use of £22 million of 'financing adjustments'. The Liberals produced an alternative budget incorporating nearly £1 million of detailed small savings. This was defeated by Labour, the Conservatives abstaining. At the March RC committee meeting the Treasurer argued that the Public Expenditure White Paper (Cmnd 9428) was as severe as its predecessor. Before accounting adjustments the Council's 1985/6 budget exceeded its expenditure target by over 10 per cent, and its GREA by nearly 8 per cent. The scope for financing adjustments in 1986/7 would be much reduced. The financial year 1986/7 would be particularly difficult.

At the county elections Labour lost its majority but remained the largest single party. The new council comprised 37 Labour, 31 Conservative and 8 Alliance members. At the annual council meeting Labour proposed committee memberships which, with the **ex officio** votes gave Labour the chairmanships and a majority on every committee. After an Alliance attempt to get 'balanced' committees, the adjourned meeting passed the original Labour motion, with the Alliance opposing and Conservatives abstaining.

Labour exercised confidently the mandate yielded them. However, they were conscious that on budget day they would be in a minority. Three different budgets might be proposed and all voted down, so each party needed a provisional fall-back position. Alliance members felt they gravitated generally towards the Labour rather than the Conservative ethos. However, it was doubtful if Labour councillors would support budget day compromises additional to those they had already accepted by not demanding more development.

Labour held the initiative; officials and the other parties had to react to them. As February approached it seemed decreasingly possible for the Alliance and Conservatives radically to influence the outcome. The Alliance painstakingly prepared amendments costed with official aid, for ultimate disclosure as a package, meantime underlining its differences from spendthrift Labour and tight-fisted Conservatives. Conservatives seemed to lack any clear budget strategy but maybe Labour jibes were overdone. Finally, the Conservatives produced amendments claimed to constitute a fully costed alternative budget, expressing moderate Conservative policies. Labour's rubbishing of tentative Alliance suggestions left diminishing room for an eventual Alliance/Labour deal and greater scope for an Alliance/Conservative rapprochement.

Officials' work fell into three parts. Firstly, departmental officers produced figures summarising the effects of continuing present service levels, plus changes as agreed by departments and committees and as

31

envisaged by the current budget. These were produced during the summer and autumn to meet the requirements of the committee cycles. The work depended on many people in many institutions, such as schools and colleges, as well as in the central departments. Secondly, the fairly routine work of the Treasury budget officials, checking the preparation of estimates by departments, going through the detailed 1985/6 budget line by line, questioning divergencies and keeping the process up to schedule.

The third element comprised the Treasurer and the Financial Planning section. Besides attending to the machinery on the estimating and expenditure side, their main concern was with the macro expenditure and funding features – alerting the parties to possible strategies, their requirements and implications, in the light of unfolding government policy; to the sorts of general decisions to be made and by what point in the process; and the shape assumed by the budget as time passed; – all within a very close relationship with the ruling party's leaders and a more distant but continuous contact with committees and council.

In June 1985 the RC committee adopted a policy of continuation budgeting despite the Treasurer's warning that the implied total of £365 million would almost certainly involve the complete loss of block grant, rate increases of the order of 55 per cent and rate-capping in 1987/8. Nationally there would be a real terms reduction in RSG, particularly affecting Avon, being above target and because of a grant switch to ex-metropolitan areas. In July the Treasurer reported on the implications of the government's consultation paper on the 1986/7 RSG settlement. In place of Targets and Holdback, restraint would be secured by GREAs and steeper grant related penalties (see Chapter 1); the marginal cost to the authority of additional spending could be significantly increased (the reverse occurred). However, neither GREA nor Avon's multiplier were yet known. With expenditure at £365 million, a range of possible values for the multiplier and GREA produced a variation in grant from £0 to £80 million. Investigations into possible financing adjustments were afoot to maximise grant receipts for the financial years 1984/5, 1985/6 and 1986/7, should penalty charges affect relative grant losses between them. Moreover, the interim 'capping' arrangements to cover the changes in grant distribution mechanisms would affect Avon's optimum financial position. Work had started on the identification and costing of develpment proposals and proposed new capital projects, together with planned savings for 1986/7 and on an up-date of each committee's financial commitments. These matters were reported to the committees in September and a report made to the RC committee in October.

Masses of information and comment were considered at the RC meeting in November. The Treasurer summarised the provisional Estimates, which, with higher inflation forecasts than previously and such items as an extra £1 million towards an increased contribution to the Advanced Further Education Pool, came to £55 million or 17 per cent above the 1985/6 figure, yet only £4.8 million was due to new development proposals. Whilst the provisional GREA of £340 million had been announced, the multiplier and RSG settlement were still unknown. The rate increase could range from 25 per cent to 60 per cent, and rate capping in 1987/8 was a distinct possibility. The Labour leader agreed with the Alliance leader that capital allocations were unlikely to match those proposed in the budget so the revenue implications would be less and allowance for this should be made in committee budgets.

The Conservatives urged that committees should propose savings to offset development but Labour stuck to their policy. During November, the service committees having been allowed to go ahead, the resource sub-committees – Land, Finance and Personnel – finalised, so far as they could, the resource implications.

In November 1985 a Conservative councillor died. On December 19 the Conservative leader resigned. The Labour group now equalled the Conservatives and Alliance combined and enjoyed the chairman's casting vote. Both by-elections (in seats unwinnable by Labour) were announced for February 13, 1986. At the RC committee meeting on January 2 Labour used its majority to change budget day from February 27 to February 12, the day before the elections. For Labour a moral blow for jobs and services, this coup was to the Conservatives and Alliance iniquitous. The Alliance leader closely studied Standing Orders, consulted lawyers and evolved a counter-strategy. On January 6 the Conservative group elected as their new leader a moderate young ex-Liberal parliamentary candidate, elected to the council in May. On January 9 the county council adopted the new budget time-table on the Labour Chairman's casting vote.

The Treasurer updated spending figures and provided RSG information for the RC committee in January. Avon had benefitted. by a better multiplier, 1.08, than anticipated, though ungenerously treated. Seemingly the government had based its attitude to Avon on the original 1985/6 budget, now drastically revised. Grant was likely to be £62.3 million and the rate precept increase 32.2 per cent. Return of grant in respect of 1984/5 would increase working balances in 1986/7 to £46 million, although much of it was earmarked. Labour attacked the settlement as politically biased.

At the budget meeting on February 12 Conservative and Alliance lists of amendments were defeated. Labour's budget (trimmed to avoid rate-capping) and a rate rise of 27 per cent were adopted on the Chairman's casting vote. Next day the by-elections returned one Conservative and one additional Liberal member, putting Labour back in a minority. At the requisition of the Alliance leader, the Labour council Chairman called an extraordinary council meeting for February 24. There the RC committee membership was reconstituted putting Labour in a clear minority. Next day the Labour councillors reported to Avon Labour party and got unanimous support for their decision to adandon all chairmanships from noon the following day, refusing to take responsibility for administering their opponents' 'cuts' budget.

Much anti-Labour media attention was focused on the crisis. The Alliance leader was indefatigable; the significance of the Alliance/Conservative 'cuts' was acrimoniously debated. On February 28 the RC committee met, elected a Conservative chairman and adopted agreed Alliance/Conservative amendments to the Labour budget, including a larger, by £7 million, transfer from balances; raised charges for services such as home care; reductions in Labour development proposals such as nursery classes; made cuts in existing services like reductions in library opening hours and economising reorganisations like changes in distribution methods for the county's monthly bulletin. The proposed savings came to £5.3 million and the rate precept would rise by 21.4 per cent.

The monthly Alliance support group meeting on March 3 rapturously acclaimed their leader. Previous efforts to distance the Alliance from Conservatives, on ideological and electoral grounds, were forgotten. The leader ironically apologised for carrying out so completely the behests of the county Assembly in securing economy without cuts. The Conservatives had moved close to the Alliance position; Labour was shown up as dogmatic and wasteful. Budget co-operation implied a new Conservative willingness to help the Alliance secure 'balanced' committees and rotating chairmanships, promising them a continuing share in power. At his request the meeting ended with a standing ovation for the leader so that it could be reported in the press, truthfully.

The new council budget meeting opened on March 7, closing on March 11. Labour sought to cancel the Conservative/Alliance amendments. As at the RC committee, where the Alliance leader had confessed to his support group that the Labour Opposition was "phenomenal" and "made mincemeat" of the Alliance/Conservative propositions, Labour vigorously attacked - amendments were ill-prepared, their effects little understood, and betrayed Alliance promises. The new budget was passed. The Alliance and Conservatives had reduced their reductions to £4.7 million after the RC meeting but a windfall increase of central grant by £9 million meantime enabled them to reduce the rate rise to 17.9 per cent.

External Factors

Central government impact on the resource side was enormous; it largely made the difference between rate rises of 60 per cent and 17 per cent. Despite application and intelligence it was impossible to predict the resource outcome. Government policy importantly affected the spending. It could not be ignored, nor could it be allowed to dictate overall expenditure levels nor preferences between services. The abolition of targets sharply reduced gains to be made from marginal cuts in 1986/7 but increased the rewards from manipulating previous budgets.

Relations with the DoE were exiguous. The Treasurer has rarely visited it. Labour and Alliance viewed the DoE and especially the local Conservative MP, Waldegrave, Minister at the DoE, as two-faced and called on Conservative councillors to support 'Avon' against 'their' government and local MPs. Altogether, relationships between local and central departments were formal and distant. Avon's non-membership of the Association of County Councils was inconvenient to officers; the county tended to be late in discovering matters passing between government and the ACC, and although professional meetings helped recoup information, input was hindered.

The most influential local interests were the party organisations. The August meeting of the Avon Labour party legitimised the priorities urged by committee chairmen amongst development proposals and accepted a demand from an NUT representative for a commitment (until the Alliance took it out) to spend £2 million on converting fixed term teacher contracts to permanent ones. Also for a confused half hour a maverick vote committed the dismayed leadership to a deficit, no cuts, no rates-rise budget. The Alliance County Assembly in November influenced the priorities (roughly according with the leader's desires) in their list of amendments - making cuts, supporting developments, or raising charges - and legitimised the ultimate product. On specific items the monthly support group made decisions, for example on a subvention to the Bournemouth Symphony Orchestra if it transferred to Bristol.

Identification of specific consequences of group and consumer pressure is otherwise difficult. Pressure there was - demonstrations by trade unions and voluntary organisations, petitions, leaflets and letters distributed amongst councillors, sometimes as part of their agenda documents. Demands by governors of two colleges of further education had patent success, because they were brought to a vote in the council and helped by rebels from both ruling parties. The media had no direct influence on specific budget items but their reports and comments were usually tendentious, superficial and anti-Labour.

'Ratepayers' were not mobilised except in so far as the Conservatives could be seen as their special representatives. A statutory meeting of council leaders, plus officers, with representative commercial and industrial ratepayers took place in October The business interests argued that higher rates caused unemployment by discouraging business enterprise and raising costs. They attacked the continuation strategy and pleaded for a zero-based budget process, which was rejected by the Treasurer. The Labour leaders said their no-cuts commitment was endorsed at the polls; claimed that rate rises were less likely than budget cuts to reduce employment; appealed to the interests to specify cuts; argued that transfer of the burden to rates was government policy and invited them to accompany council representatives to discuss the issues with Avon's MPs, especially Waldegrave. Both sides reserved their positions until the next meeting, preceding budget day, which was similarly unrewarding. The business consultees legitimised Conservative arguments and represented powerful forces in society and government.

A meeting was also held between party leaders and representatives of trade unions having members employed by the county council. The Tory leader's suggestions of expenditure cuts of £10 million and a job loss not exceeding 50 were frequently to haunt her, courtesy of the Labour leaders. The Alliance leader proclaimed his determination to protect 'front-line' services, with but marginal expenditure reductions and accepted significant rate rises.

To complement the statutory business consultation, Labour repeated its policy of consultations with employees and public. The cost of these meetings, their poor attendances and the total disregard of their suggestions, excited Conservative derision, countered by Labour's riposte that the statutory consultations and the budget review exercise, were as wasteful of public money and that people did not attend because they welcomed Labour policy.

The 'electorate' was often in politicians' minds as a body of people to whom pledges had been made, who had expectations of the parties, as a group whose diverse interests had to be tended and to whom electoral appeals must be made. In the event, by May 1986, budget-making had receded into the past and its circumstances left no clear picture of who was responsible for what. After all, the Budget was not a Labour one – or was it, in some respects? The percentage rise in rate precept was less than in neighbouring Alliance-run Somerset. The Bristol District election results were muted, giving Labour a majority, just. The impact of Avon's budget in a maelstrom of national politics and multitudinous local issues, scares, problems, misgivings, scandals and confusion is hard to discern.

Conclusion

The final budget was a triumph for the Alliance, in its content and in its balance of continuity, change and development and also in the mode of politics that produced it. This, according to Alliance lights, was how it **should** have happened. To Labour it was clear there was no way it should have happened. For the Conservatives the outcome was an odd summary of an odd year for them, so maybe it was appropriate. Yet did Labour lose? The overall shape of the expenditure budget in March 1986 was very like its provisional shape in June 1985. Some eagerly sought improvements, as in welfare rights publicity, or in equal opportunities, would be harder to implement but little substantial had been cut, some desirable new benefits remained in place, one large cut was quietly acceptable. The budget did little to advance a fairer society but neither services nor burdens on the poor and weak were outrageously worsened. To a great extent, despite the damaging influence of central government, local institutions and priorities were maintained.

As an administrative device, the budget process had systematised change, queried the established, clarified the rationales, helped in re-allocation and organisational change but brought all this into a management framework, flexible, adaptable, yet supportive and firm. Officials had coped confidently and effectively with the crisis demands of February/March and were learning to live with the new 'hung' conditions and power relationships. Resources had been identified and matched to planned expenditure. Priorities had been evaluated in the light of demands on resources and the ultimate product in the light of policy goals. Nobody was in much doubt that the lowering of development sights and the imposition of new burdens was caused overwhelmingly by the economic theories and policies of central government. The expenditure side of budget-making had been a model of rationality compared with the strange kettle of fish, the crystal ball gazing, the apparent arbitrariness and caprice on the resources side. All concerned turned to the 1987/8 budget with undimmed zest.

3. Lancashire County Council

JOHN BARLOW

Introduction

On 2 May 1985 the Labour Party lost overall control of Lancashire County Council in the local elections. Needing to hang on to 50 of its 53 seats for an overall majority it managed to win only 48 seats, but with the Liberals increasing their representation from seven to nine seats and the Conservatives winning only 42 seats overall, no single party could control the County Council. In common with many other shire counties Lancashire had become a 'hung' authority - or a 'balanced' authority as the Liberals preferred to call it. The first County Council meeting after the election ended in stalemate after eleven hours of debate, during which time a Chairman of the County Council had been elected but the Chairmanships of all the committees were still vacant. The lack of an administration at that time suggested that there would be a high degree of uncertainty and potential conflict surrounding the budget process. The budget process would provide one of the major tests of the political management of a 'hung' council and is a key theme of this paper. This paper analyses the Lancashire budget process in three sections, the first sets the political and organisational context of the County Council, the second outlines the budget process itself, and the third section makes an initial analysis of the 1986/7 budget outcome and the processes used to produce the budget.

Context

Lancashire is the fourth largest shire county in England, measured in population terms (1.382 million) and contains a mixture of urban and rural communities, incorporating the textile towns of central and east Lancashire; the seaside resorts of Blackpool, Morecambe and Lytham St.Annes; the market towns of west Lancashire; the fells in the north-east of the County as well as two new towns (Central Lancashire, Skelmersdale). Unemployment in the county in recent years has tended to be slightly above the national average. Evidence of Lancashire's needs is given by its Grant Related Expenditure assessment, which at £414.11 per head of population is the third highest amongst shire counties. Lancashire also experiences a relatively low level of resources in terms of rateable values, so that in 1986/7 56.7 per cent of its rate and grant-borne expenditure will be financed by specific block grants, compared with an average of 36.8 per cent for the shire counties.

The County Council was controlled by the Conservative Party from 1974 to 1981. However, in the May 1981 elections the Labour Party gained outright control of the authority, increasing their numbers on the County Council from 12 to 53. Labour control of the authority between 1981 and 1985 led to a number of significant policy changes and to understand the current budget decisions it is helpful to look at the broad direction of Labour's budgets in that period. It is also necessary to say something about the organisational structure of the authority and the relationship between officers and members. Finally, to set the context for the 1986/7 budget process it is necessary to examine the changes that have taken place in the political management of the authority.

(a) Labour Party Control 1981-1985

"Labour's aim is to protect and improve all County Services. Our community needs jobs, our children need the best education and the elderly and vulnerable need care". Labour Party Manifesto 1985.

Between 1981 and 1985 the Labour Party was committed to the protection and improvement of many of the County's services at a time when government grants were being reduced in real terms. In this period a number of policies were developed which represented a marked shift away from the policies of the previous Conservative administrations. An early decision was taken to increase spending in the 1981/2 financial year and to do so a supplementary rate of 18p was levied in October 1981. A high priority has been given to job creation and Lancashire Enterprises Limited was created in 1982 as a development agency funded with the proceeds of the 'free twopence' under S137 of the Local Government Act 1972.

Education and Social Services have received a high priority, notably in the development of nursery classes and day nurseries. Expenditure on education has been expanded, so that Lancashire has climbed from being near the bottom of the expenditure 'league tables' to around the national average. The Youth Service has been expanded and School Meals have continued to be subsidised by keeping down prices. In Social Services the Home Help service has expanded and charges were reduced from £1.20 to 80p. Staffing in residential accommodation has been improved and various forms of community care have been developed, notably sheltered housing and access to day centres. Another notable area of policy has been the development of a county-wide public transport policy which has resulted in a considerable expansion in subsidy and the development of a number of marketing strategies to encourage increased use of public transport. The County Council actively opposed the Transport Bill proposing the deregulation of bus services.

An analysis of the four Labour budgets reveals that the rate precept has increased by 53.1 per cent over this period and that rate and grant-borne expenditure has risen by 24.4 per cent. However, after inflation has been taken into account, it can be shown that expenditure in real terms has remained constant. When Grant Related Expenditure Assessments (GREAs) were introduced it became an aim of the authority to increase spending up to GREA which was achieved in 1982/3 and 1983/4. However, in 1984/5 and 1985/6 spending fell below GREA influenced by the setting of expenditure 'targets' which were considerably below GREA. The severity of grant penalties encouraged the authority to set expenditure at around Target, thus incurring some penalties but not at the level that would have been incurred if GREA had been attained.

The management of the budget process under Labour control was very much the responsibility of the Leader of the Council and the Chairman of the Finance Sub-Committee, supported closely by the Chief Executive and the Treasurer. The Leader could not act, however, without the support of the Labour Group or the Policy Sub-Committee of that Group, which is composed of representatives of the Lancashire Labour Party, Committee Chairmen and party officers. The Policy Sub-Committee meets at every stage of the budget process to determine strategy and its recommendations are put to the Group for approval. The Labour members of each committee meet prior to Council Committees and a high degree of voting discipline is established.

(b) The Organisation of the County Council

The Committee and departmental structures of the authority are set out in Figure 3.1. The Service Committees and the chief officers that support them, enjoy a high degree of service autonomy. Although the Policy and Resources Committee receives the reports of the service committees it does not attempt to intervene extensively in the decisions of those committees. There is a Chief Executive and Town Clerk whose department provides a wide range of legal, administrative and personnel services to all other departments as well as servicing committees. The Chief Executive is not a Bains-style manager but is nevertheless very much at the centre of the organisation and consequently at the centre of the budget process. Chief Officers' reports to Committee are vetted by the Chief Executive, with a view to giving support to those officers rather than exercising a restraint over their professional judgement. Budget reports, for example the 'growth' and 'reductions' lists, would be scrutinised by both the Chief Executive and the Treasurer to ensure that there were no legal or financial problems. A more subtle but perhaps more important role of the Chief Executive is in conveying the right political signals to fellow chief officers, for he is at the centre of the relationships between party leaders and the officers. The Management Team does not have a high profile in the authority and is not central in the budget process but is used by the Chief Executive to ensure that chief officers are aware of the political culture in which they are operating. Chief Officers have developed their own relationships with their respective committee chairmen, so the Chief Executive is by no means the only source of information on political values and aspirations. The role of officers and their relationship with councillors has become more critical since May 1985 when many of the 'rules of the game' have had to be rewritten.

Committee Structure

Policy and Resources - Finance   )
                             - Land and Buildings) Sub-Committees
                             - Personnel

       Education
       Fire Service and Public Protection
       Highways and Transportation
       Library and Leisure
       Planning, Industrial Development and Tourism
       Police
       Social Services

Departmental Structure

       Chief Executive and Town Clerk
       Chief Education Officer
       Chief Fire Officer
       County Surveyor
       County Librarian
       County Planning Officer
       Chief Constable
       Director of Social Services
       Director of Property Services
       County Treasurer

Figure 3.1   Organisation in Lancashire

(c) Managing the 'Hung' Council

The key questions after the May elections centred on who the Liberals would put into power and whether there would be a formal condition between the Liberals and one of the major parties. The Liberal strategy finally became clear at the first chaotic County Council meeting in May. First, there would be no formal coalition with either party. Second, they wished to redefine the role of the Chairman of the County Council, making the post rather like that of a mayor, quite separate from the Leadership of the County Council. Third, they produced a shopping list of 67 Liberal policies which they circulated to the other two parties to see which party was more likely to support a majority of them. Consequently the Liberals decided to support the Labour lists for Chairmanships and Vice-Chairmanships of committees but to support the Conservative nominations for Chairman and Vice-Chairman of the County Council.

The Labour view was that once a Conservative had been voted into the position of Chairman they would not be able to form an administration and withdrew their nominations for the committee chairmanships. Consequently it became impossible to appoint Chairmen at that meeting. Subsequently however, the Labour Party accepted the Chairmanships and effectively formed an administration, though without being able to control the committees.

The composition of committees was altered, numbers being agreed according to proportional representation. The Liberals and Conservatives

nominated spokesmen on each committee who were to be given the right
to briefings by officers before committee meetings in the same way
that the Chairman was. By the time the budget cycles of meetings started
the new arrangements had become established but clearly the budget
would represent a major test of how a 'hung' council could operate.

The Budget Process

The formal budget process in 1985/6 for implementation in 1986/7 was
broadly similar to previous years, except where the lack of overall
political control has necessitated certain changes. The key differences
were in the preparation of the budget estimates by officers and their
relationships with the Chairmen and opposition spokesmen and the
introduction of a separate budget meeting of the County Council. The
timetable of the key events in the budget cycles are set out in
Figure 3.2.
The first stage of the process is the production of the Continuation
Estimates for each committee. These estimates represent the baseline
from which the budget for next year is constructed but they are not
simply last year's estimates repriced to take account of inflation.
The assumptions that are built into the Continuation Estimates reflect
the policies of the authority and consequently could reflect many items
of growth and decline in expenditure. The Treasurer wrote to all
departments outlining the basis on which the Continuation Estimates
would be constructed and advising them of price changes that had taken
place. The Continuation Estimate was derived in the following way:

(1) Original Estimate – Reductions   = Base Estimate for
    1985/6   1986/7

(2) Base Estimate + Increased + Committed   = Continuation
    1986/7   Costs   Growth   Estimates

The 'reductions' column incorporates non-recurring items of
expenditure, premises or services taken out of use and reduced
expenditure arising from falling demands for expenditure. So falling
school rolls would involve a reduction in expenditure, based on the
county's policy on pupil-teacher ratios. 'Committed Growth'
incorporates, for example, the full year cost of staff appointed in
the current year, increased demands on services (within existing
policies) or staffing costs associated with the opening of new
premises.
The preparation of these Estimates is carried out by the departments
and scrutinised by the Treasurer's Department. Inevitably there is
always scope to interpret items of expenditure in different ways,
although the Treasurer's Department sets out the rules very clearly.
The production of the Estimates, carried out by third and fourth tier
officers, is characterised more by co-operation with the Treasurer's
Department than by conflict. This work was eventually completed in
early December. Further impetus was given to its work by the Finance
Sub-Committee at its meeting in October which considered a report by
the Treasurer, which attempted to sketch out the likely financial
parameters that the authority would face. In his report the Treasurer
attempted to estimate the likely effect on the rate precept for 1986/7
of spending at the level of the Continuation Estimate under different
assumptions of the level of RSG. The 'optimistic' assumption of RSG

1985

May   Elections. Labour lose control.
                       Labour 48, Conservatives 42, Liberals 9

June   Liberals support Conservatives to elect a
                       Conservative as Chairman of County Council

August (15th)   Treasurer writes to Departments setting out the
                       basis for drawing up Continuation Estimates for
                       1986/7

October (10th)   Finance Sub-Committee:

                       1. Notes Treasurer's forecast of the financial
                          situation

                       2. Instructs committees to produce illustrative
                          lists of uncommitted growth projects and
                          possible reduction - of 5% of continuation
                          estimates in both cases. (These lists prepared
                          in consultation with Labour Chairmen).

December   Estimates, growth and reductons list are complete
                       and made available to opposition spokesmen

                       RSG becomes known

1986

January (15th)   Special Finance Sub-Committee meeting:

                       1. Examines revised lists for 1985/86, Capital
                          Programme Continuation Estimates and
                          Growth/Reductions lists

                       2. Aims to restrict 1985/6 expenditure to target

                       3. Asks the spending committees to contain their
                          requests for allocation to the level of
                          continuation estimates

                       Spending committees consider their estimates and
                       their growth and reduction lists

February (6th)   Finance Sub-Committee

                       Recommends a rate precept

         (20th)   Policy and Resources Committee

March (6th)   County Council - Special Budget Meeting

Figure 3.2 Lancashire County Council Budget Process 1986/7

implied a rate increase of 29.7p (18.7 per cent), while the 'pessimistic' assumption of grant implied a 45p increase (28.4 per cent). The Leader of the Labour Group stated her party's commitment to preserving services and jobs. Spokesmen for the Conservative and Liberal groups supported this statement. The Sub-Committee instructed Chief Officers to prepare, in consultation with Chairmen, lists of costed options for 'policy changes' in 1986/7 for both (a) possible reductions from the Continuation Estimates of 5 per cent and (b) top priority uncommitted growth proposals up to 5 per cent of the continuation estimates. The production of such 'growth' and 'cuts' lists has been standard practice for some years.

At this stage of the process the lack of overall political control resulted in a significant deviation from past practice. The resolution of the Finance Sub-Committee stated that these lists should be prepared in consultation with Chairmen, which has been the standard practice in the past when one party has been in control of the authority. However, the Liberals moved an amendment to this resolution at the County Council meeting on 31 October that the spokesmen of the other groups should be consulted as well as the Chairmen. The amendment was approved unanimously. Formally, Chief Officers produced the lists which were then made available to the Chairmen and then subsequently to the relevant opposition spokesmen, in mid-December. Each party was invited to discuss these lists with the appropriate Chief Officer and also to put up its own options which could be considered by the Finance Sub-Committee and the appropriate service committee.

From mid-December onwards the budget process gained momentum in the light of the 'policy changes' lists and the announcement of RSG. The political parties began to develop their detailed budget strategies in readiness for the cycle of budget meetings which commenced with the special meeting of the Finance Sub-Committee on 15 January 1986. As this cycle of meetings progressed these strategies became clearer but in the first instance there was greater pressure on the Labour Party to produce options by virtue of their holding the Chairmanships. Consequently at each meeting the Chairman would produce a set of proposals which had been agreed by the Labour Group.

At the Finance Sub-Committee on 15 January 1986 the financial parameters were set out in the Treasurer's report which took account of the capital programme for 1986/7, the latest revised revenue estimates for 1985/6 and the implication of revenue expenditure proposals for 1986/7 on the County precept, after allowing for government grants. The Treasurer estimated that if the authority chose to spend at the level of continuation estimates then a rate precept of 204.71p would have to be levied which represented a 46.21p increase (29.2 per cent). The key proposal from the Chairman was that the spending committees should be instructed to aim for a Continuation Estimate level of spending. Items of uncommitted growth would have to be balanced by reductions elsewhere. A Conservative amendment proposing a £6 million reduction in these provisional allocations was defeated. At this stage some growth was allocated to Social Services, to set up a welfare rights service for items 3-7 on their growth list.

To prepare the way for setting the rate for 1986/7 the Sub-Committee took an important decision in principle relating to the 1985/6 estimates. The Treasurer's report had indicated that the authority was projected to spend more than had originally been budgeted for in 1985/6. (Table 3.1 below).

Table 3.1
BUDGET 1985/6

	Original Estimates (£'000)	Revised Estimates (£'000)
EXPENDITURE	582,445	587,095
Rates	226,055	227,307
Specific Grants	67,000	65,243
RSG	280,570	277,280
	573,625	569,830
Appropriation for Balances	-8,820	-17,265
Balance at 31/3/86	14,685	12,170
Excess Expenditure over 'Target'	5,098 (1%)	7,442 (1.5%)
Grant Penalties	8,787	13,601

On this estimate the authority would be 1.5 per cent above Target and would incur £5 million more in grant penalties than had originally been anticipated in setting the budget. The Sub-Committee decided to reduce expenditure in 1985/6 to the level of the Government's expenditure target and to do so by changes in the "financial and accounting policies and practices" of the authority. If the Target were to be met then there would be some £31 million in balances at the end of March 1986. A key factor in developing this strategy was the less punitive grant regime for 1986/7 in comparison to 1985/6, i.e. it made sense to avoid heavy penalties in 1985/6 by transferring some items of expenditure into 1986/7.

The January cycle of committee meetings dealt with the detailed budget proposals for each service. The Finance Sub-Committee had set an expenditure guideline but within that guideline each committee was free to determine its own priorities. At each committee the Labour Chairmen presented their proposals for growth and reductions, taken from the lists prepared by the officers. Two things became clear as this cycle of meetings progressed. First, that many of the committees breached the expenditure guideline by incorporating growth items which were not totally compensated for by reductions and second, that there was a wide measure of agreement with the lists produced by the Chairmen. The number of amendments proposed by the Conservatives and Liberals were few and amounted to very marginal changes in expenditure.

New growth was being built into the estimates of all committees and was justified in each case for a specific reason. For example, growth items of £55,000 were approved in Libraries and Leisure to support the arts to compensate for the abolition of the Metropolitan County Councils. In the Fire and Public Protection Committee the Chairman argued that essential new staff needed in the County Analyst's department should not be funded by cuts in the Fire Service. On these issues the Liberals supported Labour to defeat Conservative opposition to breaches of the 'no growth' guideline. Net growth had already been accepted in Social Services for the operation of a welfare rights service and to allow the committee to have the benefit of a windfall gain resulting from a change in the DHSS's rules governing private nursing homes. Growth was accepted in the Planning, Industrial Development and Tourism Committee to expand tourism promotion and in the Education Committee to allow for the development of a curriculum-led staffing policy.

Party political disagreements were few. The Liberals were successful in making some amendments to the budget proposals e.g. the introduction of a trailer library and additional expenditure on highway maintenance (funded by leasing vehicle and plant replacement). On these issues the Labour Party supported the Liberals and received their support on a number of Labour proposals. The single issue which did provoke overt party political conflict was on the level of charges for the Home Help service. The Conservatives proposed an increase of 20p from 80p to £1 in order to expand the service. This amendment was supported by the Liberals but strongly opposed by the Labour Group who defeated it on the casting vote of the Chairman. (Two Conservatives were absent from the Committee).

The final phase of the budget process commenced with the Finance Sub-Committee meeting on 7 February at which the Chairman presented his proposals for the rate precept in the light of the expenditure decisions of the service committees. In previous years it would have been possible to state precisely what the rate precept would be as overall political control would ensure that the Finance Sub-Committee's recommendation would go through Policy and Resources Committee and full council. However, no such certainty prevailed in 1986 particularly as the Liberals did not reveal their hand at this meeting and also because the Labour Party enjoyed a majority in both Finance and Policy and Resources which they did not have at the budget meeting of the County Council.

The Chairman's proposal was to accept the expenditure plans of each committee, despite the Finance Sub-Committee's guideline being breached (n.b. the Finance Sub-Committee's budget also incorporated net growth). That level of spending implied a rate increase of 51.2p which was clearly unacceptable, so to maintain expenditure and at the same time bring down the rate precept two financial decisions had to be made. First, to reduce the budgeted expenditure by making changes to the financial and accounting policies and practices of the authority. These changes reduced expenditure by £11 million. Second, to appropriate some £10.2 million from balances, a decision which was predicated on the achievement of reducing 1985/6 expenditure to the level of Target. The Conservatives moved an amendment, proposing that a larger sum be taken from balances (£16.6 million). The effect on the rate precept of these two proposals was a 30p increase from Labour (+18.9 per cent) and a 25.5p increase from the Conservatives (+16.1 per cent).

The Conservative argument centred on the decision to achieve target in 1985/6, suggesting that Labour had taken more from the ratepayers than they had needed in 1985/6 and therefore the ratepayer should benefit in 1986/7. The Conservative spokesman also argued that the figures for 1985/6 were too pessimistic and therefore more could be safely taken from balances than Labour were proposing. The Liberals chose not to present their own preferred option but voted against both the Conservative and Labour proposals. Consequently the Conservative amendment was defeated but the Labour proposal was passed on the casting vote of the Chairman.

A week later at the Policy and Resources Committee the Labour proposals were approved with one modification. The Conservatives again put their amendment to raise Home Help charges to £1 and were supported by the Liberals but defeated by Labour opposition. The Labour Group then proposed the extension of the service wanted by the other parties but at the existing charge of 80p. This amendment was supported by the Liberals and an extra £170,000 built into the budget. The Liberal Group did not put forward any amendments on the rate precept despite having issued a press release indicating that they thought a 28p increase was desirable.

By the time the County Council met on 6 March to approve the budget the rules of the game had been changed by the Government's announcement that extra grant would be available which meant an extra £3.2 million for Lancashire. Consequently in the days leading up to the County Council meeting the parties were forced to revise their estimates of the rate precept. The Policy and Resources Committee resolution recommending a 30p increase was the substantive proposal which was put by the Chairman of Finance in his report to the Council. Three amendments were then put to the Chairman of the County Council: (a) Conservative - 25p, (b) Liberal - 25.5p, and (c) Labour 27p. The extra RSG had produced a shift in the position of each party as follows;

Labour from + 30p   to   + 27p

Liberals from + 28p   to   + 25.5p

Conservatives from + 25.5p to   + 25p

The Chairman took the amendments in ascending order. The Conservative amendment was defeated by Labour and Liberal opposition (41 votes for, 57 against). The Liberal amendment was then put and supported by the Conservatives, being passed by 50 votes to 48. The Labour amendment was then defeated. So the rate precept approved by the County Council was 184p, an increase of 25.5p or 16.1 per cent.

To sum up, although the final rate precept was set by the Liberals and Conservatives, the Labour Party had managed to get through virtually all their spending proposals set out in committees in January. Consequently, to fail to get their rate recommendation through was not such a setback as to warrant resigning from the Chairmanships. At the same time there was broad acceptance of most of the Labour proposals by the other two parties and the differences between them in the final analysis came down to judgements about the use of balances. The existence of this consensus is analysed in the next section.

Analysis

Any analysis of Lancashire's budget for 1986/7 must start from a recognition that it is a growth budget, however small that growth might be in real terms. Rate and grant-borne expenditure rose by 10 per cent and the precept by 16.1 per cent, both of which were the largest increases since 1982/3. Among County Councils Lancashire ranks as the seventh highest increase in expenditure, although its rate increase was below average (18 per cent). Growth was built into the continuation estimates (£21 million) and uncommitted growth of £3.4 million was incorporated into the budget.

The description of the budget process in the previous section throws up a number if interesting issues, however space constraints necessarily limit the discussion here to two of them. First, the degree of agreement across the political parties deserves comment, particularly after the seeming impasse of the first County Council meeting. Second, Lancashire's budget process would appear to be a rather traditional incremental one. Some assessment of how well it performs is necessary if we are to learn from these case studies.

In the final analysis the difference between the three parties' budget proposals comes down to what they were prepared to leave in balances rather than disagreements about expenditure proposals. Such congruence was achieved without there being any formal coalitions or informal deals. The Liberals have aimed to establish their independence from the other two parties. Their support for Labour to take the committee chairmanships, based as it was on Labour's response to the Liberal's policy 'shopping list', suggested that there would be a degree of support for Labour budget proposals. The Labour Group, in turn, is opposed to 'backroom deals' with other parties, so there was no attempt to sit down with the Liberals to develop an acceptable budget package. However, the Labour Group had seen the Liberal 'shopping list' and was aware of the proposals that were likely to be acceptable to the Liberals. The leadership knew that the party's strategy had to be a realistic one in which judgements had to be made about what proposals were likely to succeed. At an individual informal level the positions of councillors on specific policies were known or hinted at so that by the time proposals were discussed in committee, support was assured from another party. The Liberals proposed a number of specific items for expenditure growth, for example, which were readily taken up by the Labour Party.

The willingness of the Labour Group to accept the Chairmanships and the realisation that if they informed the administration then they could probably get most of their policies through was a key factor in the resolution of the budget. The structure of the process was also important as the officers were responsible in the first instance for producing the growth and reductions lists which were then discussed with each of the parties, rather than encouraging each party to produce its own list. Neither the Liberals nor the Conservatives produced a set of options which was different from those options presented to them by officers in December. For both parties there were practical reasons which explain why very different strategies did not emerge. The Liberals were hard-pressed to do so being only nine in number and the Conservatives were fielding a new team of spokesmen. More important for the Conservatives was their strategic decision to rid themselves of their image of a party in favour of cuts, by adopting the policy stance of 'maintaining services at a price people can afford'. Consequently the Conservatives supported many of the options put up by the committee chairmen, although there was some emphasis given to the need to examine the efficiency of service provision and the Council's policy on fees and charges.

So, the Liberals and Conservatives confined themselves to

'counter-punching' strategies against Labour's set of proposals which were aimed at protecting jobs and services and seeking improvements wherever possible. Each of the parties managed to get something out of the budget and this first budget cycle would suggest that caution and pragmatism have prevailed over the desirability of making loud political noises and staking out one's position as clearly differentiated from the other parties.

As noted in chapter one a major theme running throughout the budgeting literature is the response of local authorities to financial retrenchment, both in their expenditure/taxation decisions and the way they take budget decisions. It has been argued that financial restraint and cutback in the short term encourages local authorities to take only ad hoc short term measures to cope with such cuts but that sustained financial pressure will result in more radical and rational reviews of the budget. In Lancashire's case expenditure has grown steadily each year, although in real terms many of its recent budgets are in fact 'standstill' budgets. The willingness to make changes in the authority's financial and accounting policies and practices must be seen as a short term expedient to enable services to be maintained and to evade the worst effects of grant penalties. As a tactic it has been encouraged by the Government's rapidly changing regime of penalties and targets.

There appears to be very little scope for fundamental reviews within the budget process. Each year the starting point is the preparation of the Continuation Estimates, supplemented in recent years by the production of growth and reduction lists. The latter exercise does present an opportunity to undertake limited reviews of existing expenditure (5 per cent in 1986/7) but is nothing like as radical as either output budgeting or zero-based budgeting. However, even this limited review shows up the political constraints which impinge on an analysis of base expenditure. Many of the reductions listed in the £35 million package would be politically unacceptable to all political parties, which raises the question that if radical reviews of expenditure are undertaken, would politicians be willing to take the radical options that might be thrown up by such an analysis?

One aspect of the Lancashire budget process which has not been emphasised so far, but which is important, is that it is 'policy driven'. The relationship between policy-making and resource allocation is not explicitly stated but nevertheless the budget is built upon and reflects the constantly changing policies of the authority. Such changes are built into the Continuation Estimates, as committed growth or reductions. So the construction of the budget estimates is not simply based on the repricing of existing expenditure. The policy assumptions which underpin the budget are well understood by the officers involved in its preparation but are not immediately obvious to the majority of councillors who are not centrally involved in the process. The need to make the link between policy and resource allocation decisions more explicit is perhaps being expressed in different ways by the Conservatives, with their concern for developing more analytical approaches to budgeting and the Liberals' desire to introduce zero-based budgeting. Both parties share a suspicion that it is possible to find economies and make efficiency savings and they were instrumental in the creation of "Effectiveness, Efficiency and Economy" working groups whose work ultimately is likely to have an impact on future budgets.

Finally, this paper has described the process leading up to the budget for 1986/7. The decisions taken in that budget cycle were in part influenced by previous budgets and so inevitably this budget will have an impact on future budgets. Consequently a longitudinal view is essential in developing and understanding of the budget process. In Lancshire the decisions to change financing practices over the past three years will have implications for future commitments, as will each year's committed growth, to say nothing of the capital programme which has not been discussed here. Perhaps most important of all, the budget for 1986/7 can only be fully assessed over the length of the political cycle from 1985 to 1989. Setting the budget in an election year is likely to be a very different experience as the parties stake out their ground and will provide a very different test of the robustness of the process used by the authority.

4. Birmingham City Council

CHRIS GAME

Introduction – Sweat Box Politics

"No sweat, no sweet" was one of the many maxims beloved and popularised by Samuel Smiles, the mid-nineteenth century prototype Thatcherite, preacher of the virtures of thrift, industry and self-improvement and the evils of 'over-government' (Smiles 1986, p.189). In present-day Birmingham it is a precept that might be expected to appeal to Neville Bosworth, the past Conservative Leader of the City Council (1976–80 and 1982–84) and to some of his more ideologically-minded colleagues; rather less so, however, to the present Labour Leader, Dick Knowles, and, as he would call them, his party "comrades".

Yet there is a sense in which Labour's 1986/7 budget-making process represents, every bit as much as its Conservative predecessors, an institutionalisation of Smiles' aphorism. For, as we shall see, the key to an understanding of any recent Birmingham budget lies in the notorious 'Sweat Box' procedure – a series of highly-charged and confrontational meetings of senior majority party members and chief officers, out of which emerge the final budget allocations and of course, the 'winners' and 'losers' in terms of both services and personal reputations.

The size, composition and conduct of these 'Sweat Box' sessions have varied over recent years within the party in power and with the personalities and political predispositions of the party leaders but their centrality in the budget-making process has not. Successive chairmen and chief officers have figuratively – and undoubtedly, in some cases, literally – sweated it out in the 'Sweat Boxes' in their efforts to obtain or, more usually in recent years, to retain whatever 'sweets' they can for their committees and departments.

The process sounds elitist, incremental and non-corporate and it is. Key budget decisions are confined to a small group of leading councillors and senior officers – a larger group, certainly, this year than in the past, but still an elite. Backbench majority group members are hardly better or earlier informed than those in the minority parties. As one observer described it:

> The fundamental feature of the Birmingham budget process is that outside the Budget Group – the senior members of the majority party – no one knows what's going on until January. In other authorities draft budgets go through committees first, or are discussed by service groups – that doesn't happen here.

Similarly, while there was probably a more concerted attempt this year than previously to question base budgets and more talk among members of the need for forward planning, budgeting in Birmingham remains ultimately a highly incremental exercise. That is not, however, to suggest that it is an irrational one. Rather, to use Paul Diesing's useful distinction, it is an exercise in **political**, as opposed to technical or economic, rationality (Diesing, 1962).

Perhaps not surprisingly, therefore, it tends to be more favourably regarded by councillors than by officers. The latter may comment adversely on the apparent arbitrariness of some of the financial decisions taken, the short term nature of some of those decisions, and on the absence of the more sophisticated strategic planning and the more corporate systems that may have existed in their former authorities. However, elected members from both parties, and particularly senior members who have been personally involved in the process, tend to be less critical: "What other way is there?" they may ask, almost rhetorically; or simply: "Well, this is the way we do it in Birmingham". To understand something both of the reasons for and the consequences of budgeting the Birmingham way, it is useful first to identify some of the financial and political characteristics of the authority.

Birmingham – Big but Hardly Bountiful

The first characteristic that needs to be emphasised – especially when making comparisons with other local authorities – is the sheer **size** of Birmingham. It is, of course, the country's second city – or, as it prefers to be known, its first provincial city. As a local authority, it has by far the largest population of any metropolitan district – nearly 300,000 more than Leeds, the next highest – and hardly surprisingly, the largest budget. Its estimated 1986/7 gross revenue expenditure of £885 million makes it equivalent to about the 35th biggest company in the country, while its 26,000 mortgages match those of about the 26th biggest building society. Its estimated payroll in March 1987 of 53,639, including some 2,000 transferred from the West Midlands County Council (WMCC), makes it comfortably the largest employer in Birmingham.

Low-Spending

In absolute terms the Council is a big-spender – a very big spender indeed. In relative terms, however, it is both historically and currently a low-spending and low-rating authority. As one officer put it:

"We're effectively more like a shire county than a Labour inner city in terms of our low spending and grant levels."

The full significance of this shire county analogy will be appreciated later on in the story of the 1986/7 budget, with the Council's decision to apply for judicial review of its grant allocation. For the present, it is possible to demonstrate its validity, at least crudely, by reference to the CIPFA expenditure statistics. These compare Birmingham first with the other 35 metropolitan districts and secondly with the major cities in the five other former metropolitan counties.

Some changes have taken place over the two years of Labour budgets from 1984 but not even the staunchest Labour supporter would claim that these changes have altered the essential low-spending picture. One of the consequences of the council's size is that to change its direction or priorities significantly can be like trying to turn around the proverbial oil tanker: difficult enough in favourable conditions but even more so if the prevailing forces and currents restrict your room for manoeuvre. As we shall see, the combination of central government forces and financial currents during the past two years has been such as to allow Birmingham politicians very little spare room.

On most of the principal per capita or per client expenditure measures Birmingham ranks fairly close to the average for all 36 metropolitan districts but lower than most, if not all, of the 'Big 6' city authorities. There are, however, one or two notable exceptions that deserve comment. Education, with by far the largest single share of the budget, is very much at the lower end of the metropolitan district league table on all the generally quoted service measures. So too is refuse collection, an outcome of the reorganisation that the service has undergone since January 1983, following the successful bid by the Environmental Health department and the trade unions for the city refuse collection contract. In striking contrast to these low-spending services is Economic Development and Promotion. With a city-wide unemployment level of over 20 per cent and the highest long term unemployment rate of any region in the UK, restructuring the economy and promotion of economic growth have been key aims of both the City and West Midlands County Councils. Unlike any other metropolitan district, therefore, Birmingham was spending more per capita on economic development in 1984/5 than it was, for instance, on either its environmental health or refuse collection services.

A similar profile emerges from an examination of recent GREA and target figures. The Council's budgets have consistently been below GREA, the only exception being 1981/2, the first year of Block Grant, in which various changes were introduced after the original budgets were submitted to DoE. It naturally follows that most of the Council's individual services are below their respective GREAs, for, as one senior officer pointed out:

"The fact that there isn't a GREA for Economic Development means that we must be well below on the others to be well below overall."

One of the explanations of this generally cautious approach to spending is to be found in Table 4.1.

Table 4.1

PARTY CONTROL OF BIRMINGHAM CITY COUNCIL

A - Changes in majority party control

	Majority party	Leader of the Council
May 1974 - May 1976	Labour	Clive Wilkinson
May 1976 - May 1980	Conservative	Neville Bosworth
May 1980 - May 1982	Labour	Clive Wilkinson
May 1982 - May 1984	Conservative	Neville Bosworth
May 1984	Labour	Dick Knowles

B - Recent party composition of the Council

	May 1982 Elections	May 1983 Elections	May 1984 Elections	May 1986 Elections
Conservative	60	60	52	43
Labour	53	55	61	70
Liberal	4	2	3	2
SDP	-	-	1	2
Overall majority	Cons = 3	Cons = 3	Lab = 5	Lab = 23

Since 1974 control of the City Council has switched from one major party to the other even more regularly than it did before local government reorganisation. Neither party has so far managed to hold on to its majority for more than four years and with a system of elections by thirds, there have been few periods during which the controlling party has been able to consider itself electorally safe. Birmingham is a classic case of a council whose whole character would be changed if the Widdicombe Committee's recommendation that councils be elected in entirety every four years were to be adopted. Over the years the Council has illustrated both the positive and negative features of elections by thirds, as enumerated by the Committee (Widdicombe 1986, pp.168-170). There can be no doubt that long term planning has been discouraged, that there have been examples of policy inconsistency and that difficult decisions, especially on spending, have on occasions been deferred because of the anticipated risk of an adverse electoral reaction. On the other hand, the City Council can reasonably claim to have reflected more fairly the normal political complexion of its electorate than ever the WMCC did, with its dramatic quadrennial changes in control and turnovers of members. There is also a much sharper and more immediate sense of political accountability, with members aware that sooner rather than later they will have to explain and justify their policies to the voters.

53

There is, of course, one exception to this principle of enhanced electoral accountability: namely, the 'fourth year' in which, prior to 1985, the metropolitan county council elections were held. Table 4.2 would seem to suggest strikingly, if unsurprisingly, that recent Labour administrations have taken some advantage of the relative breathing space offered in these off-years by levying higher percentage rate increases or retaining higher levels of balances than they might otherwise have done.

Table 4.2

ELECTIONS, RATES AND BALANCES

Financial Year	Election Year?	Party setting Rate	General Rate (p in £)	% change	Variations in balances (original budget estimate)
1981/2	No	Labour	152.75	+41	− £0.9m.
1982/3	Yes	Labour	165.80	+ 9	−
1983/4	Yes	Con.	154.10	− 7	− £10m.
1984/5	Yes	Con.	149.10	− 3	− £29m.
1985/6	No	Labour	196.80	+32	+ £8m.
1986/7	Yes	Labour	226.32	+15	− £8m.

Labour's counter-argument — if one were felt to be needed to justify this utilisation of political common sense — would be that their Conservative predecessors in both 1980/1 and 1984/5 had so depleted the City's balances in their efforts to minimise rate increases in sensitive election years that substantial increases in succeeding years were unavoidable, whichever party had found itself in control.

There are strong feelings — as well as some substance — behind this party rhetoric but not, on the whole, bitterness. The closeness of the political balance on the council has kept relations between the parties spirited but civilised. It has also undoubtedly been both a cause and a reflection of the notable lack of partisan extremism in Birmingham's municipal politics, dating back at least to the inter-war years, if not to Joseph Chamberlain himself. As Sutcliffe and Smith record in their comprehensive History of Birmingham, 1939-1970, the Unionist Party which controlled the City Council throughout the 1930s "retained much of the progressive outlook of their Liberal forbears" and claimed "with some pride after the Second World War that Birmingham had been the most 'socialist' of the Conservative local authorities" (p.76).

There are doubtless those today who would similarly claim that, under Clive Wilkinson and now Dick Knowles, Birmingham has become one of the most 'conservative' of Labour local authorities. Knowles in particular, however, would belligerently contest any such suggestion. "I'm far more revolutionary than many who claim to be on the left", he would retort, perhaps citing as illustration his various plans for "handing power back to the people". These plans include the 12 constituency-based area committees, started in 1984; the proposed network of 39 multi-purpose neighbourhood offices, the first of which were opened in 1985/6 and Knowles' own more personal schemes for urban parish councils and tenants' housing co-operatives, which he readily concedes are somewhat less enthusiastically embraced by some of his "comrades".

Nor, almost needless to say, do these decentralisation ideas have the support of the Conservatives, who see them as symptomatic of the "waste and extravagance introduced under Labour". On several other major policies, however, there is a genuine inter-party consensus – notably, the City's bid for the 1992 Olympics, the August 1986 'Monaco-style' Superprix motor race and the planned £106.5 million International Convention Centre, supported as it now is by EEC funding.

Capital Spending

There has certainly been more of a consensus in recent years on capital than on revenue spending. Although the capital budget did rise in both absolute and percentage terms during the two Conservative years, the fact is that **both** parties in recent years have sought to maximise their capital expenditure – by spending close to the limits permitted by the Government's borrowing allocations and its prevailing policies on the use of capital receipts. Thus the reduction in the capital budget between 1984/5 and 1985/6 (and the even greater fall in the respective outturn figures) is attributable less to a change in the political control of the City Council than to a combination of £12.9 million reduction in borrowing allocations and the introduction of government regulations restricting the use of receipts from the sales of land and council houses.

Both parties too have sought to circumvent some of these Government restrictions on capital spending by taking advantage of various 'creative accounting' devices. These include the establishment of the City's own development company – Satman Developments (Birmingham) Ltd. – which in 1986/7 and in future years will be carrying out a variety of capital projects for the City to the value of over £60 million and the sale of some £30 million of mortgages, **before** Liverpool received the publicity for doing precisely the same thing and the Government stepped in to regulate the practice under the Local Government Act 1986.

Pride of place under capital 'creative accounting', however, must surely go to the bafflingly complex scheme developed by the City Treasurer and his staff which amounts in effect to mortgaging the National Exhibition Centre to help pay for the new Convention Centre. Much admired as a piece of "financial wizardry" by at least partially comprehending officers, this scheme has also received the unstinted acclaim of councillors of all parties – not least because it has enabled them to receive EEC funding for the Convention Centre and the National Indoor Sports Arena through the European Regional Development Fund **without** having the City's capital allocation correspondingly reduced by the DoE, as would normally have happened.

The Birmingham Budgetary Process

These big prestige projects – the Olympic bid, the Convention Centre, the Indoor Sports Arena and the Superprix – are intended, in the words of Dick Knowles, to turn Birmingham into "the most dynamic city in Great Britain". Organisationally, however, the City Council itself remains distictly traditional. Back in 1977 the incoming Conservative administration dismissed the incumbent Chief Executive and until Labour regained control in 1980 the Council's administration was headed by a Principal Chief Officer and City Treasurer in the person of Bill Page. Not surprisingly, although there have been changes in both personnel and procedures in recent years - particularly since the appointment of Tom Caulcott as CEO and Paul Sabin as Treasurer in 1982 - departmentalism remains an extremely powerful force, not least in the making of the budget.

The CIPFA Financial Information Service, in its volume on Budgetary Processes, identifies three differing basic approaches to local authority budgeting: the Traditional, the Financial Plan and the Corporate Plan (see also Game, 1984).

In recent years, of course, financial pressures have severely limited the scope for any proposals for growth and have necessitated at least some examination of existing expenditure. But with that qualification, Stewart's description of the Traditional Approach quoted in chapter 1 captures the essence of Birmingham's past approach to budgeting. Certainly, until Paul Sabin became Treasurer, the City warranted the description applied to it by one officer as: "a financial backwater. There were no forward plans, no commitment forecast, no resource forecast, no formal monitoring, nothing." And as for the capital programme: "That went out of the window with the Chief Executive in the 1970s. It was only really revived about four years ago. Until then they used to do just a one-year capital budget ... that's crazy." As will become apparent from the cycle leading to the 1986/7 budget there have been some significant refinements and improvements introduced during the past three or four years. While not beginning to approach the sophistication of neighbouring Coventry's Corporate Plan cycle, with its five-year revenue budgets and ten-year strategic budgets, these developments have added to the Birmingham process some of the characteristics of CIPFA's Financial Approach, including:

1. The existence of a medium-term forecast of commitments prior to the detailed annual budget preparation;

2. The separation of committed and uncommitted growth items;

3. The fixing of some kind of expenditure limit in advance of detailed estimates.

The 1986/7 Budgetary Process

Commitment forecasts

The City Council's formal financial timetable is summarised below in Figure 4.1.

The 1986/7 budget process itself really got underway in June/July 1985, with the preparation by the Treasurer's Department of initial commitment forecasts for 1986/7 and 1987/8. These commitment projections represent one of the innovations introduced over the past three years. They do not involve the service departments, and they include no new policies. Their purpose is to indicate, on the basis of the Treasurer's assumptions regarding pay, prices, interest rates and grant, what the rate position looks like for the next two years.

APRIL - JUNE:
Closing previous year's accounts.

MAY - JULY:
Review of current year's capital budget in light of actual spending for previous year. Revision of three year capital programme.

4 WEEKLY FROM JUNE:
Monitoring of current year's revenue/capital expenditure and employee numbers against budget.

JUNE - JULY:
Revenue budget review for current year and forecasts for next two years.

JULY:
Government announces how it intends next year's block grant to work together with the level of rate support grant.

SEPTEMBER:
Reports and accounts for previous year published after audit.

SEPTEMBER - OCTOBER:
Current year's revenue and capital budgets revised. Draft revenue budget for next year prepared.

NOVEMBER - DECEMBER:
Consideration of next year's revenue budget by policy group. Consultation with representatives of industrial and commercial ratepayers commences.

DECEMBER:
Government announces rate support grant settlement.

JANUARY:
Finance and Management Committee approves revenue budget allocations to spending committees and adopts the first year of the capital programme as the capital budget.

FEBRUARY:
Spending committees approve own budgets.

MARCH:
City Council approves rate in £ for next year.

Figure 4.1   Financial Timetable in London

The preliminary forecast that emerged from this exercise in the summer of 1985 was of an overall rate increase in 1986/7 of 30 per cent, inclusive of the estimated precepts from the three joint boards that would take over the WMCC's responsibility for Police, Fire and Passenger Transport.

The Budget Group

The next stage in the process does not appear on the formal timetable. It consisted of an early meeting, held in September 1985, of the Budget Group of senior majority party members, to receive and respond to the Treasurer's commitment and rate forecasts. As already indicated, this Budget Group constitutes the political policymaking body in the Birmingham budget process, whichever party happens to be in power, although its size and composition have altered considerably under recent Leaders. Under Neville Bosworth the Conservatives in both their periods of office have favoured a small Budget Group, or 'Hatchet Committee', as they sometimes call it. In 1982-84 the Group consisted of Bosworth himself, the Deputy Leader, and two senior advisers, with wide experience but without any major service committee responsibilities. The Chairman of General Purposes might be brought in on occasions, but the Group would never consist of more than five.

Dick Knowles' leadership style is much more democratic and collective - more so than Bosworth's, but also very much more so than those of most previous Labour leaders, from Sir Albert Bradbeer and Harry Watton in the 1950s and 1960s to Clive Wilkinson in the 1970s and 1980s. Throughout the 1986/7 budget process, therefore, Labour's Budget Group numbered no less than 15: all the officers of the party group on the council, together with the Chairs of the major service committees - Education, Social Services, Housing, Urban Renewal, and Planning.

The fixing of an expenditure limit

Having presided over a 32 per cent General Rate increase in 1985/6, the Budget Group will have indicated in no uncertain terms that a further 30 per cent increase, especially in an election year, would be politically out of the question. The earliest guidance that officers received from the Budget Group, therefore, was that they should aim for a single-figure rate rise.

Imprecise and indirect though it was, this guidance can reasonably be interpreted as one of the features of the Financial Plan Approach: "the fixing of some kind of expenditure limit in advance of detailed estimates". Other terms for Labour's approach to fixing that limit would be A.H.Marshall's "pre-determined rating" (1974, p.85) and Hepworth's "rate rationing" (1984, p.215). Hepworth in particular does not conceal his reservations about rate rationing as a budgetary strategy, in which "the primary consideration is the size of the rate levy, which is determined without real regard to the implications for the policies of the various services" (p.215). For politicians of all parties, however, the size of the rate levy frequently is the primary consideration - quite possibly, as for the Conservatives in Birmingham in 1982, the central pledge in a winning manifesto. The same is rather less likely to be true for Labour groups, although in recent years a concern to avoid or to minimise grant penalties has often resulted in a very similar process of settling early spending ceilings. For 1985/6, however, the early political guidance from the Labour Budget Group has been to implement the major priority areas of the party's manifesto - i.e. more of an 'expenditure-led' approach than this year's 'rate-led' one.

Preparation of draft revenue budget

Following the receipt of that early political guidance from the Budget Group, the draft budget was then drawn up by accountants from the Treasurer's Department and staff from the various service departments.

At around the same time a letter went out from the Leader to the Chairs of all spending committees, asking them to identify any areas of their budgets where money might actually be saved, those lower priority areas from which at least some funds might be reallocated and finally any new spending they wished to undertake for which no money at all was available at present.

In an ideal world the three lists of prioritised items resulting from the Leader's letter would have constituted the agenda for the next stage of the process - the "monastic weekend", as Knowles himself terms it. The reference is to a weekend in early December spent at Wast Hills House - a former Cadbury family house on the outskirts of Birmingham - during which the Budget Group, together with a small number of senior officers, had its first collective and extended discussion of the draft departmental budgets and the slightly revised rate forecast that had emerged from the preparation of those budgets. In this instance, however, 'discussion' seems very much an apt description of what took place, for the Leader's letter, not unexpectedly, had failed to flush out anything like as many proposals for spending cuts as there were new bids, and as a result few, if any, hard decisions were taken. In the phrase used by more than one of the participants, it was largely a "talking-shop".

The Sweat Box Procedure - Part One

In Birmingham, as already indicated in the Introduction, the arena in which the really tough talking and bargaining take place and the key political decisions are made is the 'Sweat Box' - a series of private meetings between, on the one side, the Budget Group, the Treasurer and the Chief Executive and on the other, the committee chairs and their chief officers, with the departmental accountant. The terminology may be Birmingham's own but in essence the approach is that which Greenwood has described and labelled as the 'Spanish Inquisition' form of budgeting (1980 and 1983). As Greenwood writes (1980, p.163):

"Often these meetings well involve only the leader, the treasurer and the chief executive officer, although in some authorities one or two other leading politicians may attend. More frequently it is just the 'triumvirate'."

In the past five years Birmingham has seen three different variants of the 'Sweat Box'. Under Clive Wilkinson, the previous Labour Leader, it took the form of Greenwood's 'triumvirate'. As one senior officer put it: "He did the whole thing completely on his own, particularly in that last year (i.e. 1982/3)." Then, under the Conservatives, Neville Bosworth was assisted by the other three members of his 'Inner Cabinet' or 'Hatchet Committee'. And finally, under Dick Knowles, the whole Labour Budget Group is involved:

"Traditionally it was two sides or two ends of the table. Now it's become more of a round table."

In the 1986/7 budget cycle the first set of these 'Sweat Box' sessions took place over two days at Highbury - the former Moseley home of Joseph Chamberlain - in mid-December 1985. The Budget Group, together with the Treasurer and the Chief Executive, went through, with committee chairs and their respective chief officers, all the departmental draft budgets, with the purpose not of cutting any items at this stage, but "to draw up a kind of balance sheet for each committee - things that weren't in the budget that they wanted to do, things that perhaps could come out and some in between that they wanted to discuss further." As at the Wast Hills weekend, the former items still greatly outnumbered any proposals for spending reductions but by the end of the two days the Budget Group had at least agreed upon certain definite priorities - 'sacrosanct' policy commitments which were to be protected throughout all subsequent budget debates. These priorities included the decisions:

* to put extra money into housing repairs and to finance it by means of a rent increase;

* not to increase school meal charges;

* to maintain pupil/teacher ratios at current levels;

* to provide additional resources for mental handicap services;

* not to reduce the neighbourhood office programme.

Base budget examination

There was not, either at these Highbury 'Sweat Boxes' or in subsequent meetings, anything that could technically be defined as 'base budget analysis'. Nor had there been in any previous years. Indeed, there was almost certainly more questioning of base budgets by members than ever before, including the two Conservative years of rate reductions. Before they came into office in 1982 the Conservatives had given some thought to zero-based budgeting and had even discussed its possibilities with the Treasurer. No concrete proposals were ever formulated, however, partly because of the acknowledged complexities of introducing anything like zero-based budgeting in an authority of Birmingham's size but mainly, in the end, because of a political concern about the implications of getting into a public debate about compulsory redundancies.

Rate Support Grant Settlement

The next two events in the budget cycle - the Government's formal announcement of the RSG settlement and the Council's statutory consultation with representatives of commercial and industrial ratepayers - should, in the 1986/7 cycle at least, be considered together. They took place within a couple of days of each other - on 18 and 20 December respectively - and the one constituted the major item on the agenda of the other.

The RSG settlement, although described by Kenneth Baker himself as "broadly neutral", was certainly not neutrally received. The total sum available, £11.8 billion, represented an increase significantly below the rate of inflation and was thus in real terms the seventh successive grant reduction announced by Conservative Secretaries of

State since 1979. For Birmingham the accumulated grant loss over those years amounts to some £175 million but this problem was compounded by the other main policy behind the settlement, which was to switch the distribution balance in favour of the cities, particularly London and away from the predominantly Conservative shire counties - in an effort to persuade ratepayers of the financial benefits of the abolition of the GLC and metropolitan counties. As already noted, however, Birmingham is in some of its financial characteristics more akin to a shire county than to a Labour inner city.

There were also some other features of the RSG settlement which seemed to operate to Birmingham's substantial disadvantage. First, it was clear and demonstrable that those WMCC services due to be taken over by the City were not attracting their fair share of grant compared either with that previously given to the County Council or with that being given to the three new joint boards.

Secondly, although formal spending targets and penalties were to be abolished, the grant mechanism was adjusted so as to act as a disincentive to local authorities to increase spending - by steepening the slope on the grant related poundage in the block grant distribution formula. In addition, there was the impact of 'capping' - not 'rate-capping', from which a relatively low-spending authority like Birmingham had been comfortably immune - but **'grant capping'**. Any individual authority which stood to gain block grant as a result of the abolition of targets and penalties would have a 'cap' placed on that gain at a Government-determined base spending level.

In Birmingham's case, according to the Government's figures, this combination of a steeper poundage schedule and the grant 'cap' produced a 'negative marginal rate' of -108 per cent. In other words, for every £1 million spent (above a very low threshold), the City would **lose** grant of £1.1 million, thereby costing the ratepayer £2.1 million.

The complex details of the multiplier mechanism by which the grant 'cap' would be applied took some time to emerge from the DoE. When they did, they proved to have particular significance for Birmingham, resulting in a successful court case against the Government and eventually in yet another piece of local government finance legislation - the Rate Support Grant Act 1986.

What the City Treasurer's staff discovered, when they came to examine the detailed multiplier calculations in January, was that the Secretary of State and his civil servants, in arriving at what is termed the 'base position' for the City, had made a basic error but one with profound implications for the whole 1986/7 grant settlement - although **not**, as the Minister was later to claim, for every **previous** settlement back to 1981/2. Instead of the 'cap' being applied to the City's 1985/6 **actual** grant entitlement of £165.2 million it had incorrectly been applied to the **notional** grant figure of £158 million producing an immediate grant loss of £7.2 million and a higher and more penalising multiplier. In total, it seemed likely that approximately 160 authorities had been similarly, if not as severely, disadvantaged. The great majority of this 160, however, were low-spending, Conservative-controlled shire county and district councils, which rather limited and qualified the support from other Labour authorities that Birmingham received in pursuing its case.

Despite representations to the DoE both on this matter and on what the City claimed was an incorrect distribution of grant arising out of the abolition of WMCC, the Secretary of State gave no indication

that he was prepared to reconsider Birmingham's grant allocation.
In February, therefore, on the advice of the Treasurer and with
effectively all-party support within the council, the Labour leadership
decided to apply for judicial review of the Secretary of State's grant
determination. The case was set down for a hearing in the High Court
on Tuesday, 15 April and as reported in that day's Birmingham Evening
Mail, Mr.Justice Mann made an order declaring that the Secretary of
State had indeed acted illegally. However, as is also reported, five
days **before** that hearing, in a statement that seemed to bear distinct
signs of panic, the Minister for Local Government, William Waldegrave,
announced to Parliament that the Government would be introducing
legislation "to maintain the status quo in the block grant system"
and thus to circumvent any possible decision by the Court. That
legislation, the Rate Support Grant Act, confirmed the City Council's
powerful moral but - in the Evening Mail's words - financially hollow
victory.

Returning, however, to mid-December 1985: in the absence of the
full official figures and with the statutory consultation with
ratepayer representatives scheduled to take place almost immediately,
the Treasurer's Department had to make a preliminary estimate of the
impact of the grant settlement. The estimate produced was that, if
the Council were to spend at the level of its 1986/7 GRE of
£502.4 million, its block grant entitlement would be £136 million,
instead of the £165 million being received on its 1985/6 budget; the
City rate increase would have to be 54 per cent and the General Rate
increase 34 per cent.

These figures were, as it happens, slightly less daunting than those
projecting a 60 per cent City rate increase that had been produced
(on the basis of a slightly lower GRE estimate) two weeks earlier,
for a meeting at which Dick Knowles briefed an all-party group of
Birmingham MPs, prior to what was fully anticipated to be an
unfavourable RSG settlement.

Not surprisingly, this 60 per cent figure quickly became public
knowledge, both in Parliament and in the local press. The Birmingham
Post report was typical of its kind - conveying the impression that
it was the **General**, rather than the City, rate which might rise by
60 per cent and omitting to mention the crucial fact that this
"forecast" was predicated on the Council's rather improbably deciding
to spend up to its GRE level.

First Statutory Consultation

The first statutory consultation with representatives of commercial
and industrial ratepayers was deliberately designed and timed this
year to link in with the City's wide-ranging lobbying campaign against
what it regarded as its extremely unfair - although not at that time
illegal - grant settlement. In addition to the briefing of MPs, and
a direct correspondence with Kenneth Baker personally, the Council
went out of its way to encourage the business organisations to exert
any influence they were able to upon the Government. This was not
the form that the previous year's consultation had taken, when the
ratepayer representatives (from the regional CBI, Chamber of Industry
and Commerce, Chamber of Trade, Engineering Employers' Association,
etc.) had been presented with at least some provisional expenditure

figures but as Councillor John Charlton explained from the Chair, the Council were not in a position to discuss expenditure at this stage, because decisions still had to be taken by the majority party group.

The representatives were not unsympathetic to the Council's case, or to the suggestion that they make some kind of approach to the Government. One of the Chamber of Commerce representatives in particular, Noel Burne, was very supportive, and he agreed "to visit the Treasurer's Department for a few days to learn more about .... the complexities of the system" but it seems doubtful whether anything more tangible than sympathy and increased understanding resulted either from this meeting or from the second phase of the consultation exercise in mid-February. The general view of members and officers alike seems to be that the meetings are:

> a waste of time ... a total waste of time, really. They have little or no effect on the real decisions of rate-making and spending. They (i.e. the representatives) totally disagree with any increases in spending being proposed. They say rates should be kept down, but we don't get too much in the way of concrete suggestions about how we should do that.

It might be argued, however, that the intrinsic nature of the exercise is more to blame than the representatives themselves. As one officer put it:

> Even though they are now much better informed, they still only have one-line figures for each committee and employee numbers by each committee. They don't know what's really behind those figures, and I just wonder whether we can really expect much more from them.

The Sweat Box Procedure - Part Two

The key spending decisions that had still to be taken at the time of the December statutory consultation meeing constitute the climax of the budget-making process. The likely percentage rate rise, the allocations to committees, the provision for inflation, the levels of balances to be maintained - all of these crucial decisions are argued out and effectively settled at a single 'Sweat Box' meeting. It is traditionally held in the Treasurer's office in the Council House and it took place this year on 9-10 January - one protracted meeting, starting early on the Thursday afternoon and finishing around one o'clock on the Friday morning.

The underlying agenda for the meeting was somehow to reduce the Treasurer's latest available rate forecast - an overall increase of approximately 24 per cent - to something at least as close as possible to the Budget Group's original single-figure objective. The early part of the meeting is structured and fairly orderly: a timetable is followed; departmental budgets are presented in turn by their respective chairs and chief officers and then scrutinised by the Budget Group; flipchart diagrams, prepared in advance by the Treasurer's Department, are updated as decisions are made and further spending reductions identified.

After this initial round, though, proceedings became - not to put too fine a point on it - somewhat less structured. Some members found, for various reasons, that they had to leave the meeting for a time; chief officers either returned to their offices or went home and remained on call and still the percentage rate rise remained unacceptably high. Several of the councillors and particularly the chairs of the major spending committees, wanted to take virtually all the balances, on the ground that the City in the past has invariably underspent its budget but this idea was swiftly quashed by a "health warning" from the Treasurer, saying that, particularly with the uncertainties that existed regarding pay and interest rates, it was quite unacceptable to try to run a city with a turnover of over £1 billion on nil balances.

By the late evening, therefore, to quote one of the participants:

> it had become virtually impossible to get down to a single-figure rate rise. The nearest we were going to be was about 11 per cent and we could still have been looking at a bit over 20 per cent. That range was too broad, so after nine or ten hours the Group decided to look for some more expenditure cuts and it was in the early hours of the morning that we finally found them - another £3 million off the draft budget, and that brought the increase down to the range of 11 to 15 per cent. That was the range we went public on.

So, after the weeks of attempted prioritisation and careful calculation, some of the most critical allocation decisions were actually taken quite literally at the eleventh hour in a "short, sharp round-the-table exercise": "Right, we'll have a million and a half off Education, half a million off Social Services, so much off Consumer Protection, and so on - that's how it was finally done." As one leading member recalled, it was "all a bit bloody frayed" and there is no doubt at all that some of the Budget Group did not grasp the full implications - in either financial or service delivery terms - of the decisions that were being taken at this late stage of the meeting. It should, however, be emphasised that the key political priorities which had been identified at the earlier Highbury 'Sweat Box' meetings were all protected; of the big-spending services, therefore, Housing gained at the expense of Education and to a much lesser degree, Social Services. 'Rough justice' need not be 'fair shares for all'.

Transferred Services

It should also be mentioned that the 'transferred services' which the City was taking over from the abolished WMCC - Highways, Waste Disposal, Trading Standards, etc.) were not as harshly treated as might perhaps have been expected - since it was these services which were causing some of the most serious financial problems and which also, at that time, lacked any direct advocate. These transferred services did, however, constitute a major topic of debate in the January 'Sweat Box'. The Chief Executive in particular "really homed in on two or three chief officers who he felt were pulling the wool over the Budget Group's eyes by pitching their draft budgets for transferred services too high - they were geared to producing much higher levels of service than the County would have provided." Partly as a result of this intervention by the CEO, Consumer Protection was one of the services which seems to have emerged as a 'loser' in the 1986/7 budget but the Highways budget, the biggest among the transferred services, survived more successfully than, for instance, Education, while Economic Development continued as one of the City's 'high-spenders'.

The general feeling among both members and officers is that the City's public claim to be delivering a standard of service broadly comparable to that provided by the WMCC is a fair one:

> Certainly, if you look at the transferred services part of the budget, we're way above the spending level that the Government said we needed, way above - both in GRE terms and in the breakdown for block grant purposes which they did. And that's why we made such a song and dance about getting no block grant for these services. We were taking on £57 million of expenditure and lost £1 million of grant.

Finalisation of budget allocations

Despite the late night atmosphere in which some of the toughest decisions were taken, virtually all of them were adhered to and eventually confirmed in a further Budget Group meeting towards the end of January. There were certainly sections of the District Labour Party which were unhappy both about some of the decisions themselves and about what they regarded as a lack of proper consultation but there was never a serious possibility of any motion to reopen the whole budget package gaining a majority within the Budget Group. Formally, therefore, the provisional budget allocation to committees of £501.8 million (£444 million for existing services plus £57.8 million for transferred services) was approved by the Council's Finance and Management Committee on 18 February.

It was at this meeting too that committees were "requested" to prepare and submit estimates to the March meeting of the Finance and Management Committee in accordance with these provisional allocations. As emphasised in the Introduction to this chapter it is only at this relatively late stage in the cycle that the service committees see their budgets. Indeed, in many past years it will be the first sight that even committee members of the majority group have had. This year, depending on the inclination of the committee chair, some of the Labour service groups did hold earlier meetings, but the budget-making process is such that almost inevitably, "there's still a fair degree of ignorance in a Labour group on a service committee until February, when the budget report comes in front of the whole committee."

Second Statutory Consultation

On the afternoon **before** that mid-February meeting of the Finance and Management Committee (i.e. 17 February), the second statutory consultation meeting was held with representatives of industrial and commercial ratepayers - preceded in the morning by an equivalent, but non-statutory, meeting with trade union representatives who, in the past two years at least, have received very much the same budgetary information. This year, unusually, the meeting with the unions proved a rather tougher ordeal for the Labour leadership than did that with the ratepayer representatives:

> The trade union people certainly disagreed with some of the proposals when they saw them. They wanted more spending in one or two areas - social services, race relations - and they also raised questions about how the departments were run, really some quite nitty-gritty things.

Undoubtedly part of the unions' resentment, like that of some of the constituency Labour Parties, was prompted by the fact that this so-called 'consultation' was taking place at a time when there is very little left actually to consult about. The provisional budget has been settled and although the consultation papers set out alternative uses of funds and balances to give rate increases of either 11 or 15 per cent, no one listening to either the Labour members or to the City Treasurer can have been left in any doubt that 15 per cent was the very strongly favoured figure.

The ratepayer representatives are, of course, in exactly the same position but they seemed to accept it more resignedly; at least they did not attempt to put forward any detailed 'shopping list' of alternative proposals:

> They sympathised with our position, they welcomed the consultation and appreciated that they're so well informed compared to what they used to be ... they just totally disagreed with the increased level of spending and therefore with the increase in the rate.

Ironically, if understandably, the business and commercial organisations are much more supportive of the City's capital investment programme than of its revenue budget. Yet one of the major causes of the increased spending levels in each of the past two years has been precisely the size of that capital programme and the loans taken out to finance it. Those debt charges alone constitute a spending increase of approximately 3 per cent per annum and when pay awards and inflation are added in, that figure rises to between 8 and 9 per cent, without any service policy changes at all.

Finalisation of the Rate

The final stage in the budget cycle is, of course, the actual making of the rate, first by the Finance and Management Committee and finally by the full City Council - this year on 18 March. As already indicated, two principal alternative exemplifications had emerged from the January 'Sweat Box' and had subsequently been included in the information given to the unions and ratepayer representatives. The first showed how an overall 11 per cent rate increase might be achieved - mainly by running down both balances and the City's special funds down to nil. This was the strategy that the Treasurer had in fact deemed unacceptable in his earlier "health warning".

It was the second strategy, therefore, that was provisionally indicated to the February Finance and Management Committee and which, following the notification of the joint board precepts (28.38p) and the Residuary Body levy, was formally approved by the Committee on 10 March. The principal question to be decided at this stage was how much expenditure to finance from general balances and how much to charge to the City's two special funds. Both of these funds had been established in earlier years, at least partly for the specific purpose of minimising block grant losses. Similarly, it was the Treasurer's recommendation to members this year that they maximise the use of these funds, rather than balances, since this would be likely to maximise the City's block grant entitlement both for 1986/7 and, if the current grant arrangements continue, for 1987/8 as well. This recommendation was accepted and the outcome was a General Rate levy for 1986/7 of 226.32p - an increase of 15 per cent over the 1985/6 figure of 196.8p.

5. Liverpool City Council

MICHAEL PARKINSON

The financial affairs of Liverpool city council are diferent from other local authorities. When the Labour party won control of the council in May 1983, budget making stopped being a technical financial process and became instead a highly charged political act. After Labour's victory, Liverpool's financial difficulties dominated national politics as the Militant led Labour council used them to challenge the Conservative government's grant regime and force the reluctant national Labour party to support its challenge. In 1984 and 1985, the Labour council threatened to bankrupt the local authority if the government did not give Liverpool more money to balance its budget. In both years Labour eventually abandoned this threat but delayed setting a rate until several months after the financial year had started. In 1986 the council set a rate by the beginning of the financial year but its expenditure was fixed at least £37 million higher than expected income. At the end of June 1986, the money to pay for the authority's services had still not been found and Liverpool was once again on the brink of financial collapse.

The political, legal and financial consequences of these decisions were enormous. In November 1985 the National Executive Committee of the Labour party suspended the Liverpool District Party. After an internal inquiry, in June 1986 the NEC expelled several leading councillors and officers of the District Party for their membership of the proscribed Militant Tendency and abuses of party rules during their budget campaign against the government. Meanwhile, in June 1985 48 Labour councillors were disqualified from office and surcharged by the District Auditor for the losses they incurred by delaying setting a rate in 1985. In March 1986, the High Court upheld the

Auditor's judgement although the councillors made a further appeal to the Court of Appeal in July 1986. That same month the District Auditor reported that the council's financial affairs were "seriously out of hand" with unacceptable methods of decision-making and major problems on both capital and revenue budgets.

Parties, Coalitions and Budgets 1974–83: The Lost Decade

To understand the Labour council's decisions they have to be seen in their historical context. In Liverpool, perhaps more than in any other authority, annual revenue budgets cannot be seen in isolation. The conflicts and confusion which characterised Liverpool's budget making under Labour occurred in a less extreme form in many previous administrations. Bitter arguments about the city's finances dominated Liverpool politics during the decade between 1974, when the new district council was created and 1983 when Labour won the first absolute majority on the council. Until that time every budget was set by a coalition of at least two parties.

The absence of a clear party majority created enormous political incoherence on the council and throughout the decade there was constant conflict between the three parties about the right spending and rate levels for the city. Although Labour controlled the council for four years during this period it only got one budget passed, in 1980. Every other year the Liberals and Conservatives voted together for their own budgets or cut the expenditure plans of minority Labour administrations. Eventually this led Labour to relinquish minority control of the council in 1978 and to refuse to run it again, despite being the largest single party, until it won an absolute majority in 1983.

During this 'lost decade' of coalition politics the Liberal and Conservative parties competed to restrict council expenditure. The result was that although in 1973/4 Liverpool's rate level was 45 per cent higher than the national average, by 1978/9 it had fallen to only one per cent above. During this period of Liberal administration, rate rises failed even to keep pace with inflation as Liverpool's expenditure increased at a significantly slower rate than that of all the other local authorities. It also failed to increase in line with central government guidelines during that period.

The record of limited council spending during the late 1970s was central to Labour's case after 1983. It was the basis of its claim, which was publicly and strenuously endorsed by the council's financial officers, that the Conservative government's grant regime imposed an unreasonable burden upon the city. Labour claimed that Liverpool, in contrast to other authorities, had limited its expenditure during the 1970s and therefore both had less need, and was less able, to reduce its expenditure a second time in the 1980s. Yet the government gave it more restrictive expenditure targets in the 1980s than those Labour-controlled authorities who had developed large base budgets in the 1970s on which their more generous targets now rested. Since the Government cut the rate support grant of local authorities who spent over target, Labour believed that Liverpool's past virtue was being punished while others' profligacy was rewarded. This encouraged Labour's opposition to the government's grant regime.

Labour party politics during this period also contributed to the crisis. Throughout the 1970s the Liverpool Labour party moved from its traditional right of centre position towards the far left. The Militant Tendency became especially powerful, rapidly building up its membership and organisation within the city and the Labour party. By 1981 the Tendency had persuaded the Labour party that when it got power it should threaten to bankrupt the city. It should set a 'deficit' budget and refuse to increase its rates or rents, or cut its services to compensate for grant cuts, to try to blackmail the Conservative Government into giving Liverpool more money. If the Government did not acquiesce, the city would run out of money, and schools, nurseries and old people's homes would close, housing repairs would end, the dead would not even be buried. All Council employees would lose their jobs.

The city's economic circumstances were also important. Labour devised this bankruptcy plan during the late 1970s when the rapid decline of Liverpool's private sector and rising unemployment dramatically increased the political importance of public sector employment in a city where the local authority employs 15 per cent of the local workforce. Between 1973 and 1978 public employment in Liverpool increased but in the second half of the decade, as the Government restrained public expenditure, local authority employment in the city declined. In this context, local authority trade unions became increasingly concerned to protect existing council employment. In 1979 they created a Joint Shop Stewards Committee to resist further council job losses. That committee also became an important supporter of the Labour party's commitment to protect 'jobs and services' and encouraged its bankruptcy strategy.

The combination of all these forces meant that when the Liverpool electorate returned Labour to power in 1983 on a bankruptcy platform with the city's first absolute majority in ten years, the scene was set for a major confrontation between Liverpool's Labour council and the Conservative Government, with the national Labour leadership anxiously looking on.

Labour in Office 1983–86

The financial problems the Labour council faced as it made its budget for 1986/7 were the direct result of that confrontation. During its three years of office, the Labour council had engaged in a great deal of inventive creative accounting. But this had merely postponed difficult decisions. By June 1986 the council's financial options were virtually exhausted. Each of Labour's three budgets contributed to its underlying financial dilemma.

Labour's 1984/5 Budget

Labour first tried to blackmail the government into giving Liverpool more money in 1984. In March the council produced its first deficit budget. The government had set the authority a target of £216 million for 1984/5, but Labour planned to spend £269 million. In addition to this, during its first year of office in 1983/4, Labour had not made any of the economies that had been planned in the budget it had inherited from its Liberal predecessors. As a result the council had spent beyond its target of £212 million for that year, incurred £17 million in grant penalties and ended the year with a deficit of over £34 million. That deficit had to be added to the 1984/5 base budget. Although the council planned to use £7 million of its reserves, it still intended to spend £296 million. At that level, the council would only get £27 million in government grant, leaving £269 million to be raised from the rates. But Labour intended to put up the rates by 9 per cent, which would produce only £108 million. The city would inevitably run out of money before the end of the financial year and all its services would collapse.

However, Labour did not implement that budget. In April 1984, the council group split and Labour could not get a majority but at the May elections, despite its threats of financial suicide, Labour increased its council seats from 51 to 58. After this popular victory, the national Labour leadership, who had been opposed to Liverpool's tactics, pressed the government to help the city. After two months of negotiations between council officers and civil servants, an agreement was reached. The government promised Liverpool up to £8 million, which would reduce its revenue budget by £20 million once reductions in grant penalty were taken into account, if Labour abandoned its bankruptcy plan. The Labour party agreed and in July 1984 the council passed a quite different, balanced budget.

Labour had to make many concessions to the Government and drop many of its new spending plans. Most important the council agreed to transfer from its capital budget £13 million, which had been intended to pay for part of its house building programme, to the revenue budget to help pay the wages of workers who maintained and repaired existing housing. This capitalisation of revenue spending inevitably limited Labour's major housing programme and had been strenuously resisted by the council. The council also rescheduled its debt repayments, used up its various reserves, and made rather optimistic assumptions about the rate of inflation and the likely cost of its services during the year. These changes allowed it to cut planned spending for 1984/5 from its original figure of £269 million to £223 million. At that level all government penalties for spending over target were eliminated. However, the council did not increase its rents or fees. It made no effort to reduce its workforce and hence its salary bills and it only increased the rates by 17 per cent, more than the original 9 per cent but far less than civil servants had calculated was necessary to get the council's finances on a sound long term basis. In other words, the 1984/5 budget was balanced by creative accounting only. The council's underlying financial problems were simply transferred into 1985/6.

Round 2: The 1985/6 Budget

The Labour council reopened its argument with the government almost as soon as the 1984/5 budget had been agreed, four months into the financial year. This year the politics were different. In the first case, the Labour council had exploited the small concessions the government had offered in July and claimed a major political victory. This angered the Conservative government and convinced it there was no point in trying to help the city further.

In addition, in November 1985 there was a major dispute about the amount of extra money that the council claimed the government had promised for Liverpool's major housing programme in 1985/6, in return for the £13 million of revenue expenditure the council had capitalised in July to balance the books. The government denied the council's claim that it had promised a capital allocation of £130 million, in contrast to the £37 million it allowed the council. After this denial, the Labour council immediately threatened to reverse its decision to capitalise and create a budget crisis again but in 1985 the Government had decided it would not repeat its behaviour and resisted the pressure until the council eventually abandoned its threat without getting any extra money.

The second political difference in 1985 was that Liverpool had joined with a number of other Labour controlled local authorities to campaign to resist the government's rate-capping legislation. They adopted a strategy of refusing to set a rate until the government changed its legislation. The government did not and eventually all the authorities conceded and set a rate. However, Liverpool was the last to do so. It set its rate on 14 June 1985. Unlike 1984, this delay led the Labour councillors into serious legal problems. After several unsuccessful efforts to persuade Liverpool to make a rate, the District Auditor finally decided this year to take action against the council. On 26 June he informed them that his preliminary investigations revealed that by delaying setting a rate the council had lost at least £106,000. Since that figure was greater than £2,000 for each of 49 councillors responsible for the delay, he intended to surcharge them for that amount and disqualify them from office. The councillors replied to the charges on 19 July but on 6 September the Auditor rejected their defence. In January 1986 the councillors appealed against the Auditor's decision in the High Court but on 6 March three High Court judges unanimously rejected their appeal. The Labour councillors next appealed to the Court of Appeal and the case was planned to start on 7 July 1986.

The delay in setting the rate in 1985 led the Labour council into enormous legal difficulties but the budget it finally set caused it equally large political problems with the national Labour party. Throughout 1985 the Labour council, under instruction from the District Labour Party and supported by the Joint Shop Stewards Committee, had once again refused to take the steps necessary to balance its income and expenditure and on 14 June 1985 it presented its second deficit budget. Despite its expenditure target of £222 million for 1985/6, the council planned to spend £265 million. At this level, rate support grant would fall to £29 million, leaving £241 million to be paid for from the rates, which would require a rate increase of 170 per cent. Labour planned to increase the rates by only 9 per cent which would produce only £125 million and leave a deficit of £117 million. On that basis, the authority would eventually be unable to borrow from public or private sources and would run out of money at some point in the autumn of 1985.

Despite the advice of its professional officers, the warnings of the District Auditor, the recommendations of the Government and the pleas of the national Labour leadership, Labour refused to change its policy for the next four months. On 6 September the council took the step that its bankruptcy tactic had always required, but which nevertheless created political turmoil. It issued redundancy notices to all 31,000 employees. They would lose their jobs in December 1985 and be reinstated in the new financial year four months later. Meanwhile local services, except for minimal emergency ones, would end. This tactic split the local unions. Some accepted it but more rejected it. The Joint Shop Stewards Committee disintegrated as a result of it and several unions left it and never returned. The District Labour Party was thrown into confusion by the move and rejected the redundancies but also opposed any cuts in expenditure which would help avoid redundancies.

However, the national Labour leadership, which was stunned by the tactic, was clear what it wanted. The council should balance its books, in whatever way was necessary. At the annual party conference three weeks later, the national executive committee forced Liverpool to withdraw its request for support of its plan and insisted that the council allow an inquiry into its finances by independent experts from the Association of Metropolitan Authorities. In return, several of those authorities promised to help Liverpool with its capital programme by lending it some of their own capital allocations.

The inquiry was led by Maurice Stonefrost, Director General of the GLC. It reported in November 1985 - the first time that the council's finances had been exposed to extensive independent scrutiny, when it was within days of bankruptcy. In many respects the Stonefrost Report confirmed the council's claim that its problems arose at least partly from "the effect of the system of grant assessments on the council's position at a time of economic and social stress in Liverpool". It also observed that the Government's failure to provide extra money to help Liverpool's housing problems "does not appear to reflect well upon the Government." Nevertheless, Stonefrost argued that the council could and should avoid bankruptcy. It had five sources of income - grants, rates, rents, charges and borrowing - which it could vary to match expenditure. The report recommended two actions. First, the council should use some of its capital funds to pay for revenue expenditure. That would limit the scale of the house building programme but if the council went bankrupt the programme would obviously stop completely.

However, Stonefrost insisted that capitalisation on its own was not enough. The report stressed that the council faced very difficult decisions which it should start to tackle sooner rather than later if it were to establish financial credibility and avoid the crisis returning in future years. The council had to start matching income and expenditure and should trim its services, increase its fees and put its rates up by a further 15 per cent. Such a rate increase was, in Stonefrost's words, "the cornerstone to the restoration of financial credibility". Credibility "required more than arithmetically balancing the books" and could not be achieved "solely by accountancy transactions which ease the problems in 1985/6 and add to the problems of 1986/7", but this was exactly what happened in November 1985 with all the consequences Stonefrost had predicted. On 25 November, in the face of the opposition of the national Labour party, the local trade unions and growing doubts in the local Labour party, the council finally abandoned its stand a few days before the authority was due to go bankrupt. The council again agreed to capitalise over £23 million of revenue expenditure in two financial years. Once this was done, government grant penalties were correspondingly cut and the revenue budget could be reduced to £262 million, the amount that the rate levied on 14 June would finance but the rate rise that Stonefrost had argued was the cornerstone of credibility was not made. The council again balanced its books by creative accounting and the underlying problems were once more ignored.

In fact, the solution adopted worsened the council's long term problems. It had raised the money to capitalise £23 million of revenue spending by entering into a deferred payment arrangement with a London stockbroker, Phillips and Drew. Under this arrangement, a financial syndicate would pay up to £30 million to private contractors working on the council's capital programme in 1985/6. This would release the equivalent amount from existing capital resources to allow the capitalisation required to balance the revenue budget. However, the loan would have to be repaid over a five-year period. In future, the council would have to find up to £8 million a year from its capital allocation to repay the loan. In view of the Government's reductions in national housing allocations, this would make it difficult for the council to pay for any new house building or even maintain existing housing. What especially angered the national Labour leadership was that it became clear that the arrangement had first been announced at a council committee in September 1985. There was no evidence to suggest it could not have been used then. The Labour council had allowed the city to hover on the brink of financial collapse for over three months and had threatened redundancy for all its employees, when the eventual solution had apparently been available all that time. That provoked the suspension of the District Labour Party.

The Third Round: The 1986/7 Budget

The council's second budget crisis was not resolved until the financial year 1985/6 was already eight months old. Labour's strategy meant that the council lurched from one crisis to another on an ad hoc basis with hardly any long term financial planning. Inevitably, barely any attention had been paid before December 1985 to the next year's budget which was due to start in four month's time in April 1986. Little detailed information about the council's plans for the following year was released and few finance and strategy committee meetings were held to discuss plans during these four months.

This prompted the District Auditor to act once more and prepare a major review of the council's financial affairs which he released on 24 March 1986. It was a devastating attack on the Labour council which argued that its "financial and management systems are seriously out of hand and urgent steps are needed to correct the situation". The last two year's crises "demonstrated the need for realistic assessments of available resources and of realistic expenditure programmes that can be financed from them". The council needed to provide "better and more up to date financial information" to allow this to happen.

The Auditor admitted that Liverpool was one of the most socially deprived areas of the country but argued that its problems had been worsened by "the council's own style of management (which) has led to inefficiencies, diseconomies and ineffectiveness". The council's "objectives, priorities and strategies are not clearly set out in a way that will assist their achievement". The Auditor argued that the 1984/5 budget process was "inordinately lengthy, consumed a disproportionate amount of time, adversely affected the work of the city treasurer's department. Little financial benefit resulted".

The 1985/6 process was "again lengthy, time-consuming and costly." It produced no extra money. The measures finally adopted did not "address the real problem posed by an expenditure level which is higher than can be met by the level of rates the council is prepared to levy." They "could have been taken much earlier in the year ... (avoiding) much worry and distress to recipients of services and to council employees." On the capital budget he argued that "The council is entering into commitments without knowing how they can be financed. This is a recipe for future financial chaos." He continued, "The normal budgetary control system now appears to be inoperative. It may take some years to restore the financial management process to the requisite standard. It is largely through (the city treasurer's) endeavours and those of his staff that the city was able to function at all in the latter part of 1985."

These failures in decision-making had also affected budget making for the following year. The Auditor stressed that only weeks before the next financial year began, it was evident that "Production of a proper budget for 1986/7 is not going ahead on traditional lines. In the absence of such a budget the council cannot ensure that spending plans are capable of being met from available resources. The production of a properly constructed, detailed balanced budget is urgently required." A budget for 1986/7 was, however, produced on 21 March at the Finance and Strategy Committee. It did not, however, meet the Auditor's requirement.

The Treasurer's report to the committee explained that since the city had spent beyond 20 per cent of its GREA and 4 per cent of its 1985/6 target, it had been rate-capped by the government for 1986/7. In June 1985, Liverpool was set an expenditure limit of £265 million, consisting of a 10 per cent increase on budgeted expenditure for 1984/5 plus £19 million for the former county council services which the city would be responsible for providing after abolition. The authority asked for a redetermination of that figure on the grounds that in 1984/5 it had £15 million of reserves and capital receipts which had been used to reduce its base budget and which were not available in 1986/7. Its real base budget that year had been higher than the Government's assessment. In December the DoE accepted that £9 million could be added to the city's expenditure limit, which was set at £274 million, allowing a 15 per cent rate increase.

This was the technical source of Liverpool's financial problem for 1986/7. In 1985/6, the authority's base budget had been £262 million. In order to maintain its grant in November 1985 it had reduced its expenditure to £222 million, primarily by capitalising revenue expenditure with the money generated by its deferred payment arrangement. However, the Treasurer estimated that in 1986/7, given various changes in actual spending in the year and inflation, it would cost £287 million to provide the same services. He also estimated it would cost £24 million to run the former county services, not the £21 million the DoE had allowed. In other words, his estimate was that the city needed to spend £311 million in 1986/7 but was restricted to £274 million, unless further reserves and capital receipts could be found. On those figures, the council would have at least £37 million less money than it actually needed to run the city.

The deficit was reduced in three ways. £4.7 million was found by moving spending between three financial years to minimise grant penalties. £4.7 million extra government grant was gained because local government spending had been less than anticipated the previous year and every authority was getting a share of the surplus which was being 'recycled'. £1.8 million was found by transferring some costs from the council to the DHSS for elderly people in voluntary residential care. Nevertheless, that still meant that the actual gap between income and expenditure was £27.5 million and might rise during the year.

The Treasurer pointed out that there were only three areas where the authority could significantly reduce its net expenditure: employees' salaries, supplies and services and council house rents and insisted the necessary reduction had to be found "with the utmost urgency". However, the Labour council's budget which was passed on 27 March 1986 did not reduce the gap. It simply accepted those two figures, set the maximum rate the DoE permitted and began the year with a budget deficit but it set up a special committee system to identify ways of closing the gap by the second week in June.

However, the meeting of the Finance and Strategy Committee on 10 June revealed that the maximum possible savings which had been identified by the committees even if implemented would produce only £29 million during the part of the year that remained. The reductions that the committees had actually approved only added up to £4 million. There was still a gap of £23 million. The Treasurer "earnestly recommended" the committee to examine costs and rents as rapidly as possible to "avoid an unlawful deficit at the end of the year." The Treasurer also pointed out that the financial institutions were only lending money to the city because the council had stated its intention to balance its books. The council would have to start doing that in earnest if it were to continue to borrow money and avoid insolvency. The slight progress towards reducing spending made by mid-June once more left the city on the edge of bankruptcy.

Conclusion

Budgets are financial statements. They are also political gestures. In June 1986 Liverpool was on the edge of collapse because the Labour council was refusing to make the decisions necessary to balance the books but by this time its consistent refusal over three years to match income and expenditure meant its options were very limited. It required major cuts in jobs, reductions in services and large rent rises - unless the council could negotiate another deferred payment scheme which would allow the problem to be passed on in an even more severe form to the following financial year and possibly another administration.

The collapse of the local economy, councillors' reservations about the government's grant system, which were shared by the council's officers, the initial support of the electorate and some trade unions encouraged the Labour party in its policy but essentially the deficit budget was a political decision, devised deep within the Labour party. The council's professional officers consistently advised against the strategy but the Labour council did not accept their advice. The officers were accorded a minor role in policy making. Even the Labour group on the council did not make the policy alone. The theory of party democracy meant that the policy was determined by the District Labour Party outside the council chamber. The group simply implemented

it but even within the District Labour Party, power to initiate policy
was concentrated in the executive committee, whose recommendations were
always endorsed.   Within the Labour group itself power was highly
concentrated in the hands of the chairman of the Finance and Strategy
Committee, to whom extensive powers had been delegated.   In other words
the Labour party set the shape of the budget strategy but its real
contribution was limited to discussions of general principle.   The
informal concentration and exercise of political power within the party
meant that policy was made not openly but in secrecy by a narrow elite.

6. Oldham Metropolitan Borough Council

PAUL BARBERIS AND ARNOLD SKELTON

Context and Background

Oldham Metropolitan Borough Council is one on the 10 district councils within the Greater Manchester County, a major industrial conurbation in the North West of England. The Council was created upon the reorganisation of local government in 1974. It has a population of approximately 220,000, nearly half of whom live in the town of Oldham itself, a former county borough council. Oldham is situated approximately 10 miles east of Manchester and at the foot of the Pennines. It is a former mill town having risen to prosperity during the expansion of the textile industry in the 19th century. Its subsequent decline has been associated with the decline of that industry. In recent years, it has diversified its industrial activities to include electro- and aero-engineering, leather goods and paint manufacture. The borough council has been active in trying to attract new industries to the area and has, for example, established an Economic Development Unit to encourage and support industrial development.

Like many other industrial towns in the north of England, it is currently suffering the effects of economic depression. In October 1985, its unemployment rate was 14.4 per cent, compared with a regional average of 16.3 per cent and a national average of 13.4 per cent. Levels of unemployment have risen substantially over the last decade: 3802 unemployed in 1975; 8769 in 1980; and 11,925 in 1985. [1] The following figures give further confirmation of the economic and social decline and of the increasing pressure on services in the area.

Table 6.1

SOCIAL CHARACTERISTICS

ITEM	1979/80	1983/84
Job vacancies, school leavers	785	465
Job vacancies, adults	7933	6955
Unemployed adults	4854	12765
% pupils on free meals	18.8	31.4
Rent arrears as % of total rent	3.9	5.2
Average rent rebates/year	5648	18104
Average rent allowances/year	620	2662
Cap. exp. on housing improvements	£5.2m	£2.6m
No. of field work referrals	7394	8804

(Source: Economic Development Unit, Oldham MBC)

Politically, Oldham has a strong Party tradition and its style of politics is quite traditional too, perhaps best described as consensus politics. During 1985/6 Oldham was a Labour controlled council as it has been since 1979. Of a total of 60 members, 40 are Labour, 16 Conservative and 4 Liberal. The Conservatives held a majority on the Council immediately prior to the elections of May 1979. In May 1985 the Labour Group elected a new leader, a younger man, to replace the long serving and ailing (since deceased) representative of the old guard.

There are two features of particular note in connection with the immediate context to the budget. First, Oldham has a housing problem which has financial as well as social consequences. Few houses were built during the 1930s, '40s and '50s, producing a deficit that required a mass building programme in the 1960s and 1970s. There is no quantitative problem of housing provision to meet current needs – indeed there is now a surplus – but the high proportion of relatively recent develpment has meant a much higher debt burden than that faced by most councils.

Second, the Government announced that the Greater Manchester Council was to be abolished on 31 March 1986. This meant that the preceding months involved leading members and many officers in detailed discussions and negotiations to make necessary arrangements for the provision and transfer of services upon the abolition of the County Council. This itself has immediate significance so far as the budget is concerned. It has further significance for the process of the budget itself, inasmuch as there remained until an advanced stage considerable uncertainty as to how these arrangements were to be finalised. Indeed, it was necessary in the event to complete the budgetary process with some matters concerning abolition either unresolved or uncertain, in terms of finance and staffing consequences. Our study is, therefore, of an untypical year, a fact which was frequently remarked upon in conversation with all members and officers to whom we talked.

The Budget Machinery

Formally the full Council decide the Budget and it held a special meeting towards the end of March to decide the budget for 1986/7. As is common in local authorities, it has a central committee with responsibility for all matters of finance, the Policy Committee. This committee consists of 10 councillors, the majority from the ruling party, most of whom are chairpersons of major committees. Six members are drawn from the opposition parties, currently five Conservative and one Liberal. It is chaired by the Leader of the majority party. Although this Committee is of central importance to the Council, budget matters are dealt with in more detail by one of its sub-committees, the Strategy and Resources Sub-committee. This sub-committee was set up in June 1985, a fact which is significant to our study in three ways. First, this sub-committee was established to enable a synoptic and long term view to be taken of the budget. This implies that participants were aware of some inadequacies in previous budgetary procedures. Secondly, its creation was initiated by the Chief Executive and Treasurer - a suggestion accepted by the newly elected leader in 1985, after having been resisted by his predecessor. Thirdly, the creation of this sub-committee for these reasons provides us with a bench mark against which we can survey the actual procedures adopted in making a budget for 1986/7: we can compare intention with outcome.

At officer level the Council is served by a Chief Executive and Treasurer, roles that were combined upon the appointment of the present incumbent, in January 1983. He is present at all meetings of the Policy Committee and of the Strategy and Resources Sub-committee. He also attends meetings of the Labour Policy Group, the inner circle of the Labour Party: but he does not attend Labour Group meetings. Reporting to the Chief Executive and Treasurer are a Deputy Treasurer and a Chief Accountant. Within each of the service departments, there is a Group Accountant, namely a member of the Finance Department who acts on its behalf in overseeing the financial arrangements of each particular department. This provides a vital link to co-ordinate the budgetary process.

The Budgetary Process

The Finance Department is involved in preparing a budget which contains three elements. First, a revision of the current year Estimates; second, a forecast of the expenditure for the forthcoming financial year; third, a general estimate for the year after that. This process, taking place at officer level, begins in the Autumn of each year.

The starting point is the current year budget, adjusted to account for inflation, underspending, new policies, changes in interest rates and unforeseen items of expenditure. These elements provide the basis for a revised current year estimate. The process for establishing calculations for the forthcoming year's budget is initiated by the Finance Department who send appropriate forms to each spending department. This process begins in October and is followed by detailed discussions and negotiations between the Finance Department and officers of the spending departments so that by Christmas a committed budget figure is established. In so doing, officers work through two processes concurrently; one concerning the original estimate and the other concerning the revised estimate for salaries and wages. Interestingly, the Chief Accountant described the latter process as zero based budgeting, inasmuch as salaries and wages estimates are built up, post by post and calculated as an out-turn figure. The computer print-out of all salary posts provides information at mid-year point (i.e. September) and all figures for salaries and wages are agreed between spending departments and the Finance Department by mid-November. The procedure is not, however, zero based in that there is no detailed scrutiny of the need for each post, merely a detailed financial calculation based upon each member of staff in post rather than a general estimate based upon establishment figures.

Immediately after Christmas these calculations begin to take on a more global focus, with consideration of a number of broad manoeuvres: for example, to defy the Government's expenditure targets; to increase charges; to use existing balances; to engage in creative accounting; to increase rates; and to cut services.

Oldham had no wish to defy government spending targets and thus incur heavy penalties. Just before Christmas, the Council was notified by the Department of Environment of its grant related expenditure, showing a cash standstill of £94 million, and £97.8 million allowing for inflation at 4.3 per cent. This compares with a Grant Related Expenditure Assessment (GREA) figure for Oldham for 1986/7 of £106.5 million. This seems to have been received with some horror by the Leader, seeming as it did to imply either a massive rate rise or savage cuts in services. Interestingly, the Chief Executive and Treasurer appeared more phlegmatic about the decision and its likely consequences.

Early in January the Labour Policy Group called for calculations on the basis of an "external measure" (i.e. the Government's figures) as a bench mark for decisions. Having already discussed the implications in detail with the Leader, the Chief Executive and Treasurer told the Policy Group that a 7 per cent cut would be needed in the likely estimate, as things then stood, for 1986/7. This would bring the Council close to the Government's inflation-inclusive figure of £97.8 million. It was agreed that spending committees be 'asked' to produce budget options to achieve these reductions, a call for 10 per cent cuts to meet the 'no-inflation' level of £94 million having been defeated within the Policy Group at the wish of the Leader and on the advice of the Chief Executive and Treasurer.

Increases in charges were not expected to provide much relief. The greatest potential source is normally that of housing rents; but Oldham's rents were already higher than any other in the Greater Manchester area, and the possibility of further increases was dismissed by the Labour Leader, although no full debate took place in the Labour Group. Instead, committees were expected to look for smaller scale yields from increases in other charges.

The possibility of using existing balances was virtually pre-empted on the advice of the Chief Executive and Treasurer, advice which matched the disposition of the political leadership. Similarly, there was no overt decision to engage (or not engage) in techniques of 'creative accounting'. This is perhaps a matter typically (though not always) left in the hands of officers. The Chief Executive and Treasurer was adamant that creative accounting had not been used in this or previous years. Instead he referred to financial practices which were "in the best interests of the town". For example, where there had been natural underspending, debts had been prematurely settled. Also, the revenue account had been used where possible to finance capital housing expenditure, thus attracting a 75 per cent subsidy. Interestingly, another senior officer interviewed did refer to the use of creative accounting. To some extent the discrepancy may be a semantic one. Certainly there was no evidence of non-charging of expenditure.

Some local councils have responded to financial crises by selling assets to bring short term yield. Such disposals are once and for all measures which, when exhausted, cannot be repeated. In Oldham the position is more complicated. Two council estates were sold in the 1980s. These sales, according to the Chief Executive and Treasurer, were driven not by financial considerations (the yield was under £1 million) but as a matter of housing policy. Others to whom we spoke were less certain about the distinction. Whatever the motive and whatever the policy (if any), Oldham had gone as far as it could or was prepared to go with asset sales when it prepared its budget for 1986/7. Thus the main variable factors were to be cuts in services and/or increases in rates. We now concentrate our analysis on these two areas of decision making.

The call for 7 per cent cuts was received calmly by spending committees. It was noticeable that at no meeting of the Policy Committee, or of its Strategy and Resources Sub-committee, or of the Labour Group were these cuts specifically debated. Spending committees responded to the request by specifying the implications of a 7 per cent reduction, the identification of potential sacrifices being the work either of senior officers in the departments, or of senior officers in conjunction with chairpersons. This activity took place during January and February. On the surface (i.e. in formal meetings) the budgetary process seemed to enter a period of interregnum; whilst below the surface much detailed preparation was taking place. There was no 'star chamber', no 'Spanish Inquisition', nor even what Greenwood describes as a 'sweat-box' of hyperactivity in which inflated departmental priorities are hastily and sometimes crudely trimmed. Indeed it was not possible to observe and we can only imperfectly reconstruct, the process of events. Equally, we are reluctant to imply scenarios of conspiracy, counter-conspiracy and intrigue. The reality, we suspect, was more mundane.

It is clear that the Labour leadership had no intention of implementing 7 per cent cuts. This explains the calm. In the event, 'budget options' (items of increased or reduced expenditure) brought a nett overall reduction of nearly 1 per cent, the main area of cut-back being highway maintenance ($£\frac{1}{4}$ million reduction). [2] The 'options' for education showed a nett **increase** of over £400,000. These decisions had been put to and endorsed by committees before the end of February - decisions ratified by the Policy Committee which also had a few relatively insignificant but unresolved committee 'options' to determine.

The meetings of the Policy Committee and of the special budget meeting of the Strategy and Resources Sub-committee which immediately preceeded it, were consequently low-key affairs. The Chairman (the Council Leader) and the Chief Executive and Treasurer, both engaged elsewhere on 'vital Council business', were absent from this theoretically important meeting. The Deputy Chairman observed that the budget was a "complicated business" - a sentiment evidently widely shared as members approved without debate the main expenditure proposals. The meeting was one of the shortest we attended.

This low-key approach was certainly a political triumph for the Labour leadership. The prevailing style of politics in Oldham impels the opposition parties - and even the back-benchers from the majority party - towards a passive role. Through sheer lack of detailed information it may be difficult for those not directly involved to make a contribution. In addition many back-benchers seem more interested in constituency and related matters - perhaps because these are more tangible and manageable. The Chief Executive and Treasurer works closely with the Leader of the Council, meeting on a daily basis. He also meets leaders of the opposition parties, though much less frequently, more as a matter of courtesy and to provide general information than to engage in detailed discussions. So it is inevitably difficult for those outside the 'circle of the informed' to penetrate the orbit of the budget process, even if such is their wish. The politics of consensus, with its implication of broad trust and acceptance, generates little momentum to disturb the pattern. It was notable how little the opposition parties sought, during the months of preparation, to relate specific policy proposals to any macro perspective on the budget, aside from periodic expressions of the need to protect ratepayers. Indeed in one case, the Conservatives, in an effort to protect local traders, opposed a proposal intended to reduce costs - a gesture from which Labour members made maximum political capital.

Not until the special Council Budget Meeting on 19 March 1986 did opposition parties present detailed alternative plans. The Liberals presented a package of miscellaneous savings which would have reduced the proposed rate by 1p in the £. The Conservatives proposed increased rents to council tenants whose dwellings had been improved with installation of gas central heating. These proposals were easily defeated in the vote. The Labour leadership described these proposals as "scratching around for savings", savings which would in any case have been financially insignificant. Labour's trump card was the fact that this meeting was the first occasion upon which specific opposition proposals had been made - a charge which was only half-heartedly denied.

Two more general observations made by the Conservative opposition at the Council Budget Meeting are worthy of mention. First, it was claimed that committees had examined only savings that would have brought unacceptable sacrifices, such as the closure of cemeteries, a moratorium on housing transfers, or the withdrawal of educational maintenance and clothing grants. The implications were that such cuts were unacceptable to the Conservatives as they were to the other parties, but that (perfunctory) consideration of them had pre-empted examination of other possible savings that would have been more acceptable (to the Conservatives at least). Second, it was claimed that this had been done deliberately. To this the Leader of the Council made the interesting remark that many of the 'policy options' had been determined by officers, upon whose integrity the Conservatives' challenge was therefore an unwarranted smear. This was sufficient to silence the opposition, a further manifestation of the prevailing consensus and perhaps, of the lack of assertiveness of an opposition heavily outnumbered.

The Labour leadership were nevertheless sensitive to the political consequences of the 20 per cent increase in rates (from 202p to 244p in the £), the inevitable outcome of its disinclination to respond to other possible manoeuvres. A few days before the Council Budget Meeting, the Policy Committee had approved a revised schedule of increases in discretionary charges, the effect of which was to reduce the proposed rate for 1986/7 from 245p to 244p in the £. Moreover, at the Labour Group meeting on the eve of the Council Budget, one of the councillors expressed his misgivings at the extent of the rate increase, calling for re-consideration. This was easily defeated, mainly on the grounds of the impossibility of making 'eleventh hour' changes, and of the need for consistency and solidarity. In deference to the latter, it was decided that the Council debate should be carried by the Leader and chairpersons, a decision which perhaps reflects a lack of complete confidence and trust by the leadership in some of their back-bench supporters. Indeed, in our informal conversations, we learnt that the one dissenter represented the views of others among a silent minority of Labour back-benchers. In moving the recommendation for a rate of 244p in the £, the Council Leader was unequivocal and uncompromising:

"It is an horrific increase and I have no pleasure in recommending it to the Council tonight. The bulk of the increase is, however, outside the control of the Council. We have therefore no alternative but to face this (increase)..."(3)

The twin reasons for the increase, he said, both lay in Westminster. First, the Government had abolished the GMC, and this accounted for 24p of the 42p increase. Second, there had been a reduction in the Rate Support Grant leaving Oldham with a grant of £59.1 million or 57 per cent of its budget for 1986/7, a reduction of 4 per cent. This, the Leader said, accounted for a further 6p increase. This left a 12p (roughly 6 per cent) increase, only slightly above the level of inflation. He was able to claim that Oldham's budget of £105.1 million was within the Government's 'notional' (i.e. Grant Related Expenditure) figure for the Council of £106.5 million, albeit attracting a penalty loss of £2.6 million for planning to spend above the stipulated £94 million. Oldham was therefore being penalised for spending less than "the Government's own assessment of our need to spend." (4) And so the rate for Oldham was duly fixed.

Analysis and Conclusions

First, one of the most notable features of the style of politics in Oldham is its consensual nature - an initial impression consistently confirmed in all our observations. At Council and committee meetings there was predictable cross-barter banter but nearly always within accepted parameters. Members of opposing parties retained a general cordiality, so that even personal political attacks were laced with elements of humour. The Conservative leader's solicitor's practice was the subject of repartee on a number of occasions, especially during debates about proposals to make donations to other local authorities to help defray costs incurred by litigation. Towards the end of the budget cycle, the Labour leader publicly recounted a conversation with his wife. He threatened to return from the dead to haunt her: to which she replied that she would then at least have the chance to see him. On another occasion, the Deputy Labour leader delayed the start of a meeting he was chairing while proceeding to arrange for one of his colleagues to give a Conservative member a lift home afterwards - on the understanding that the Conservatives behaved themselves during the meeting!

Although the Labour Group had elected a new Leader in 1985, which may have brought about a new style of political leadership, this should not be interpreted as having been a challenge to the consensus style of party politics. The new Leader was by no means the obvious choice; it appears that he was the consensus candidate who triumphed against more prominent figures. With little experience of political leadership and an undeveloped support base within the party, it is probable that his approach during his first year of leadership has been borne of the need to establish and consolidate his position. While others might have adopted a more aggressive, confrontational approach, he chose a more low-key, consensual style.

Politics in Oldham are traditional as well as consensual. There was little evidence of the extreme right or hard left, though the latter have a small presence on the Council following local elections in May 1986. Oldham, as one 'moderate' Labour member told us, is usually about "5 years behind the major cities".

Second, there was little evidence of explicit budget strategy in meetings of the Council, or in any of its central committees, or indeed in the Labour Group. As noted above, there were particular proposals which had budget implications but which, during debate, remained unconnected to any broader canvas. Thus, either a budget strategy was being conducted at another level, perhaps within the Labour Policy Group or informally by the Leader in conjunction with the Chief Executive and Treasurer; or else there was no strategy at all. The Chief Executive and Treasurer was adamant that there was a strategy: namely to follow Government expenditure guidelines, and to protect education, housing and social services. Others to whom we spoke seemed less confident in identifying a strategy. No doubt the definition of a strategy may vary among the participants. What the Chief Executive describes as strategy, others might call a response to exigencies. What everyone was agreed upon was that the Strategy and Resources Sub-committee did not, during its first year, operate in the way intended. Those at the centre of the budget process - the Leader and the Chief Executive and Treasurer - were particularly emphatic about this. The Sub-committee was, after all, their 'baby'.

Following this observation about the lack of overt strategy was made another: that whether or not there was a strategy, much detailed and routine work was going on beneath the surface (the 'black box') mainly at officer level. Officers worked to a well ordered schedule of procedure and events. The serving up of the 7 per cent options was almost a diversion from the routine of budget preparation, an (intentionally) unproductive diversion as it turned out. The outcome of the budget, resting mainly on rate increases to balance competing constraints, was in a sense a line of least resistance, involving no cataclysmic turning point. It would be a distortion to say that the budget 'made itself' but as Mackenzie (1967, pp.232-4) has noted, we often search in vain for the locus of a decision as much because there is no recognisable locus as because it lies hidden from our attention. Nonetheless the overriding impression is of a centralised system, in which the Leader and Chief Executive played the dominant parts, supplemented by a strong Finance Department dealing on a one-to-one basis with each of the spending departments.

Our fourth observation is that the majority of councillors in Oldham adopt a parochial perspective of their roles. The interests of their electoral wards and particular hobby horses are uppermost, often to the exclusion of broader issues of strategy. This is hardly an original observation (Maud 1967, Corina 1974) but it suggests one of two possibilities for the future: either the attempt at strategy in Oldham will remain frustrated; or else there will be a heightened tendency towards oligarchy and a schism between leaders and followers.

This possible schism may either be bridged or exacerbated in the light of our fifth observation: that any possibility of clear strategy was pre-empted by the abolition of the GMC. Quite unintentionally, the central committees turned out to be the formal mechanism through which abolition matters were handled. It would be facile to cite abolition as the overriding factor to explain the discrepancy between intention and outcome in the way Oldham produced its budget. We have already referred both to the general disruption and to the financial consequences for the rates. The latter were created in part by a shift from rateable value to population as the basis for calculations of certain ex-GMC functions – a shift which disadvantages Oldham, while benefiting other near-by districts such as Manchester and Trafford. Moreover, Oldham was informed, on the day of the Council Budget Meeting, that it would have to raise $£\frac{1}{4}$ million in addition to the amount notified earlier to cover insurance premiums inherited from the GMC. For some time to come, matters concerning abolition will continue to exercise leading members and senior officers but these considerations should be less of a distraction during preparations for the 1987/8 budget. It will be interesting to see whether the Strategy and Resources Sub-committee is able to fulfil its intended purpose and if so, whether it draws all members towards a more strategic perspective, or whether the roles of the leaders (of the majority party) will become further divorced from those of the rank and file. The implications will be equally interesting at officer level, where already the Management Team consists of an elite from among the Council's chief officers.

There is no doubt that abolition was a nuisance and a distraction, and adversely affected Oldham's budget for 1986/7. However, senior figures were able to make political capital out of this, claiming that abolition was the major cause of the eventual rate rise. Indeed, throughout the process the Labour majority took every opportunity to highlight the difficulties created by the Conservative Central Government – not only abolition, but also their setting of punitive Targets and their failure to allow financing of the 'necessary' GREA. Eventually the Labour leadership was able to 'blame' the Government for 30p of the 42p rate rise.

Although relationships with the GMC dominated this budgetary cycle, other external groups were also involved in budget discussions – notably local unions and Chambers of Commerce and Trade. Such groups offered clear but partisan advice and this appeared to have little impact. One senior officer told us that he was disinclined to accept the advice of those who had no electoral mandate. For this officer at least, requirements for external consultation seemed tokenist and time consuming. A much more important influence was the EEC. Oldham has regularly claimed and received EEC funding for local projects and the Council has recently agreed the appointment of an officer whose full-time responsibilities will be to maximise financial aid from Brussels.

Finally, we comment on the roles of the Leader of the Council and of the Chief Executive and Treasurer. These two men, using in harness the authority of their respective offices, gave broad shape, if not strategy, to the budget during the crucial period of January-February. The Leader, as noted, often played a 'ring holding' role during meetings but he was able to assert his authority at crucial moments, as when he silenced the Labour group in January with a warning of rate rises of up to 30 per cent. Many Labour councillors believe that his position as leader, initially fragile and widely seen as short-term, became more secure as the municipal year proceeded. It is accepted that his role in the budget has been mainly responsible for this transformation.

The authority of the Chief Executive and Treasurer was never in doubt. On a number of occasions he intervened (with or without prompting from the Leader) during committee (but never in full Council) meetings. He was not afraid to deal head-on with issues raised by the opposition parties sometimes on matters of political sensitivity. His interventions were nearly always accepted as authoritative. Where his advice excited discussion, opposition members were usually careful to express acknowledgement of his political neutrality before pursuing further questions. Only once was there a half-hearted suggestion that he was impregnated with the colours of the majority party. He succeeded in playing a major and positive role in the budget, while drawing and maintaining universal respect. Here again, the climate of consensus played its part.

Inasmuch as the budget was "made rather than bequeathed" and inasmuch as it is possible to penetrate the 'black box', we conclude that it was made primarily by the Leader and the Chief Executive and Treasurer each with a select supporting cast. This powerful nexus, working through and within the Labour Policy Group is surrounded by an outer orbit of committees, sustained by a galaxy of mostly willing back-benchers and ably assisted by a cadre of central finance offices: herein, if anywhere, lay the dynamics of Oldham's budget.

Notes

[1] Economic Development Unit, Oldham MBC.

[2] Joint Meeting of Policy Committee and Finance Sub-Committee, March 1986: papers, to which we were given access, are not available for publication.

[3] Budget 1986/7 Presented by the Chairman of the Policy Committee Councillor J.B.Battye, at the Council Meeting 19 March 1986 Speech text p.1.

[4] Ibid. p.4.

7. Harrow London Borough Council

STEPHEN COPE

Introduction - Harrow in Context

Harrow is a relatively small and prosperous borough in London. Its Council has been dominated by the Conservatives for many years, although after the last May election they now have the smallest of majorities. It is a high-spending Conservative-controlled local authority.

The purpose of this report is to describe and explain how budgets are made in Harrow LBC. The research project involved a perusal of a vast array of Council documents, the conduction of many interviews with leading actors in the budgetary process, the monitoring of the local press, and some general reading on budgeting in local government.

The focus of the research was the financial year 1985/6 which saw the making of the revenue budget for 1986/7 and the review of the capital programme for 1985/6 to 1988/9. This report gives an approximate chronological version of the budgeting process and focuses on the decision-making rather than the more formal decision-taking process.

The Making of the Revenue Budget

Traditionally revenue budgets have been made on an annual basis in Harrow LBC, like most local authorities. The budgetary cycle was characterised by several key stages:

(a) Analysis of the government's public expenditure plans.

(b) Establishment of initial budget targets for spending committees.

(c) Review of the Value-for-Money Programme.

(d) Assessment by the committees of the financial and service implications of the targets.

(e) Review of the budget strategy in the light of the announcement of the Rate Support Grant settlement.

(f) Preparation of detailed budgets by the committees in line with the revised budget targets.

(g) Consideration by the Policy and Resources Committee of these budgets and the recommendation of the final budget and rate levy.

(h) Setting of the rate by the whole Council.

Many Conservative councillors believed that this conventional one-year budgetary cycle was inadequate. First, there was much concern that the Council has spent consistently in excess of its expenditure target. Given the present government's commitment to reduce local government spending, these councillors wanted a budget strategy that would bring Harrow down to target. They favoured some form of budget planning whereby savings could be made which would maintain and even enhance the level of services, rather than the usual annual trimming exercise where cuts were made without sufficient regard to service provision. They argued that many potential savings, such as those stemming from school closures and computerisation require a longer period of time than one year if they are to be realised. Second, several Conservatives were concerned that there was very little pressure to be efficient. Consequently, they argued that a longer-term budget strategy designed to reduce Harrow's spending would create a climate conducive to the pursuit of value for money. Third, rates in Harrow have not risen for several years because the Council's funds and balances have been used to hold the rates down. This situation could not last because the funds "will run out pretty soon" and therefore either the rates would have to increase or money savings be found. Many Conservatives were alarmed at the already high level of rates and thus preferred to adopt a budget strategy which would produce substantial savings.

The opportunity to implement a longer-term budget strategy arose when the Conservative Group changed its leader, although it was not this issue which precipitated the change of leadership. The former leader, Brian Clark, was reluctant to embark on such a strategy since he felt that the financial situation of the local authority would improve in the near future. The new leader, Donald Abbott, entertained no such hopes and assigned to Ron Grant, the Chairman of the Forward Budgeting Sub-Committee, the task of bringing Harrow's spending in line with government guidelines.

The thinking of the Conservative leadership corresponded with that of the Finance Department and by October 1984 the Medium Term Budget Strategy (MTBS) was developed with the overriding purpose of reducing the Council's spending to the Government's expenditure target over the next four years. The MTBS required that for the first year (1986/7) spending was to be reduced by 2.5 per cent, and for the next two years by 2.75 per cent. (1) At this stage, these target savings were only provisional because there were several major uncertainties which could undermine the budget strategy - for example, the then proposed abolition of the Greater London Council (GLC), the future of the target system and future grant settlements.

It was also decided that for social services there would be an adjustment to reflect demographic changes. This 'demographic money' was justified because of the rising elderly population in Harrow and the consequent increasing demands on social services. Other services were not subject to this adjustment. This situation gave education, in particular, an inbuilt advantage over other services in meeting its target because the savings from falling school rolls would count towards the required savings of the MTBS rather than being discounted as a demographic adjustment.

Although the target savings required by MTBS were applied across-the-board (save for social services), their effects would not be felt equally by services because they faced different pressures and constantly changing circumstances. Also, committees were free to vary the incidence of their targets between the different services within their remit providing that the aggregate level of savings made reached target. For example, the General Public Services Committee required the refuse collection service to find more savings than highway maintenance and the trading standards service.

The MTBS received widespread support within the Conservative Group, although several councillors had reservations regarding its effects upon services. They were comforted with the assurance that the strategy was designed to maintain, not reduce service standards. Most Conservatives saw the MTBS as a way of making spending reductions through efficiency savings rather than service cuts. They envisaged that most of these savings would stem from the Council's value-for-money programme but were aware that several "tough operational decisions" needed to be taken, such as the decision to close schools. The distinction between efficiency savings and service cuts was critical for the purpose of implementing the budget strategy because much of its political support would evaporate if services were adversely affected by the MTBS. Also, this distinction softened the opposition of the chief officers of the service departments to it. The MTBS heralded "a start of a change of attitude amongst chief officers", since the debate now focussed upon savings rather than cuts. The reaction of the officers to the MTBS was mixed. The 'administrators' broadly welcomed the strategy but those directly concerned with service delivery were worried about its disruptive effects upon services. The Opposition - the Liberal Alliance and Labour Groups - were also alarmed at the possible adverse consequences upon service provision of the MTBS. Likewise, the trade unions were also critical of this strategy and were concerned that the Council might have to abandon its no compulsory redundancy policy in order to produce the required level of savings. Given the substantial political support for the MTBS and the dominant position of the Finance Department, the strategy was adopted and it was agreed that its general service implications should be reviewed early in the following year.

In January 1985, the Government produced its annual White Paper presenting its plans for public expenditure. These plans are of little value to local authorities because they are based on unrealistic assumptions and forecasts (especially the inflation base) and have required "some upward discounting of the announced figure to become an unspoken convention" (Adams 1986). Furthermore, these plans are presented for local government generally and are not broken down for individual authorities. Nevertheless, the Finance Department assessed the general implications of these public expenditure plans for local government, the most important of which was the forecast that local authority spending would contract in real terms.

By March the Finance Department had calculated the budget targets of committees for their review of the MTBS, which were later endorsed by the Policy and Resources Committee. During this month committees considered the budgetary and service implications of the strategy and identified a package of savings which was very roughly in line with those required. This exercise consisted of no more than a broad review and the implementation of the savings identified was not considered. Following this review the Policy and Resources Committee concluded that the MTBS was feasible but several committees had difficulties in identifying the required level of savings. The Education and Leisure Committees were unable to find their share of savings and the Director of Education was required to put forward a set of proposed savings in September. Conversely, the Social Services Committee found that for at least the first year the MTBS would be relatively painless to implement because of a windfall. The Committee had made an explicit decision to encourage elderly people to live in private or voluntary homes where the rents would be met by the Department of Health and Social Security rather than in Council-run homes. This DHSS money is substantial and has gone a long way towards meeting the target for social services. The Director of Social Services, Alan Holden, commented that "it has all been too easy in some ways" but believed that for the remaining years of the budget strategy social services will find it very difficult to produce the savings required of the MTBS.

The Council operates a value-for-money programme and as part of the initial review of the MTBS, committees examined their contributions to this programme. Its objective is to generate savings that lead to service improvements. The programme is run by the departments, which report twice yearly to committees and is coordinated by the Finance Department. For the Conservatives the value-for-money programme is integral to the success of the MTBS. The Finance Department is more modest about its value and regards the programme as a useful way of securing political support for the process of making savings but acknowledge that departments could perhaps pursue more vigorously their projects within the programme. Departments generally are more sceptical of its usefulness and see the programme as little more than a public relations exercise which identifies savings that would have materialised without all the fanfare of the programme.

During September, committees considered the detailed budgetary and service implications of the MTBS for 1986/7 and more generally 1987/8. These reviews were based on reports prepared by the service departments in conjunction with the Finance Department. (2) The influence of the Finance Department varies between departments - it exercises greater influence over the content of the budgets of the Engineer's and Leisure Departments than those of the Education and Social Services

Departments. These budget reports were largely endorsed by committees. Several committees identified more savings than required but overall there was a significant shortfall of the savings needed to comply with the MTBS. To a certain extent this shortfall was anticipated because of the problems of planning several years ahead and more important because education was expected to be "where the significant resistance lies". Given that education acounts for well over half of the Council's net expenditure, it was always apparent to everyone concerned that Education was the key to the success of the MTBS. As Education accounted for most of the shortfall of savings required it is worth exploring in detail the reasons why Education was unable at this stage to achieve its target level of savings.

First, the Education Department has very little control over its budget in the short term. About one-third of its spending and most of its income are outside its influence, for example teachers' pay and mandatory student awards. Also, the Council has decided to protect pupil/teacher ratios and capitation allowances and to operate a no compulsory redundancy policy. Therefore, though the Education budget is large, only a relatively small proportion of it can be examined in order to find savings. Second, many savings require a long lead-in time to be implemented, which creates greater difficulties in finding the required savings within a short time. For example, the Council must follow a long and tortuous procedure before a school can be closed. Third, there is very little commitment to the MTBS in both the Education Committee and Education Department because of its potentially adverse consequences upon education provision. On this point, the Director of Education believed that it was "irresponsible for the Council to set financial targets without having regard for the consequences for services." Furthermore, the Education Department claimed that previous cost-cutting exercises have "squeezed the pips" and further savings could be achieved only by abandoning certain policies which the Education Committee would be reluctant to cancel. Finally, with the forthcoming local elections in mind and the importance attached to education locally it is not surprising that the Education Committee was resistant to making the required amount of savings. (3)

This shortfall caused considerable concern within the Finance Department. The Chief Executive and Director of Finance wanted a clear political choice to be made regarding the position of education in the budget strategy in order to maintain the credibility of the MTBS. After much heated discussion between Donald Abbott and Brian Clark (the Chairman of the Education Committee) it was agreed in October that the £411,000 shortfall from 1985/6 carried forward to 1986/7 should be written off in order to ease the burden on the Education Committee. It was also agreed that committees should have to absorb the revenue costs of the capital programme within the targets set under the MTBS.

By Autumn two developments affecting the MTBS had unfolded. The first concerned the abolition of the GLC. It was agreed earlier that the services transferred from the GLC to the Council would be treated separately for budgetary purposes. (4) For those services where the costs of provision were known (e.g. travel concessions for the elderly, blind and handicapped), they would be incorporated into the relevant committee's budgets but for those where the costs were not clearly known (e.g. the London Residuary Body Levy), they would be funded from the contingency fund which is calculated by the Finance Department. The reasons for this special budgetary treatment of the transferred services were twofold. First, the Conservative Group and the Finance Department were determined that the abolition of the GLC should not threaten the MTBS. Second, the Finance Department did not want to give the service departments the opportunity of using abolition as an excuse for inflating their budgets far in excess of what they needed. The Finance Department wanted to keep tight control of the budget-making process, particularly as it was not clear whether the Government would sufficiently compensate the Council with more grant for taking over services from the GLC.

The second development was the announcement by the Government that the target system was to be disbanded from April 1986. The Conservative Group and the Finance Department held the view that the MTBS should continue to be implemented although its basis was the now defunct government target. They argued that whatever the effects of the new system of expenditure control and they were not clear, the Council would still have to reduce its spending if it was to avoid being penalised for 'overspending' by the government.

In December the government announced the Rate Support Grant settlement. This announcement came later than usual because of a court challenge against the Department of the Environment which threatened to undermine the entire target system. One of the many problems of the block grant system highlighted by the Audit Commission is the lateness of grant decisions. (Audit Commission 1984). Their lateness inhibits local authorities from financial planning. This problem is particularly felt by Harrow LBC because of the longer timescale of its budget strategy. The Chief Executive commented:

"Everyone agrees that effective management of local services requires a degree of medium term financial uncertainty. Successive block grant settlements have undermined service and financial plans with arbitrary rate changes based on unexpected grant swings." (1986)

Overall, the grant settlement for Harrow LBC was favourable compared with previous years and it included an estimated £11½ million as additional funding to compensate the Council for taking over functions from the GLC. (5)

By January 1986, revised budgets for committees were produced by the service and Finance Departments. The budget was prepared originally at November 1984 prices and was now amended to reflect November 1985 prices, as well as to take into account any agreed policy changes, the revenue consequences of the capital programme, the cost of the transferred services from the GLC, savings, growth items and other financial adjustments (e.g. those which were the result of inaccurate estimates). The contents and the changes of these budgets were inspired generally at officer level following discussions with the respective chairman and were then approved by committee. The committees also undertook a mid-term review of the value-for-money programme and reviewed many of the charges under their remit. (6)

Service departments submit their spending estimates at current levels of provision. The Finance Department alone is responsible for calculating how much is needed for contingency purposes. The level of contingency (i.e. the amount set aside to cover for pay and price increases) will not concern service departments too much because they can legitimately claim for any pay and price increases to carry out Council policy. It is only in circumstances when the amounts set aside which are cash-limited prove to be insufficient that departments will be affected as they will probably have to make compensatory savings. The Finance Department forecasts the amounts required for both foreseen and unforeseen contingencies. The Department makes a realistic forecast but tends to err on the cautious side by adding about one-half per cent on top. It has a good 'track record' at forecasting future levels of inflation and for the financial year 1986/7 a six per cent rate of inflation was assumed, plus an estimated provision for settlement of the teachers' pay dispute. For this year only some of the contingency funds were to be used to finance certain services taken over from the GLC.

Towards the end of January the Forward Budgeting Sub-Committee considered the budget review undertaken by the committees and concluded because of the uncertainties surrounding the abolition of the GLC the budget for 1986/7 could not be predicted accurately. It warned that further budget amendments might be required. There was particular uncertainty over the distribution of GLC monies and the levy of the London Residuary Body which was set up to oversee the winding up of the GLC. By this time there was much concern over the position of Education in the budget strategy. Education was "a little behind" but there was little agreement over what course of action, if any, needed to be taken. The Finance Department and Ron Grant, the architect of the MTBS, were very aware that the outcome of the strategy rested on Education and despite "a few fudges" were very determined that education be kept in line. However, the Education Department and the Chairman of the Education Committee believed it was informally accepted that Education was running one year behind but would over time fall into line with the budget strategy. The problem of Education finding its share of savings was exacerbated because the savings it had found were based on very optimistic assumptions. For example, the level of recoupment money from other local authorities who send their children to Harrow schools was budgeted on the high side. Last year the Education Committee decided not to pay the transport costs to parents who send their children to schools outside Harrow in the hope that this move would encourage them to send their children to schools in the borough, thus reducing the amount of recoupment money paid to other local authorities. Also, favourable forecasts were made for the level of contributions to and benefits from the national pooling arrangements for higher education, which are notoriously difficult to predict. The Education Committee hoped that these savings would materialise rather than their having to find further savings. If they were not realised and it was not known until the following year, then there may be a shortfall in savings of up to £200,000. With regard to the way the Education budget was produced, the Director of Education maintained that "the whole thing was fudged by the Conservatives". He believed that there was "a degree of conjuring about the whole exercise" which amounted to no more than "a measure of pretence". For 1986/7 Education appears to have met its target but in reality the budgeted savings may never materialise, which would in the event seriously jeopardise the future of the MTBS.

In early February the members of the Forward Budgeting Sub-Committee met with the representatives of local industrial and commercial ratepayers under the Rates Act 1984. Although these business representatives were consulted, their influence was "pretty minimal". They tended to focus on management rather than service issues but had "no tangible effect" on the Council's budget plans. In addition to this statutory consultation of local business representatives, a variety of other bodies were consulted throughout the budgetary process. At various stages the views of the relevant trade unions were canvassed but although they are "handled very carefully" on industrial relations matters they had no influence over the budget. Also, the Housing and Education Committees consulted respectively the various tenants' associations and school and college governing bodies. These bodies have a more specific influence upon the budget than the local business representatives. [7]

Also in February several bodies announced their precepts, which Harrow LBC are obliged to collect on their behalf. The Finance Department had an approximate idea what these precepts would be towards the end of last year following discussions with the Fire and Civil Defence Authority, London Regional Transport and the Metropolitan Police. However, the annual grant settlement contains the most accurate indicator of the likely level of these precepts.

At the same time several outstanding matters regarding the abolition of the GLC were settled. The London Residuary Body announced its levy. The lateness of this announcement was caused by the GLC decision not to cooperate with the LRB over the transfer of its services. Also it was now possible for the Finance Department to estimate how much was needed to participate in the grants scheme run by the London Grants Committee and how much was required to operate the concessionary fares scheme for the elderly. Most important was the matter of distributing GLC monies. The LRB had agreed that the GLC's balances should be distributed to the boroughs on a pro rata basis, consequently the Council received just over £2 million. It is likely that another substantial cash transfer from the GLC will be allocated to the Council because the GLC has not yet closed its accounts and appears to have underspent dramatically in its last year of existence.

With the detailed committee budgets prepared, the various precepts announced and several issues about the abolition of the GLC resolved, the Finance Department produced several reports outlining the budget situation. By this time the likely level of rates was taking shape.

Before the rate levy could be set the Conservative leadership and the Finance Department had to decide on the level of funds and balances that the Council was to hold and whether any of them should be used to hold the rates down. In 1981/2 two funds were set up for the explicit purpose of using them in future years to avoid grant penalty and thus maximise block grant. This widespread practice of creative accountancy allowed the Council to spend the money in subsequent years without incurring penalty because the funds counted as expenditure in the year they were established for the purposes of the target system. [8] These funds and the Council's balances have been used in previous years to hold the rates down but this year there was some disagreement between Ron Grant and the Finance Department over their use.

In the past the Conservative Group and the Finance Department have been in rough agreement over their use despite holding different priorities on how they should be used. The Conservatives are more concerned with bringing the rates down and with averting any adverse electoral consequences, whereas the Finance Department are more concerned with leaving sufficient levels of funds and balances to safeguard against any unforeseen circumstances and to provide a certain level of services. Previously these differing priorities could be met because of the abundance of funds. This year, however, these differences were aggravated by dwindling funds. This situation led to "verbal fisticuffs" between Ron Grant and David Adams during the earlier stages of the budgetary process. This dispute receded as it became evident that the Council was to receive a large cash transfer from the GLC. The Conservatives decided to make a small change to the recommendation of the Chief Executive and reduced the balances to allow for a 1p. reduction in the rate levy. During the year 1986/7 it was budgeted to use over £6 million in balances but no funds.

On 27 February 1986, following recommendations from the Policy and Resources Committee and despite a Liberal Alliance amendment, the Council approved a revenue budget which would reduce the rates by over two per cent. With the May elections looming it would be tempting to conclude that this rates reduction was a cynical electoral ploy but it must be seen in the context that this year was the fifth in succession in which the rates had not risen. Although the May elections may not have had a decisive effect on the level of rates they had a more significant effect upon the content of the budget. Many of the savings proposed were designed by chief officers and committee chairmen to be the least damaging to the electoral fortunes of the Conservatives. For example, there was no attempt to reduce the generous pupil/teacher ratios, which if happened would lead to "political death". The decision to cut library opening hours was overturned because of widespread opposition. These measures fitted in with the Conservative strategy of not making decisions which would have adverse electoral consequences.

The budget for 1986/7 meant that in relation to the MTBS the Council had "more or less made it" but there remained substantial doubts whether the strategy would last its course. These doubts were held by many leading councillors and officers - even Ron Grant, the founder of the strategy is "not totally confident" of its future success. This depends on the level of savings that Education is able to produce. The Council proposed to embark on a school closure programme in order to generate the required savings but the threat to three schools has been lifted, which casts much doubt over the Council's ability to implement the budget strategy. The Director of Education sees that "the nub of the problem lies in the political will" but believes like many others that the political commitment to the MTBS has waned significantly over the last year.

There are several reasons why the level of political commitment has diminished. First, the outcome of the May elections reduced the Conservative majority on the Council to only one. As a result the Conservatives are more reluctant and less able to implement unpopular cost-cutting decisions, such as the closure of schools. Second, many councillors serve on school governing bodies and sit on the Education Committee. They therefore tend to adopt a protective attitude to the Education budget. There needs to be a high level of support for the MTBS if this 'parochialism' is not to become an obstacle to finding the required level os savings. Finally and most important, there is much national debate over local government and education in particular, which may have a considerable effect upon the future of the MTBS. With the coming General Election there has been speculation that local government spending will increase, which will ease some of the pressure upon local authorities to make spending reductions. Also, this view has been reinforced by the signals sent out to local authorities by the recent appointment of Kenneth Baker as Secretary of State for Education and Science that education is about to receive a substantial injection of money in the wake of the widespread concern about the effects of the teachers' pay dispute. All these uncertainties have challenged the thinking of those who predict a worsening financial situation for local authorities and who therefore formulate budget strategies which lead to large money savings. Future events may make the MTBS redundant. Financial planning is only possible if events can be controlled or predicted. If they cannot, there is the danger that a budget plan such as the MTBS will be overtaken by these events and become obsolete.

The Making of the Capital Programme

The Council operates a four-year rolling capital programme. This programme is reviewed annually. The current year's programme is monitored continuously and amended to reflect slippage and other changes. These annual and regular reviews of the capital programme ensure that it is both up-to-date and realistic.

Each year the Government announces its authorisation of capital spending in five blocks - education, housing, social services, transport and other services. The amounts assigned to each of the blocks reflect only the priorities of the government and a local authority is free to spend its authorisation as it sees fit, provided that it falls within the definition of prescribed capital expenditure under the Local Government, Planning and Land Act 1980 and does not substantially exceed its aggregate block authorisation. (9) Despite this flexibility, it is Council policy to follow the block allocations decided upon by the government. (10) This course of action was adopted to reduce the level of friction between committees and departments, since there is no competition for resources because the allocation process is determined outside the Council.

The annual review of the capital programme began in May 1985, although the block authorisations for 1986/7 were not notified to the Council until much later. The Finance Department drew up various guidelines for the review which were based on the assumption that local authority capital spending would continue to contract. This assumption was derived from previous block authorisations and the government's plans for public expenditure. These guidelines were later endorsed by the Policy and Resources Committee. For example, they required that high priority should be given to those projects which would incur minimal revenue costs or yield substantial income because these revenue consequences have to be absorbed within the MTBS. Capital projects also had to be restricted to those which could be undertaken by existing staff resources. Furthermore, it was agreed that the Housing Committee should have exclusive use of its capital receipts generated from the sale of council houses and that the use of other capital receipts was to be confined to various priority schemes such as the development of the town centre.

Following the issue of these guidelines, the capital programme for 1986/7 to 1988/9 was prepared by the Finance Department and the relevant service departments. (11) This process is very much an interdepartmental exercise with little councillor involvement. By November an array of officer groups - the Capital Programme Group, the Programme Review Group and various client groups - had compiled the capital programme within the guidelines and also had submitted bids to the respective government departments.

In November the review of the capital programme was considered by committees in order to ensure that their programmes reflected their service and project priorities and the level of available resources. For the Housing Committee there were several significant changes to its capital programme because of a change in the interpretation of the rules governing capital expenditure and the use of capital receipts. Capital receipts used to finance housing repairs do not constitute as prescribed capital expenditure under the provisions of the 1980 Act and as a result more funds were released to finance major housing repairs programmes.

During December 1985 and January 1986, the government had notified the Council of its block authorisations for 1986/7 and indicated provisional pointers to the authorisations for the next two years. The authorisations of the five blocks are generally calculated on the basis of past spending and measured needs. For example, the housing block is based on an index measuring general housing needs and the past spending of local authorities. The other services block for London is allocated to the London Boroughs Association which then distributes it to boroughs according to a formula of population and past spending.

Service departments have varying difficulties in forecasting their respective block authorisations. Social Services, for example, submitted a bid of over £750,000 but was authorised to spend only £289,000. The Council then applied to the Department of Health and Social Security for more authorisation but its request was turned down. As a result, the Council is now seeking a meeting with the minister not to obtain more authorisation for 1986/7 but to shape the climate in which subsequent decisions are made. Social Services can live with a low allocation for one year but its capital programme would be wrecked if future authorisations remain at this low level. Conversely, Housing has consistently been authorised to spend about £4 million in its Housing Investment Programme and the only uncertainty lies at the margins.

Following the notification of the block authorisations, the guidelines underpinning the review of the capital programme were reviewed by the Policy and Resources Committee on the advice of the Chief Executive. In January committees modified their capital programmes to keep them in line with their block allocations and the revised guidelines. The Social Services Committee were compelled to delay many large projects because of its low allocation and the Education Committee also considered postponing several schemes because of an unfavourable other services block for London. When this annual review was completed, the Finance Department advised the Council on the financing of the capital programme and its revenue consequences.

The making of the capital programme is largely an officer exercise. The service departments determine the priority list of projects to be undertaken within the guidelines set by the Finance Department.

Councillors fine-tune the order of the 'shopping list' of schemes to be programmed. The Conservative Group, generally, are not very concerned with the contents of the capital programme save for certain priority projects but are more concerned with limiting the revenue consequences of the programme in order to protect the MTBS.

There are several formidable problems encountered in the making and reviewing of the capital programme. First, there are severe financial constraints imposed by both the Government and the Council itself. The Government applies strict limits on the overall level of capital spending of each authority. The Council in its adoption of the MTBS has created pressures to limit the revenue costs of the capital·programme and thus tends to undertake those schemes with minimal revenue consequences. This pressure has had a significant effect on the kind of joint financing projects which the Council undertakes and it is now reluctant to embark on projects with recurring revenue commitments. Second, there are staffing constraints. Not only are the numbers of staff tightly controlled but the Council allows only those schemes which can be undertaken within existing staff resources to be programmed. The Assistant Controller of Housing saw this constraint as a greater limitation than the lack of funding. Finally, the most critical problem is the "lack of certainty of the future" over levels of funding and other key factors. This problem was stressed by the Controller of Architecture when he reported that "undertaking a review of the Capital Programme in advance of notification of block authorisations for the coming year is a speculative exercise and surrounded by many uncertainties." These uncertainties include the level of future funding, changes in the capital programme, slippage, the availability of staff and the negotiation of tenders. These indeterminate factors make planning the capital programme a very complex and precarious task. Therefore, it is only feasible to budget for one or two years ahead, and as a result short term rather than long term projects tend to be undertaken.

Conclusion - Budgeting in Perspective

There are many uncertainties inherent in the budgetary processes of local authorities - the block grant system, rate-capping, the proposed reform of the rates, the block allocations of capital spending, the current review of the capital expenditure control system, the abolition of the GLC and the Metropolitan County Councils, new policy developments, service demands, the teachers' pay dispute, the level of inflation, local elections and the looming General Election. These uncertainties pose major difficulties for budget-makers in planning ahead. One of the objectives of the MTBS was to remove some of this uncertainty in budgeting.

However, there may be some value in uncertainty within the budgetary process. This uncertainty does not necessarily lead to an unfavourable budget. Out of the milieu of uncertainty a favourable series of events may emerge. Such an outcome occurred with Harrow LBC in its making of the revenue budget. The Council, this year, was able to reduce its rates because of the advantageous outcome of the abolition of the GLC (that is, cash transfers and generous grant funding). Uncertainty may make for difficult but not necessarily unsatisfactory budgeting. An uncertain situation requires flexibility where adjustments of position and the unfolding of events do not threaten whatever strategy is adopted. Despite claims to the contrary there remain doubts about whether the MTBS is flexible enough to survive the future.

Finally, a prominent trend of budgeting in local government is the move from policy planning towards cash planning. This trend is manifested in the way Harrow LBC budgets for both revenue and capital spending - for example, the decision to reduce Council spending; the quantitative nature of the MTBS; the application of across-the-board money savings; the rigidity of targets; the lack of attention to measuring demands, needs and performance of services; the acceptance of the government block allocations and the priority given to those capital projects which incur minimal revenue consequences. Many officers in the service departments lamented this trend especially as there are now diminishing opportunities to switch money between budget headings but acknowledged that the making of policies cannot be divorced fom the availability of resources. Budgeting is no longer a reflection of need save for the 'need' to reduce spending.

Notes

(1) The base to be used was the budget for 1985/6 which was prepared at November 1984 prices.

(2) The close budgetary relationship between the service and Finance Departments averts the likelihood of departments adopting such strategies as padding their budgets, proposing politically unacceptable items as savings in order to scare off councillors and putting forward unnecessarily damaging savings which if implemented would embarrass councillors.

(3) In the local elections of May 1986 education and in particular the proposed closure of several schools were by far the most dominant local issues in the campaign.

(4) After 1986/7 these services would be integrated into the main budget process.

(5) On 22 July 1986 the Government announced that all financial assistance given to those local authorities bearing extra responsibilities as a result of the abolition of the GLC and the Metropolitan County Councils is to be withdrawn.

(6) There is a general policy to increase charges in line with the rate of inflation. However, the Housing Committee charges the highest rents possible on Council homes because two-thirds of the tenants are in receipt of housing benefit and therefore do not pay or pay only part of the rent charged and because it is Council policy to keep the Housing Revenue Account in balance without making contributions from the General Rate Fund.

(7) The school and the college governing bodies have certain budgetary powers contained in their Articles of Government.

[8] The District Auditor was approached for his approval of this
     accounting change, as with other changes (such as the change
     from a five to a ten per cent sinking fund contribution of
     interest payments, which reduced earlier payments but increased
     later ones).

[9] Although there is some concern that if a local authority does
     not spend its block on the authorised purpose it will lose some
     of that block in subsequent years.

[10] The other services block is used by the Council for those services
     who have no block and as a support to the education block.

[11] The influence of the Finance Department varies considerably
     between departments in the making of the capital programme.

8. Sheffield City Council

DAVID MORRIS

To countless generations the name of Sheffield is synonymous with steel; an industry which provided the city's economic infrastructure and which was a source of employment to many of its workforce in a population of a little over half a million persons. The steel industry has, however, suffered a severe recession over the last decade due to a worldwide surplus capacity in steel manufacturing occuring at a time of far reaching economic stagnation in the industrial nations. Traditional markets for domestically produced steel products have also been threatened and not infrequently lost to rival overseas steel producers, especially those from Japan and South Korea. British Steel, the nation's largest provider of steel to industry, has been obliged to undertake a considerable rationalisation of its activities in the face of challenges by market forces and in the process has reduced its workforce by 150,000; from 210,000 in 1979 to a figure of 60,000 at the present time. Sheffield has taken a proportionate cut in the numbers employed in its local steel producing workforce and in industries allied to it.

Matching the decline in the city's much vaunted reputation as the centre of British steel production there has developed Sheffield's new identity as the "capital of the Socialist Republic of South Yorkshire". Sheffield has an unparalleled local political pattern with a continuity of one party political dominance in the management of its public affairs which cannot be rivalled by any other English city of comparable size. Since the mid-1920s the City Council has been almost exclusively in the possession of the Labour Party; the single notable exception being a twelve month period in 1968/9. The consequence of that political continuity has been that the planning of local authority service provision has taken place in the certain knowledge that, barring the intervention of central government, the implementation of policy was assured. This very political stability, whilst calling forth the criticism of opposition politicians of political stagnation and the nullification of political initiative, has been viewed by the electorally successful Labour Party as having provided continuity in all aspects of the local policy making process; formulation, enactment, implementation and monitoring. Inevitably, this stability has been reflected in the city's budgetary process.

Continuity in policy making undoubtedly stems initially from the electoral record of the Labour Party in local electoral contests but has been strengthened by the city's management structure which is, itself, a determinant of the influence that various actors can exert upon the budgetary process. Sheffield's management structure can best be explained in terms of the following headings:

(i)   Chief Executive - The Chief Executive was appointed in line with the Bains Committee proposals and acts as Chairman of a group of senior Chief Officers which normally meets fortnightly, or more frequently if required, to approve corporate management plans and budget changes. In theory, this is the management team of the MDC, but in practice it only rarely fulfils such a central role and spends much of its time on relatively minor matters.

(ii)   Programme Committee - In 1982 the then committee structure was reorganised into Programme Committees accountable for like activities. There are now Programme Committees and Programme Chief Officers who act as "supremos" for the group of activities for which they are accountable. These Programme Committees are responsible for monitoring developments against the Labour Group's political manifestos in their areas. Currently there are Programme Committees covering education, employment, environment and planning, family and community services, housing, libraries and arts, municipal enterprises, general services and recreation. The Programme Committees are one of the methods of implementing policy in a coherent and consistent manner.

(iii) Policy Committee - Chaired by the Leader of the Labour Group and which plays the formative role in directing and coordinating Council policy. The Chairmen of the Programme Committees are heavily represented in its membership.

(iv)   Budget Sub-Committee - Chaired by the Deputy Chairman of the Policy Committee and exhibiting a high degree of overlapping membership with the Policy Committee.

Certain implications for the budgetary process follow from this management structure. In many local authorities there is still adherence to a division of functions between politicians and officers; politicians determine policy and officers implement it. In Sheffield, Chairmen of Programme Committees have been provided with permanent offices and secretarial services and are undertaking more and more day-to-day management, with authority to call officers before them.

It is interesting to speculate whether this system will, in the long term, affect the quality of Chief Officers applying for posts in Sheffield because of the confusion of roles which inevitably results when policy-makers become heavily involved with the administrative process on a daily basis. The recent necessity to re-advertise the post of City Treasurer might be taken as evidence that this is already occurring. Since the introduction of Rate Support Grant Penalties, which are determined on a progressive sliding scale, so that the level of penalties increases with the level of City overspending of the financial targets set by Central Government, the Policy Committee has had to indulge in "creative accountancy" in order to even out the level of expenditure. Its ability to maintain expenditure below the higher level of penalties is advantageous to the City Council. Alongside this role of the Policy Committee there is evidence of a change instituted by the City Treasurer in the role of the Internal Audit Division. Its "tick and tell" role has been delegated to the Programme Committees and the audit role has become more and more a value for money investigation to ensure that resources are used effectively to meet stated objectives. This change is not without political significance as it serves the function of highlighting to the Audit Commission that it is not only Central Government which has a monopoly on value for money investigations and that Local Government is fully aware of its needs and responsibilities in this area.

As suggested above, the City's budgetary process has not been the exclusive preserve of its politicians and officers. The election in 1979 of a Conservative Government pledged to reduce public expenditure has also played a formative role in shaping the city's finances. The influence that Central Government policy was to exert upon Sheffield's budget began to be discernible in the 1980/1 financial year and by examining the following four financial years it is possible to see a clear pattern emerging, characterised by a reduction in the percentage of the city's income derived from Central Government grants and matched by a corresponding increase in the percentage of income derived from rates.

It will be seen that the overall income from these two sources increased from £225 million to £285 million over the period. Adjusting the former figure for inflation gives:

$$\frac{225}{270.2} \times 355 = \text{£296 million}$$

which indicates that overall there has been a reduction in Sheffield's expenditure in real terms of about £11 million.

The massive increase in income required to be raised from local rates (from £95 million to £195 million - a doubling) is caused not by increased spending but wholly by the reduction in Grants from £130 million to £95 million. Allowing for inflation only, the latter figure should have been:

$$\frac{130}{270.2} \times 355 = \text{£171 million}$$

Table 8.1

SOURCES OF INCOME

	Retail Price Index (September)	Government Grants (General & Specific) £ million	% of Total Income	Rates £ million	% of Total Income
1980/1	270.2	130	57	95	42
1981/2	301.0	115	45	134	53
1982/3	322.5	108	40	159	58
1983/4	339.5	100	35	181	63
1984/5	355.0	95	33	190	67

and the equivalent rates figure would then have been:

$$\frac{95}{270.2} \times 355 = £125 \text{ million}$$

It is clear that 1981/2 was a crucial year within this five year period in the swing from Grants to Rates. For this year the Government deemed that the grant settlement would assume pay awards of 6 per cent and price increases of 11 per cent. In the event pay awards were about 7.5 per cent and price increases about 12 per cent. At this time the Government warned that local authority expenditure must be brought into line with Government plans. Penalties were introduced where targets were exceeded by 4 per cent or more.

Expenditure targets continued to be determined by Central Government, and the 1983/4 level was set at the 1982/3 original budget less one per cent in cash terms. Failure to spend at or below this target incurred penalties such that spending above the target of two per cent incurred a grant loss of £1.20 for each additional £1 of spending. This meant that the cost to the Sheffield ratepayer of each £1 million of any "excess" spending was £2.2 million.

These severe penalty clauses meant that local authorities which were reluctant to cut services had to make financial provision from rates or balances to make up the losses. This, then, was an additional factor in local authority budgeting which inexorably led to the Government's decision to rate-cap so that authorities could not defy the Government's intentions in this way.

The analysis of expenditure over the five years provides information on the savings between services, and the central provision for specific needs.

Because Sheffield was a "second-tier" authority until the abolition of the Metro Counties, it was required to meet a proportion of South Yorkshire County Council's needs by precept. A "high" of £53 million (23 per cent) in 1980/1 was followed by lower precepts of between 15 and 17 per cent until 1984/5, by which year the precept had increased to £54 million, equivalent to 19 per cent of total expenditure in Sheffield.

The reduction in inflation from the high peak of the mid 1970s was reflected in the reduced provision from 13 per cent in 1980/1 to the more modest levels of subsequent years. This central provision was for specific pay and price increases anticipated but not then known precisely. Some provision for general inflation was also made in the budgets of the individual services.

In reviewing the percentage budgeted spending for the various services, it must be borne in mind that the City Council's philosophy was and is to maintain and develop its social services. The changes over the five years reflect this approach, as shown below:

Table 8.2

£m ON MAJOR SERVICES

	Inflation R.P.I.	Education (including Polytechnic)		Family and Community Services		Recreation and Arts		Employment	
		£m	% increase	£m	% increase	£m	% increase	£m	% increase
1980/1	270.2	91		23		10		−	
1981/2	301.0	117		30		13		2	
1982/3	322.5	126		33		15		2	
1983/4	339.5	135		36		15		3	
1984/5	355.0	134	+47	37	+61	16	+60	3	+50 on 1981/2

The allocations to Committee services from the Rate Fund are determined after taking account of fees and charges levied by these services on their users. Clearly these charges have to be reviewed annually as one important source of finance. Over the five years under review this estimated income has increased from £108 million to £172 million - a rise of 59 per cent. The two major income-earning services were Housing and Education - the former in respect of tenants' rents and grants, etc. and the latter charges for school meals, contributions from other local authorities, tuition fees and the allocation from the "Pool" for advanced further education. The changing pattern of Sheffield income and expenditure for the financial years 1980/1 through 1984/5 is identified in tables 8.1 and 8.2.

Sheffield MDC's Budget - 1985/6

As a consequence of the Conservative Government's reduction in grants to local authorities, many Councils have sought to offset that reduction in funding by increasing their local rate income. With the stated intention of protecting ratepayers - house occupiers, industry and commerce - from excessive rate increases in 1985/6 compared to the previous financial year, the Government obtained Parliament's approval for legislation which empowered the Secretary of State for

106

the Environment to set a maximum rate in the pound. In the case of Sheffield this maximum was 207.07p. In addition to Sheffield, a further seventeen local authorities also found maximum rates being prescribed for them in 1985/6; a process which became universally known as "rate capping".

Before considering Sheffield's dilemma in 1985/6 it is necessary to bear in mind two points:

(i) If councillors are in breach of Section 2(i) of the 1967 Rates Act by actions which result in losses to the ratepayers totalling more than £2,000 for each councillor, then they may be required to personally make good that loss or be declared bankrupt and they then face disqualification from office.

(ii) Delay in setting a rate in any financial year may result in losses because money may have to be borrowed to tide the Council over until a rate is set and ratepayers know what is due, and the subsequent additional interest on this borrowing is a "loss" to the ratepayers.

During February 1985 a series of meetings was held by Sheffield's Labour Councillors to establish a budget that would maintain jobs and services whilst also providing for some expansion in both of these areas. Conservative and Liberal Councillors were not invited to attend these meetings and when the Leader of the Liberal Group on the Council attempted to do so he was physically restrained. By late February there were indications that a budget of £249 million had been agreed by the Labour Group.

On February 25th the Secretary of State for the Environment confirmed a maximum rate of 207.7p in the pound (permitting total expenditure of approximately £220 million) for Sheffield. This led to the Leader of the Labour Group forecasting that the City Council would set a budget on March 7th which would ignore this limit. He said: "What is at stake goes far beyond the intricacies of local government and right to the heart of democracy". During the following eight weeks the Labour Group openly and vociferously exhibited its opposition and hostility toward rate capping by refusing to set a rate and by appealing to the Courts against the procedure to be used in determining grant aid to Councils. In opposition to this stance by the Labour Group the opposition leaders on the City Council demanded urgent intervention in the City's financial affairs by the District Auditor. The City's Chief Executive and the City Treasurer warned all 87 Councillors in writing that delay in setting a rate would reduce the City's income to such an extent that the extra cost of borrowing to replace the consequent loss in income might well run at a figure of up to £20,000 per day.

In early May the Labour Group again refused to set a rate and the Labour Group Leader predicted that the Secretary of State for the Environment would find it both politically and practically difficult to permit the District Auditor to disqualify Councillors for honouring their ballot box promises. At this time also action by the City Council in the Court of Appeal for the right to challenge the level of grant to Sheffield was dismissed. The City Councillors were now confronted by a choice; either they could set a rate for 1985/6 in accordance with directives from the Secretary of State for the Environment or they could hazard their own political careers and personal finances by refusing to comply. This stark choice was evident on May 7th.

At a marathon sitting of the City Council on that day the Labour Group Leader saw both the moderate and left wing factions of the Labour Group vote against him. The first rebellion from the moderates came at 2.00p.m. when the Chairman of the Budget Sub-Committee proposed a legal rate and said that Councillors owed allegiance to the law and were obliged to offer a realistic protection of the electorate which had voted them into office. It was emphasised by the moderates that defiance of the law would lead to surcharge and disqualification of individual members of the Labour Group and would also leave the Opposition free to implement spending cuts until such time as substitute Labour Councillors were elected to office. This proposal secured the support of 18 other Labour moderates and that of 17 Conservatives. However, 38 Labour Councillors of a left wing persuasion voted against the proposal and it was lost. Significantly perhaps, Liberal Councillors refused to vote on the proposal until they were given representation on the Budget Sub-Committee.

After hours of further debate the Chief Executive warned that abstention by members would be tantamount to voting against making a rate and could render Councillors liable to penalties. At a further vote the 9 Liberals then voted with the moderate Labour faction and the Conservatives, and the moderate proposal was then carried by 46 votes to 38.

The debate was then suspended so that the Labour Group could consider its position. Its closed meeting voted for "deficit budgeting" by 29 to 27. The Labour Group Leader then returned to the Council chamber to put forward an amended proposal for deficit budgeting and to appeal for Labour unity. Now, however, the Labour "left" condemned deficit budgeting as merely a token gesture of defiance of the Government's policy and contended that jobs and services could not be maintained with a rate of 207.07p. Eventually 22 of the Labour "left" voted with the Conservatives and Liberals against the deficit budgeting proposal and the amendment was defeated by 48 votes to 36. Finally, at about 11.00p.m., after a nine hour debate, the Labour "moderates" together with the Conservatives and Liberals approved a substantive motion setting a maximum legal rate of 207.07p in the £ together with a budget within the Council's restricted means.

On 9 May, seven "moderate" Labour members were stripped of their chairmanships or deputy chairmanships of influential Council Committees by the Labour Group "to ensure that the policy of the Labour Party and the Labour Group is carried out." Despite the City Council vote on 7 May, the Policy Committee re-affirmed an expansionist budget of £250 million, with a short-fall of funding of about £32 million. The local newspaper editorial commented that: "the Sheffield Labour Party resents honest dissent rather than welcoming and respecting it. Councillors are not so much representatives of electorates that send them to the Town Hall as delegates mandated by the party organisation." The Labour Group Leader vowed to fight for an expansionist budget despite the City Council's decision to set a legal rate. Deficit budgeting was, therefore, to be imposed on the City although it had been rejected both by the Labour "left" and "moderates" and the opposition parties.

Sheffield now had a legal rate but an expansionist budget far in excess of anticipated income, for the first time. In accountancy terms deficit budgeting (i.e. budgeting to spend in excess of income and reserves) is unworkable in the long run because employees have to be paid and goods and services have to be purchased with **real** money. Borrowing to meet the short-fall incurs high interest and repayment costs. In 1985/6 £20 million of the deficit could be met from reserves and marginal savings but using up reserves merely passed on the problem to 1986/7. Because of the financial dilemma, a formal budget presentation for all services had not been produced at December 1985 for 1985/6. It is understood, however, that there is provision for an additional 300 jobs and expansion of the home helps service and of schools maintenance.

In August 1985 the Secretary of State for the Environment proposed a change in the targets and penalties system of grant aid for 1986/7. The Rate Support Grant was to be maintained at the same level as 1985/6, which means a cut in real terms equivalent to anticipated inflation – at least 5 per cent. He announced that 12 local authorities would be rate-capped in 1986/7 – 10 from the 1985/6 list plus Liverpool and Newcastle. Sheffield City Council does **not** appear on the 1986/7 list because it had set a legal rate in the 1985/6 financial year.

In early October the Court of Appeal complicated the issue for 1985/6 by declaring that the Department of the Environment, in determining the level of grant, had acted contrary to the 1980 Planning and Land Act Section 59(11a) by not treating all authorities equally. This response to a challenge by Nottinghamshire County Council and Bradford Metropolitan District Council may yet have far-reaching consequences which cannot be fully assessed at this time. Yet there are indications that the majority of the Labour Group in Sheffield no longer regards the more extreme options of defiance as politically viable. The example of Liverpool, which had exhausted all its funds by the end of November 1985, showed that the Government expects local authorities to plan within their resources, and does not intend to bail them out.

It appears that Sheffield has rejected once and for all the option of bankruptcy and plans "a continuous re-assessment of services." It is possible that a collection of financial options can be devised which will allow the maintenance of jobs and services. There appears to be substantial reliance on the City Treasurer's ability to meet part of the shortfall by creative accountancy, which includes 'switching' between capital and revenue accounts and it is also planned to defer as much revenue spending as possible until 1986/7. As mentioned earlier, this merely defers problems by twelve months.

Given a strong Conservative Party majority at Westminster pledged to reduce public expenditure and a strong Labour Party majority in Sheffield Town Hall pledged to protect jobs and services against any centrally imposed constraints, it was perhaps inevitable that the financial aspect of the central-local relationship would become the focus of conflict, and equally that it would be a highly politicised question. Notice of the difficulties that lay ahead for the City was given in a letter to its Chief Executive from the Department of Environment on 11 December, 1984 which stated that....

"The Secretary of State for the Environment in accordance with section 4(i) of the Rates Act 1984 hereby gives notice that he proposes to prescribe a maximum of 207.07 pence in the pound for the rate to be made by the City of Sheffield Metropolitan District Council for the financial year beginning on 1 April 1985."

This letter followed in the wake of the announcement that Sheffield had been designated for selective rate limitation in 1985/6 under the Rates Act of 1984. As previously mentioned Patrick Jenkin confirmed 207.07 pence in the pound for Sheffield's rate in February 1985.

Sheffield District Labour Party had, however, taken action on budgetary matters long before receipt of the formal letter from the Department of the Environment. In January 1984 a meeting of its Executive Committee had approved the establishment of a Budget Working Party, a group equivalent to its existing manifesto/subject working parties. The Budget Working Party's terms of reference were:

"1. To become familiar with the present budgetary process and timetable and to produce an easily understood outline and presentation for the party.

2. To discover exactly how this process has taken place ...(how) decisions have been made about priorities and the overall balance of resource allocation (between departments...).

3. To analyse what the budgetary process...implies for the political process and for policy implementation....

4. ... suggest ways in which the budgetary process can become a positive means of socialist planning (rather than an annual accounting system)."

The DLP's Budget Working Party's first report concluded:

"1. The Party needs to understand the Budget not merely to obtain information about it.

2. The **political** implications of the technicalities like incremental budgeting must also be understood.

3. It is necessary to influence the **whole process** of the **budget's formulation** and not merely approve or modify budget proposals when there is little opportunity to alter them substantially.

4. If treated politically, the budget can be a valuable exercise in socialist planing. This is particularly true in its long term aspects, as well as in the yearly budget preparation. By looking at the long term aspects, the party ... can begin to shape the future so that the budget reflects party priorities more clearly.

5. Resistance to the Government's attack on local financial independence will be greatly assisted if the District Labour Party has more knowledge about, understanding of, and influence over the budget."

Later in 1984 and as the strictures to be imposed by the Department of the Environment were announced it was agreed that DLP delegates should attend Special Budget Sub Committee meetings and that a Special Working Party be set up consisting of members of the Council's Budget Sub-Committee and members of the DLP's Budget Working Party. In short, political determination of the budget was increased and it became ever more politician led.

The trauma which Sheffield City Council and individual councillors endured during 1985/6 reflected the determination of some political elements to "fight the Tory Government for its attacks on the working class", even at the expense of the ratepayers they are supposed to serve. The Chairman of Liverpool District Labour Party, has claimed his City's actions as "an historic step in the directorship of the working class." Sheffield's Labour Group Leader took the more pragmatic line that it is for a future Labour Government to right the perceived wrongs of the present relationship between Central and Local Government.

Sheffield MDC's Budget 1986/7

Out of the turmoil associated with determining the City's budget for the financial year 1985/6 two clearly discernible principles emerged, namely that the Labour group which dominated the City Council was pledged to the maintenance of jobs and services whilst at the same time being unprepared to offer itself as a hostage to fortune by stepping outside the law and setting an illegal budget. Political expediency could be said to have prevailed over deeply held political preferences and inclinations. Yet the delay in establishing a budget until so late in the day in 1985/6 meant that many of the Council's departments were rapidly approaching the new financial year with no clearly established expenditure targets and the Council found it necessary to draw upon its reserves and other funds to support its electoral pledge to preserve jobs and services whilst at the same time complying with the strictures of the law. Such action did not, however, create a precedent because in 1984/5 the Council had been delighted to dig deep into its reserves to the tune of £11,885,000. In 1985/6 similar sources of income were drawn upon almost three times as deeply, the final figure being £33,321,000. In some ways more disturbing for the City's Labour Council than its need to bring its financial reserves into play has been the statement made in the House of Commons on 22 July 1986 by the Secretary of State for the Environment, Mr.Nicholas Ridley. In announcing the annual rate support grant for 1987/8 Mr.Ridley stated that the total grant provision would be £25.2 billion or £2.5 billion more than for 1986/7 which, allowing for inflation, means a real increase of £1.1 billion over present financial year. Of particular significance from Sheffield's viewpoint was Mr.Ridley's announcement that for rate-capping he had lowered the expenditure criterion from 20 per cent above Grant Related Expenditure (a resource equalisation device) to 12.5 per cent. This change automatically drew in a further eight Labour local authorities and one Liberal authority. Sheffield was among the eight Labour authorities now caught in the rate-capping web. This leaves the City facing a financial shortfall of £11 million for the next financial year which will widen to £25 million when account is taken of inflation

111

and the cost of new projects. A further and obvious implication for the City Council is that it will, if it is to remain within the law now that the Government has outlawed forward funding of capital projects, at the very least have to halt a wide range of planned housebuilding and renovation schemes using deferred purchase arrangements (a device whereby a council uses a bank to carry the effects of prescribed capital expenditure into future years) and will now have to account for all of its capital spending plans within the year in which the work is undertaken.

The Labour Leaders of Sheffield City Council responded to this announcement from the Department of the Environment by saying that the prohibition of forward funding was a vicious act designed to cut the lifeline authorities had been using to keep local communities afloat and that Sheffield City Council had made efforts to abide by current spending rules only to find itself again a victim of Central Government dictates. Whether or not the fact that Sheffield has now joined the list of rate-capped authorities will mean further financial and political turmoil and the prospect of a renewed confrontation between City Hall and Westminster or whether it will entail a further round of "creative accountancy" remains to be seen.

9. Kingswood District Council

STEPHEN WILLIAMS

The Political History

Kingswood District Council is a new authority created in 1974 by the reorganisation of Kingswood UDC, Mangotsfield UDC and Warmley RDC, inheriting members, officers and practices which were substantially to influence the running of the new authority. Geographically Kingswood itself is largely a Victorian urban development on the outskirts of Bristol. The other two former authorities contribute a greater suburban and rural character to the new district, with boundaries further from the sprawl of east Bristol. It is bordered by two larger, more rural district councils, Northavon and Wansdyke. A two mile strip through Wansdyke divides Kingswood from Bath, whose proximity, like Bristol's, has come to influence Kingswood's attitude to capital and revenue expenditure during the last decade. Despite the efforts of the authority to foster local identity with Kingswood District Council and its services, there is the unavoidable and dominating presence of Bristol, an authority some four times bigger than Kingswood and the largest non-metropolitan district established in 1974.

The political composition of the authority has been an important element in its development since 1974. Not until 1983 did a party (Conservative) secure a majority. Initial political instability was caused not merely by the failure of a party to win overall control; the need to integrate disparate political factions from the former authorities was also a factor. This problem was heightened by the continuing presence of powerful local independent members. However, the tradition of local government independence had been eroded to the point where, by the late 1970s, the Conservatives declared they would contest the seat of any such members who had not by then joined the Conservatives through a gradual process of absorption. Indeed, several leading members of the current Conservative group were Independents before accepting group membership, and its attendant party discipline. Between 1976 and 1979 very loose political control existed. Labour (always, since 1974 a substantial, identifiable and organised group), Liberals (who as a numerically small group exerted considerable influence) and Independents attempted collective leadership. Chairs were shared between these groups but disunity prevailed, with policy inconsistencies between service committees, policy committee, and full council. Between 1979 and 1983 tighter political control emerged with the Conservatives taking chairs and working with the Liberals in an alliance which attempted to develop more coherent policy. The 1983 election proved decisive in giving the Conservatives a majority. Labour became an opposition with 'shadow chairs' and an agreement that they be provided with agenda briefing by officers before committee meetings. However, by-elections in 1985 and early 1986 eroded this majority, and by the completion of the 1986/7 budget cycle in March 1986 Kingswood was again a 'hung council'. During the Autumn of 1985 however, when the key budget decisions were taken, the Conservatives still held a small majority. In taking the chairs of the committees, they operated a members ratio of 10:6:1.

A Financial Tradition

Kingswood was developing in the 1970s a tradition of low spending even before central government's attempts to curb local authority spending. It is proud of being a "prudent authority and careful in the way in which it uses its financial resources". [1] There are several reasons for this parsimony. Lack of political control in the early years of the authority, with conflicts between committees and council, meant that many schemes and projects were never developed. The authority also devised policies in the tradition of an 'enabling state'. There was enthusiasm for 'pump priming' expenditure in working with voluntary groups and a limited use of the authority's resources in assisting local recreational and leisure schemes, such as an 'open spaces' programme of 'green areas' for walking, cycling and horse riding. The capital expenditure programme has been influenced by the proximity of Bristol (and Bath). Members realised that many facilities were already in existence, provided by the former Bristol County Borough and that the city would maintain them, continuing their availability to Kingswood residents. This low-spending tradition and recent changes in government rules on grants and on spending meant that until 1985/6 Kingswood had never approached either GREA or 'target' levels of expenditure. Although there had been, in anticipation of local elections in May 1983, an expansion in spending for 1983/4, the majority Conservative administration re-imposed tight financial controls on taking office after the election. For 1984/5 resource-led and member-led features of the budget process clearly emerged. For that budget the Conservative group imposed pre-determined budget figures, rather than allowing officers to 'build-up' expenditure proposals. The authority committed itself to a level of revenue expenditure well below a government guideline which reflected the previous year's growth budget. For 1985/6, with a 'target' set well below GREA, the authority for the first time budgeted to the maximum before possible grant penalty. Again the officers were presented with overall budget figures which represented the priorities of the ruling group.

The 'Four Year Plan 1983-1987' [2] had been published as a statement of policy objectives after the Conservatives' electoral success. The initiative for this document, however, lay with officers, who did the initial drafting. What emerged, after amendment by the group, was a brief and general statement. Policies were related to service provision by individual committees, stating little on overall strategy. However, Objective 6 for the Policy committee remains central to the budget process:

"The government's main policy objective is to contain and if possible reduce public expenditure. To conform to this and to assist local businesses, expenditure will be carefully monitored and rate increases kept to a minimum." [3]

An important input to the budgetary process is the attitude to the rate levy. The strategy of the Conservative group has been to hold increases to the minimum. A concomitant policy has been to maximise government grant, by avoiding levels of spending which incur penalty. During the 1980s, by drawing on substantial balances in the General Rate Fund, the annual rate increases remained lower than otherwise would have been necessary to maintain services. As the balance diminishes policy changes may be necessary in the late 1980s. A similar use of balances influenced policy on rents. Substantial balances in the Housing Revenue Account allowed the authority to fix rent increases below Government advisory levels. There were two years free from rent increases in the 1980s and only an average 60p. increase for 1985/6. By 1986/7 this strategy was no longer possible and proposals for bigger rent increases for 1986/7 led to a bitter row between the Conservatives and the Labour opposition. The depletion of these balances during the last three years had reduced the account to a level where changes in rent policy became unavoidable.

The Formal Structure

A sense of Kingswood's budget process can be grasped by a description of its progress through the formal structure of the authority. However, as demonstrated later, informal relationships are probably of greater importance in determining the final outcome.

This formal structure reflects the recommendations of the Bains Committee (1972). Since its creation in 1974, Kingswood has had a Chief Executive Officer. His main role is defined as:

"to co-ordinate the work of the chief officers so that the Council's policies and targets are met." [4]

This management role extends over the Council's seven departments, each led by a chief officer. Noticeable is the lack of direct correspondence between the functions of these departments and the organisation of committees, a factor which assists a corporate style of management. Committees thus have responsibility for budgets which overlap the work of different departments. This arrangement helps

115

to strengthen the position of key officers in the budget process, such as the Chief Finance Officer, dominant members, such as the Leader and senior committee chairmen. The Chief Executive's responsibilities are for management services, personnel and industrial relations. The Chief Administrative Officer handles the authority's internal business, such as committee agendas, electoral matters and legal affairs. The Chief Financial Officer exercises overall financial control, including loans, investments, rate and rent rebates and the financial aspects of house sales. The other four departments are more oriented to the direct provision of community services. The Housing Department deals with rents, housing allocation, including homelessness and is responsible for overseeing the construction of elderly peoples dwellings within the housing capital programme. Environmental Health monitors pollution, noise, and has responsibilities for pest control, statutory inspections, safety licensing and housing renovations. The Planning Department deals with all planning applications, displays and tree preservation. Finally, there is a large department under the control of the Chief Technical Officer. Its services include recreation and leisure services, highways and street lighting, drains, refuse collection and the modernisation and maintenance of a stock of more than 5000 council dwellings. His responsibility extends to the Direct Labour Organisation, which deals with routine council programmes. Large projects are subject to competition and put out to tender. The sections within the Direct Labour Organisation concerned with building repairs and with highways and sewers, are both profitable; they exceed the 5 per cent statutorily required return on capital. It is a contracting element of the authority's activities but the Conservative group is not opposed to the Direct Labour Organisation per se. The refuse collection serice has been the subject of audit scrutiny and is under current examination by the authority to see where savings can be made.

The key committee in the authority is the Policy Committee, established consistent with the view that local government requires organisation likely to strengthen policy co-ordination and resource management. The relationship of the service committees with the Policy committee and with the departments, indicates Kingswood's attempt to pursue efficiency and establish priorities, through a corporate style of decision-making.

The formal cycle of budget preparation involves each service committee considering estimates during October and November. These then pass to the Policy committee before Christmas and are presented to full council for final approval in January. The Personnel Committee considers the budget dealing with all establishment costs. However, it is difficult for this committee to control expenditure beyond general levels of manpower. This is because employees in each department calculate the percentage of their time spent on work budgeted by each of the service committees. The overall manpower costs, as considered in total by Personnel, are then re-allocated as 'Net Expenditure Transferred to Other Services' and recharged proportionately to the estimates of the various service committees as appropriate. Similarly, on a pro-rata basis, other establishment costs on transport, printing, postage, telephones, insurance, repairs, maintenance, gas, electricity, rates, water rates, car allowances, staff training, cleaning and non-capital equipment are also allocated to the budgets of the service committees, after initial presentation in total to Personnel. The four committees overseeing service provision are Recreation, Environmental Health, Housing and Planning. A six week cycle of meetings is the norm for the council and its committees, (although Planning sits more frequently) and use is made of several sub-committees. This structure mirrors an ethos of service provision which has a considerable bearing on the size and distribution of Kingswood's budget. A very high percentage of the authority's revenue budget is committed to the provision of statutory services, for example in housing and in planning. Additional council spending takes the form of assistance to local voluntary groups in supporting activities and facilities generated within the community itself, for example, small grants to a local wildlife trust, to local sports clubs, and the charge of a peppercorn rent to a local railway preservation group.

The Informal Dimension I: Political Leadership

Political leadership has now become the key element in Kingswood's budget process. It is member led with key decisions taken by the core of the Conservative group. The Council Leader is de facto a full-time politician, regularly working at the Council Offices from early morning. An emphasis on informal structures of decision-making demonstrates the effectiveness of central control. The Leader is able to hold impromptu discussions with chief officers and call ad hoc day time meetings with other key members. This enables him to guide reaction to budget-related problems throughout the period from the initial compilation of estimates in the Autumn to rate setting in March. His main political adjutants are the deputy leader, Council chairman, and the committee chairmen. The rest of the Conservative group play a strikingly passive role in the budget cycle. Although vice-chairmen attend agenda briefing meetings with corporate teams of officers several days before committee, they rarely contribute more than back-benchers to budget decisions. Relationships between leading members and chief officers are central to this informal dimension of decision-taking. Negotiations and bargains frequently involve the Chief Finance Officer. His professionalism dominates not only interpretation of complex rules of local government finance; his role as policy adviser is such that the Leader and other members are dependent on his guidance for the development of any techniques of cutback management employed by the authority. His role is perhaps comparable with that of a Whitehall Mandarin. Corporate management also contributes to the Chief Finance Officer's influence over decisions on pruning estimates exceeding initial resource allocation, or justifying exceptional growth items in a nominal 'standstill budget'. Despite apparent multi-lateral bargaining at officers' meetings and at chairmen's briefings, what prevails is the centralised political and financial control of leading members, as advised by the Chief Finance Officer. Other officers regularly attend pre-committee meetings, including the Chief Executive Officer, the Chief Administrative Officer and, as appropriate, chief officers from Technical Services, Housing, Planning and so on. Despite their contributions and occasional special pleading for budget items, the group leaders and the Finance Department officers dominate. Informal structures reveal an inequality of power amongst chairmen. Departures made from the initial September resource allocation to committees indicated the ability of some chairmen to protect more effectively their committee's spending, through a capacity to negotiate bilaterally with the Leader and his financial advisers.

The progress of budget proposals through the formal structure does not weaken the control of the political elite and key officers. In committee and council the only contributions to the defence of budget proposals come from the Leader, his deputy and chairmen. At committee usually the vice-chairman's role is restricted to moving formally the acceptance of Estimates. Conservative back-benchers do not contribute to debate on committee budgets, nor do they respond to challenges on policy or on specific items, from the opposition. Group discipline is impressive with members attending and voting reliably. Back-benchers appear more interested in ward issues and seem not well informed on the intricacies of local government finance.

An articulate and critical Labour group failed to change budget proposals for 1986/7, meeting disciplined voting in committee and council. They attacked committee budgets in general terms and on specific items, maintaining criticism throughout the cycle. But attempts to expand committee budgets, protect deferred projects, or challenge policy met with consistent defeat at the hands of the majority group.

The Informal Dimension II: The Budget Process for 1986/7

In Kingswood, the process of setting the budget, within this formal and informal framework, is essentially resource-led. In the late summer the Chief Finance Officer advises the leading Conservative group members on likely local implications of the latest Department of Environment statement on Rate Support Grant levels for the following year. Calculations are then made about possible levels of resources, based on varying assumptions about Kingswood's rate levy, (same as current year, raised by 1p. etc.). The leading members of the group then meet to take what are the effective decisions about the total level of the authority's expenditure and its allocation between committees. The process is also member-led, although decisions are taken by an elite, with the majority of council members' playing little significant part. Some officers, especially the Chief Finance Officer and the Chief Executive Officer, are also closely involved at this stage. In early September an informal meeting of the leading members of the Conservative group, with these two officers, determined a policy of 'nil growth' for 1986/7. They also voted the key decision on non-housing capital projects - that the whole budget would be concentrated in a single scheme, an extension to the swimming pool to create a new sports centre. This was a political decision, representing the view of some group members that such a visible achievement would prove electorally advantageous.

Several strategies underpin decisions on revenue spending. In the first place the group were unflinching in their commitment to keep within government controls. The approach is ideological, and consistent with the resolve to maximise government grant. They also wanted to hold rate increases to the minimum possible. The extent to which services could be maintained rested upon resource availability within the confines of these strategies. 'Nil growth' was a political statement, rather than an accounting exercise and in practice the size of the committee budgets did alter during the cycle. This again reflected the concentration of power in the hands of the Leader, Chief Finance Officer, other leading Conservative members and some departmental chief officers. The style in which these adjustments were made reinforces the significance of the informal structure.

There is no detailed analysis of the 'base' or 'committed' budget. So much expenditure is tied to the provision of statutory services, in housing, and planning, that the scope for substantial re-allocation is very limited. Initially, the formal process involves the Chief Finance Officer making assumptions about inflation, interest rates and wage settlements. Departments move from the recording of existing expenditure to a submission of new estimates to the Finance Department by early Autumn. The Finance Department then allocates a senior officer to each departmental budget. In this way many problems are resolved bilaterally between Finance and other departments prior to the involvement of chief officers at corporate levels of management. The limited role for committees and full council in the financial control of an authority led by a small but well disciplined majority is demonstrated by the brevity of discussion on budget issues. Committees rarely spend more than twenty minutes in approving budgets. The opposition uses these opportunities to criticise and to introduce amendments but do so knowing that the majority will consistently out-vote them. The capital budgets go to committee about one month before revenue estimates, so the revenue implications of capital spending can be integrated into final estimates (an exception being the Personnel committee which deals with both as establishment spending). For 1986/7 the decision to put all non-housing capital raised by loans and receipts into the sports centre project meant that virtually all other capital projects were deferred. Where final choices had to be made and cuts imposed, decisions were effectively taken in corporate style at meetings held before committee. Most projects anticipated in the previous year but not started by 1986/7, were deferred by meetings of officers, decisions confirmed when the same officers attended a chairman's agenda briefing a few days before committee. These were the opportunity costs of the sports centre scheme supported by the elite group earlier. In these discussions the initiative for keeping budgets within agreed totals lay with the Finance department and priorities for the tiny amount of possible capital spending emerged from negotiations with appropriate chief officers. Officers whose departmental spending was under analysis had to defend priorities. The Chief Technical Officer, for example, argued which vehicles had to be replaced and which possibly could be maintained for another year, as budgets for vehicle leasing for Recreation and Environmental Health, were pruned. Other projects delayed during the current year, such as a public convenience, were lost from the 1986/7 budget, despite opposition attempts to restore them at committee. This corporate investigation of committee budgets, however, probably approaches the embryonic 'Spanish Inquisition' style of establishing priorities identified by Greenwood (1983). Policy Committee was the only forum where all capital projects were discussed before council approval. Labour argued that the cycle did not permit an effective assessment of overall capital spending priorities. They felt items were steam-rollered through and that government policy was responsible for deferment of projects like the public conveniences, car parks, a district crematorium and restrictions on improvement grants. The housing programme was limited to starts on elderly people's dwellings and the improvement scheme concentrated on central heating conversions on the council's housing stock. The Conservatives expressed the view, shared by officers, that Kingswood does not have a serious housing problem and that present funding is adequate. Opposition members do not share this opinion and see housing investment as evidence of how controls on raising loans and spending receipts have cut services. The housing waiting list has grown from 900 to approximately 1400 during the last three years. Housing need indicators are internally generated and a rule of thumb guide based on experience and a profile of the list, suggests that about 40 per cent are 'in need'.

The passing of the revenue budgets also focused attention on the informal power exercised by the leading actors. The 'no growth' policy in practice expanded to accommodate inflation allowances but some committee budgets increased by as much as ten per cent over base, while others correspondingly contracted. The Recreation committee budget increased because of the seniority and drive of its chairman and his ability to win support from the Leader. Many officers felt that where estimates exceeded the initial resource allocation, responsibility lay with members to make final decisions on cuts. These were taken in a style similar to what Greenwood (1983) has elsewhere labelled the 'sweat shop', where a central group imposes cuts once it is apparent that insufficient resources exist for the programme. In Kingswood these key actors are the Leader, the Chief Finance Officer and leading chairmen. They meet secretly just before the estimates finally go to committee. Budgets are accordingly reduced, as illustrated by the deletion of grants to some local sports organisations.

Kingswood makes little attempt to plan budgets beyond an annual basis. The 1986/7 capital programme is exceptional as the sports centre commitment of all non-housing capital ties up resources for a two year period, to include 1987/8. Uncertainty about future levels of Rate Support Grant and possible changes in government rules on spending, further contribute to the absence of longer planning. Additionally lack of flexibility in the committee base budget and the authority's limited policy objectives [5], provide little incentive for budget planning.

Middle managers play no decisive role in decision taking. Some felt unnecessary work was involved in identifying jobs (sports pavilions needing decorating for example) but found a 'standstill policy' meant such aspirations did not leave their department, or disappeared in bilateral negotiations with Finance. 'Growth items' needed identifying for later corporate consideration but middle managers found no precise definition to work to in labelling such items.

Drama surrounded the rate-setting meeting which had been postponed from 5 March to 11 March 1986, because of Avon County Council's failure to agree a rate, thus delaying the districts. (See Chapter 2). On 7 March Labour won a by-election. This left the Council composition as:

Conservative   22

Labour   19

Liberal   3

Independent   2

Vacancy   1

A death and resignation had cost the Conservatives their majority of one held at the outset of the budget process. The revenue budget required the support of an Independent and the chairman's casting vote for approval, although the capital programme was opposed only by the Labour group. Even at this late stage, government-created uncertainty still impacted on the decisions. The re-allocation of grant by the Department of the Environment just before rate-setting provided an increase for Kingswood sufficient to reduce the proposed increase in the rate, so it moved from 15p. to 16p., instead of a rise to 17p. as assumed since September.

Responses to Financial Constraint

In the early 1980s Kingswood did not feel the need to revise dramatically the process of preparing its budget. However, it was already under sufficient financial pressure to begin devising innovative techniques as a response to government imposed constraints on resources. The first reaction of the authority to tighter limits on grant aid was the depletion of balances. This was an alternative to either a significant cut-back in services or increases in the rate levy. Since 1981/2 the General Rate Fund balance has diminished from £1.3 million to £0.2 million estimated for 1986/7. During the same time the Rate Support Grant has declined from 67 per cent to 53 per cent of net expenditure. During this period the rate income remained below what would have been necessary to fund the established levels of spending. It can thus be seen that balances have been an important buffer protecting the level of service provision, at a time when grant and rate income declined proportionately to the authority's spending. A politically controversial feature of the 1986/7 budget was the switching of money from the Housing Revenue Account to the General Rate Fund, a policy new to the authority. Diminishing the Housing Revenue Account by up to £400,000 per annum had been a feature of the authority's finances in the 1980s, as rent increases were kept low. To avoid a deficit of £500,000 in 1986/7 rent increases averaging £2.20 were necessary to keep the account in surplus. Also the Conservative Leader proposed switching £80,000 to the General Rate Fund to offset costs of rate-borne housing services. This move provoked a bitter attack on policy from Labour which was sustained from the Housing Committee, to the Policy Committee and full council, so strongly did they oppose this change.

One important response to constraints on grant has been a review of fees and charges set by the authority. Since 1980 it has had an index-linked policy written into its procedures. For 1986/7 the Leader, with the chief officers, agreed increases in charges exceeding the inflation element. Ad hoc increases were imposed by the Environmental Health committee on cemetery services, pest control, trade refuse disposal and licensing and inspection services. The basis of these increases was a 'rule of thumb' assessment based on comparing charges for services by neighbouring authorities. It was agreed that Kingswood lacked the scale of operations to attempt to increase income by developing these services as purely commercial enterprises. For the Recreation Committee a more systematic review of charges was proposed during the current budget cycle, which may lead to higher increases in the future. The Chief Finance Officer and officers from Leisure Services sought agreement on a form of cost-benefit analysis of all sports facilities. This would explore the feasibility of raising charges to 30 per cent of authority costs of football pitches, tennis courts and the like.

Evidence of accounting innovation can be found in the capital programme. Until 1982/3 the authority had operated a Renewals and Repairs Fund which was used to finance vehicle acquisition. Contributions to the fund were made each year from the service accounts of the authority in a similar way to paying debt charges. For 1986/7 the main aspect of 'creative accounting' is the use of leasing arrangements. These cover the smaller items of vehicle acquisition, photocopy machines and car-parking meters, which were charged to the revenue accounts. Until 1986 the authority had also engaged in creative accountancy, not at the time of budget setting but at the end of the financial year. Any underspend by committees was used in rescheduled early debt redemption, a reason being the desire to maintain revenue account spending at a level which continued to maximise central government grant.

Internal audit is still an important method in the pursuit of efficiency. Recently an Invoices Sub-committee was established which randomly examines invoices, checking for error or excessive charging. Membership of a purchasing consortium is seen as a method of restricting expenses, while external audit led to the examination of the refuse service.

The Impact of External Factors

The most important external factor influencing Kingswood's budget process is central government. As already indicated, by 1983 the authority had a policy objective consistent with the government's desire to reduce public expenditure. There appeared to be harmony between the traditional prudence of Kingswood's Conservative group and the Government's aims. Budgets were prepared within the prevailing rules on GREA or 'target'. However, by 1986/7 pressures were building up in containing spending, given the assumptions of resource availability. For this budget uncertainty about the level of grant aid prevailed in the Autumn. This was replaced in December by frustration and incredulity when the Department of the Environment's figures on Rate Support Grant became known. The relevance of comparisons with other authorities is important because not only were members and officers disappointed at the level of Kingswood's grant, they were astonished at levels elsewhere. It was noted that Bath was to receive grant exceeding its proposed budget. Confusion about procedures in constructing GREA led to representations to ministers at the Department of the Environment. However, members were angered by a feeling that the authority was being penalised by an assessment system beyond their comprehension and also unfairly for being a 'good' authority in central government's terms.

Further evidence of the impact of uncertainty caused by central government occurred with the capital budget. When Estimates were prepared at departmental level and submitted to the October Housing committee and Environmental Health committee, members were uncertain of the outcome of bids to the central government under the Housing Improvement Programme. Apprehension also existed about possible changes of rules controlling the spending of capital receipts.

The potential for harmony between local authorities and central government, particularly where the same political party controls both, can however be seen with Kingswood's attitude to council house sales. Even before 1983, the Liberals were prepared to support the minority Conservative group's policy to sell council dwellings.

The electoral cycle is the other significant external factor in the budget process. There was a growth in spending before the 1983 district elections (and a contraction in spending in the following budget). There was also a belief among some leading members of the Conservative group that investment in the sports centre would prove to be an electoral asset for the 1987 election.

Few other external factors have much impact. The statutory consultation with non-domestic ratepayers yielded little. A large multinational engineering firm responded on behalf of the CBI, as did one of two local Chambers of Trade. These two written comments conveyed broad indifference so that at the rate-setting meeting members of all parties questioned the value of these consultations.

No other groups influenced decisions. The NALGO branch secretary has aspirations for union consultation but this does not currently occur. Political leadership is highly concentrated in the majority group and the Labour opposition was consistently out-voted, so there is negligible impact by parties outside the council.

Conclusion

In concluding it seems that Kingswood's political marginality strengthened the political input into the budget process. Decision-making was centralised, with power concentrated in the hands of a few politicians, themselves heavily dependent on professional and strategic advice from key officers. The post-Bains style of corporate management made this possible, although as a traditionally low-spending authority responses to the need for cut-back still tended to be incremental and marginal, rather than involving a thorough review of policy. Its approach to 1986/7 spending was resource led. The response to constraints on government grant, given its own policy of minimum rate increases, has been depletion of balances, spending to GREA levels and maximising grant aid. Services have largely been protected but the scope for maneouvre under existing legislation seems much more limited than at the start of the decade.

Notes

[1] <u>An Introductory Guide</u>,Kingswood District Council, 1986, p.21.

[2] <u>Policy Objectives 1983-1987</u>, Kingswood District Council

[3] Ibid, p.12

[4] Kingswood District Council 1986, op.cit., p.10

[5] <u>Policy Objectives</u>, op.cit.

10. Portsmouth City Council

SYLVIA HORTON

Introduction

Portsmouth is a non-metropolitan district situated on the south coast
of England. Its geography is a significant factor in its social,
economic and political structures. It is mainly an island and is
entirely urban. It has a population of 179,600 concentrated into an
area of 15 square miles and occupying 73,700 units of housing, 14,745
(20 per cent) of which are Council units. There are also overspill
estates in Havant and Waterlooville.

Portsmouth's economy is mixed, relying mainly on tourism, the service
sector (public and private), retailing and distribution, shipbuilding
and marine engineering and light industry. The naval dockyard, which
at one time dominated its economy continues to support the marine
engineering industry throughout the area. In order to broaden its
employment base and shift its emphasis away from the Dockyard, which
has been affected by changes in the Government's defence policy, the
City has vigorously encouraged new industry and commerce since the
early 50's, establishing 8 new industrial estates within the City.
Since the mid 60's office development has also been encouraged as
a means of further employment diversification and there is now over
two million square feet of new office floorspace. Two major
international organisations located themselves in the city in the
1970's and smaller national insurance and finance companies followed.
Although manufacturing industry continues to decline new "high tech"
firms are moving into what has become a centre of the British micro-
electronics industry.

Although the local economy is generally buoyant, Portsmouth has a higher than average level of unemployment for the south-east and a hard core of long term unemployed.

Political Structure

Portsmouth is a Conservative controlled area. The Conservatives have dominated in both general and local elections since 1945. With an almost unbroken period of office over 40 years, Portsmouth is probably the most strongly Conservative of Britain's medium sized cities. Support for the Conservatives is falling, however, and in no election since 1979 have they received an absolute majority of votes. After the local election in May 1986, the composition of the Council was Conservatives 22, Labour 10, the Alliance 6 and Independents 1. This gave them an overall majority of five, their smallest since the District was established in 1974.

Unlike many one-party dominated authorities Portsmouth is member led. The most important political structures are the Conservative caucus, which includes the chairmen of all major committees, the Conservative group (all Conservative councillors) and ad hoc meetings between the Leader and Conservative members. It is within these groups rather than the formal Council committees that the most important policy and political decisions are made. Informal meetings with the Leader and Committee Chairmen are often attended by the Chief Executive and his management team.

Structural changes in the organisation of the Council, the creation of Leader of the Council and the emergence of a number of strong political leaders since 1974 has resulted in member direction. Both Councillors and officers acknowledge that the Leader and the Chairmen have the principal influence on the policies which the Council adopt.

Member control has emerged also as a consequence of the existence of a few leading politicians who are prepared to devote a considerable proportion of their time to the work of the City Council.

Council Structure

Portsmouth incorporated most of the Bains proposals in the new organisational and administrative structures which were created in 1974. It has a Policy and Resources Committee with six sub-committees for Administration, Personnel, Property, Commercial Docks, Licensing and Employment and Training. There are five programme committees and certain other special committees.

The Policy and Resources Committee has 12 members including the Leader and Deputy Leader of the majority party, the Leader of the opposition, the chairmen of standing committees and four elected by the Council. All programme committees have 12 members with the Conservatives holding all the chairmanships and vice-chairmanships and having a majority of councillors on each.

The City Council's management system at officer level is based on a directorate structure. The Chief Executive is head of the paid service and the Council's Managing Director. He leads a team of Directors which comprise his Management Team, each of whom is responsible for a programme area of activity. Within the directorates, 12 Chief Officers head departments responsible for the provision of particular services.

The Chief Executive has close links with the Leader of the Council and leading politicians of all parties and is responsible for ensuring that the policies adopted by the Council are effectively implemented.

Functions and Expenditure

Portsmouth has a limited range of statutory responsibilities but it exercises a wide range of permissive powers. It is not a typical shire district. It has a high population density and a level of need which is closer to the metropolitan areas than to the county shires. It has undertaken major investment programmes to stimulate economic activity and to generate wealth in the community which have been expensive. Portsmouth has consistently been amongst the highest spending shire districts with one of the largest per capita debts. Between 1978/9 and 1984/5 its gross expenditure increased by 83.7 per cent, well in excess of the cumulative inflation rate.

Before 1981 the major areas of rate fund expenditure were housing, followed by leisure services, environmental health and planning. Since 1981 there has been a relative decline in housing and a proportionate increase in tourism and tourist related activities. Other areas of increase on port health, consumer protection, housing allowances and Housing Act advances reflect mainly new statutory responsibilities.

Portsmouth is classified as a "big spender" - in the top ten of the shire districts. Its high expenditure has brought it into conflict with the Government's policy to reduce local spending. From 1981, when the new block grant system was introduced, Portsmouth's planned expenditure was consistently above its GREA and exceeded its Target expenditure. This led to rate-capping in 1985/6. Portsmouth suffered under the grant system based on GREAs because the latter reflected average expenditure within the category of shire districts and did not adequately accommodate "deviant" authorities. The highly interventionist role of the District in tourism and its expenditure on related services such as museums and art galleries bore no relation to its GREA. For example, in 1984/5 Portsmouth's GREA component for museums and art galleries was £196,000, whilst its planned expenditure was £1,029,000. Another area where large discrepancies occurred was in debt charges. Portsmouth had a large capital debt in 1979 and this has grown because of its many investment programmes. Table 10.1 shows the absolute size of the debt and the cost of servicing it as a percentage of rate fund expenditure. Although rate fund debt charges have declined significantly since 1983, the absolute size of debt remains very high and this is not allowed for in its GREA.

Furthermore, Portsmouth's housing expenditure, which is amongst the highest of all shire districts, includes an exceptionally large GIA programme [1] which the GREA does not take into consideration.

As a result of these factors, Portsmouth became an "overspender". Unwilling to change its policies the Council's planned expenditure continued to be above both its GREA and its Target although its out-turn expenditure was lower and it only incurred penalties in 1982/3 (see Table 10.2).

In spite of the fact that it was Conservative controlled, Portsmouth was clearly in line for rate-capping in 1985 as its planned expenditure was 34.57 per cent above GREA and 5.26 per cent above Target.

Table 10.1

SIZE OF DEBT AND COST AS A PERCENTAGE OF GROSS EXPENDITURE

Year	Absolute Size* £m	Cost of Debt as Percentage of Rate Fund Gross Expenditure
1979/80	131,000	43.1
1980/1	139,000	36.1
1981/2	145,000	40.4
1982/3	150,000	42.3
1983/4	160,000	19.0
1984/5	170,000	20.58
1985/6	177,000	19.22

*This is total debt including non-rate fund capital investment. Approximately £60m is on rate-borne services.

Table 10.2

PORTSMOUTH'S EXPENDITURE, GREA'S AND TARGETS 1981/2 - 1986/7

Year	Expenditure *Original Estimate **Revised Estimate ***Actual £m	GREA *Original **Revised £m	Target £m	Block Grant £m
1981/2	*15,042 **14,280 ***13,460	*15,299 **15,445	–	7,910
1982/3	*16,052 **15,754 ***15,146	*13,137 **12,970	14,294	6,954
1983/4	*16,383 **15,646 ***15,687	*14,977 **14,993	15,788	9,186
1984/5	*16,863 **16,020 ***16,021	*12,531 **12,529	16,021	8,601
1985/6	*16,511 **16,511 ***16,511	*13,852 **13,861	16,511	8,577
1986/7	*17,675	*16,483	n/a	9,614

128

Also its budgeted expenditure for 1984/5 represented about £88.75 per head compared with £71 per head for the ten largest shire districts and £51 per head for the shire districts as a whole. When the Council was informed that it was to be rate-capped it vigorously disputed the reasoning but did not apply for re-determination or consider not setting a rate. The council appealed against rate-capping on the grounds that the GREA construction had failed to take into account the City's massive debt charges, its exceptionally large GIA programme and its large expenditure on tourism and tourist related activities. The appeal was overruled and Portsmouth was rate-capped for the financial year 1985/6.

Rate-capping had an effect on Portsmouth's expenditure but not as much perhaps as for the other 17 rate-capped authorities. The Council's estimated expenditure for 1985/6 (prior to the rate-capping announcement) had been £18,600,000 or £1,415,000 above its rate-capped limit of £16,751,000. A reduction of £1.4 million was necessary therefore to produce a legal budget. The Council decided to officially spend at its target of £16,511,000 but to finance its excess of activities by drawing upon other funds. These included £600,000 from the City-owned commercial docks account and £146,000 from its Direct Labour Organisation account. In addition the Council raised £300,000 by increasing council house rents. The only 'real' cut was £400,000 by deferring certain items of capital expenditure.

Rate-capping did however have an effect on the rate levied by the Council which fell by 1.2 per cent over 1984/5 or by nearly 7 per cent allowing for inflation. Portsmouth's rate has been very volatile since 1979 and there is no relationship between the rate and the Council's level of expenditure which has risen consistently (with the exception of 1985/6) throughout the period. Unlike the County rate, which has increased every year since 1979, the District rate has risen and fallen with regularity. The pattern is understood only when it is related to the rate support and block grant. A comparison of rates and block grants shows that there is a correlation between the rate and the level of central government funding. In the first year of the operation of the new block grant in 1981 Portsmouth came out of the settlement as the most favoured authority in England and this settlement allowed the Council to reduce the rate by 18.5 per cent over 1980/1. A reduction in the grant the following year, however, combined with inflation, led to a 22.6 per cent increase. The instability in both the City's GREA and its grant have thus led to the instability in its rate since 1981. Portsmouth tends to give support to the Audit Commission's (1984) view that the new block grant system has created uncertainty and led to higher rates than necessary. Clearly the system has not been conducive to forward planning, although Portsmouth has not been severely constrained in its expenditure because of its independent sources of revenue and its accumulated capital funds. Although always conscious of the need to watch the rate, especially during election years, the Council has been willing and encouraged to spend. The local Chamber of Commerce has generally supported high expenditure as much of it is seen as wealth and revenue-creating and beneficial to the economy of the City. Regular re-election of Conservatives indicates support too from ratepayers. Since 1984 however the Council has resorted to other means to stabilise the rates.

Rate-capping paradoxically removed some of the uncertainties which had come to characterise the Council's budgetary process throughout the 1980s as it actually had a hard figure to work on early in the budget cycle. Planning the budget for 1986/7 however, saw a return to the previous uncertainty since it was not clear whether the Council would be rate-capped again or what the implications of yet further changes in the central government grant would mean for its expenditure. With the Government's decision to abolish the target system and to place the emphasis on GREAs it looked as though the Council might be even worse off than under rate-capping. Budgeting for 1986/7 therefore took place partly in the dark until December 1985 when the Government announced its new grant policy and published the GREAs for the District.

Budget Making

Portsmouth had an established formal procedure within which the budget for 1986/7 evolved. A programme of deadlines for reports, statements and meetings was drawn up in June 1985 and there were no substantial deviations from the plan which is set out in Figure 10.1. Estimates started very early within the Departments which were asked for information on their capital schemes by May. The forecasting of trends in price and wage inflation began in June and there was some early indication of grant levels by July. The Treasurer sounded out the views of the Leader of the Council before drawing up his own financial projections which were presented to the Conservative Group Caucus in June. He made predictions about the target to be set by the DoE, inflation rates and movements in wages and salaries. He outlined the Council's ongoing and new expenditure schemes, the cost of servicing the Authority's debt and the revenue cost of existing programmes. He forecast that revenue expenditure would probably be about £400,000 above target. He recommended that the policy of the Council should be to keep within an expenditure plan which would avoid any severe penalties or further rate-capping. In this he was clearly expressing the view of the Leader of the Council and the Conservative group. Very little action at member level occurred between June and September but within the Departments bids for increased revenue expenditure were being drawn up.

The formal budgetary process began again in early September when a second report was produced by the Treasurer and presented to a chairmens' meeting. This reiterated the continuing uncertainties surrounding the budget including changes in the block grant system, the new grading structure for manual workers and the consequences of the deregulation of public transport. It gave formal guidance, however, on the assumptions to be made about base line rate-borne expenditure and on the availability of contributions from other Council funds and balances. It was clear that most growth in the budget would come from the cost of financing the capital programme and therefore tighter control of new capital expenditure was essential. Some new revenue costs were identified as well as areas where pressure was likely to come from outside bodies for additional funding.

Areas for revenue saving and generation of new funds were also listed and committees were urged to look closely at charges as a source of extra income. Revenue contributions from "other funds" [2] were identified but the Treasurer urged caution in "milking" these funds

September — City Treasurer produces forecast of financial
variables and "GUIDELINES"
↓
Policy and Resources Committee approve Guidelines
↓
Meeting with Chamber of Commerce
↓
October — Guidelines sent to Departments
↓
Departments submit details of new capital
programme bids and new revenue growth to City
Treasurer and Chief Executive
↓
November — Departments draw up base estimates assuming
continuing level of service, incorporating
inflation factors, with full effects of
growth/cut items and capital programme
↓
December — Final base estimates to City Treasurer, Chief
Executive's Management Team consider **new** capital
and revenue bids
↓
Mid/End — Treasurer/Chief Executive consider general rate
December fund summary and capital programme
↓
Block Grant Settlement announced
↓
Discuss with Leader and Deputy Leader
↓
Chairmen review programme estimates with chief
officers
↓
Late December— Chairmen's Committee consider draft estimates
January and rate
↓
January — Programme Committees approve estimates
– February ↓
Meetings with Chamber of Commerce and Trade Union
representatives
↓
Policy and Resources Committee approves final
estimates
↓
March — Council approves the Rate

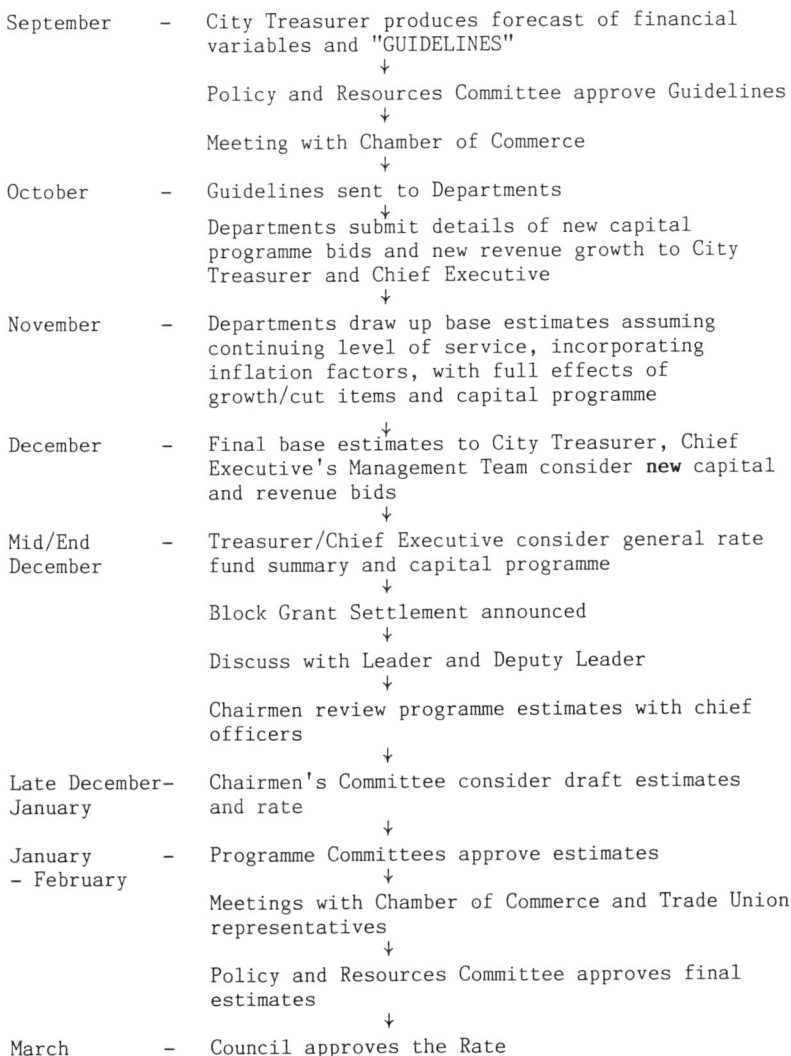

Figure 10.1 **The Planned Formal Procedure for the Budgetary
Process**

for short term expediency over long term financial planning. Finally, the likely effect of grant changes on the City, which was currently spending 19.2 per cent above GREA, were assessed. Priority was to get down to GREA or the threshold which the Government set for 1986/7 and to avoid excessive grant penalties. The speculative growth rate set by the Treasurer was 1.7 per cent.

Because of the uncertainties surrounding the financial situation the Policy and Resources Committee decided not to issue formal guidelines to the committees. The Treasurer's report was issued to all Departments and met with the "unofficial blessing" of all committee chairmen and Directors. In addition, a joint memorandum from the City Treasurer and the Chief Executive was distributed to all chief officers in October giving instructions on the final preparation of capital and revenue estimates which in fact amounted to guidelines. But no cash limits on capital or revenue were set for Departments or committees.

The timetable set for the submission of final estimates and bids was a very tight one. Chief officers were requested to update the current approved capital programme for inflation and slippage, submit a revised programme on an outturn base for schemes to be completed in 1985/6 or still in progress in 1986/7, and submit a list of prioritised bids for new capital items, by 8 November. Second, Directors were requested to provide information on all slippage to the Chief Executive by 1 December with "sound information". Although no targets were set for particular programme areas, Directors were asked to keep bids down to realistic levels and every bid had to be individually submitted with a clear justification, close costing and identification of any staffing implications. Officers were given detailed inflation figures for specific elements of expenditure (some 24 in all) and they were directed not to engage in incrementalism but to examine all base expenditures to identify where economies could be made. All new areas of revenue growth had to be prioritised and submitted to the Treasurer by 8 November **after** discussions with the Chief Executive. Wherever possible revenue expenditure and new growth were to be matched by savings, increased efficiency and elimination of waste. Management reviews were to continue with the aim of cost saving through better management or contracting out. In anticipation of a possible adverse Rate Support Settlement officers were asked to prepare contingency plans for a one per cent, two per cent and four per cent cut in budget. All capital and revenue budgets had to be approved by the appropriate chairman and discussed with the committee accountant who was the link between the Treasurer and the Department.

This timetable gave the Departments and Directorates two weeks in which to finalise their budgets and prioritise their capital bids and revenue expenditure. Some preparatory work on revenue estimates had already been done as advance notice of the inflation factors had been given in September and the capital programme had started in May – identifying costs, hardening up options and putting them into the cycle. Nevertheless, the short time-scale for the final submission inevitably had an effect on the process of prioritising and ordering new bids and officers felt under pressure.

Most proposals for new initiatives – both capital and revenue – emanated from Departmental working groups. New bids or existing bids carried over from the previous year were classified as (a) essential,

(b) highly desirable or (c) desirable. The vetting process which began in earnest from October onwards first of all removed the totally unrealistic bids, secondly eliminated those bids whose size excluded them from consideration, and thirdly, produced a list which was considered realistic both in terms of the money required and their justification as essential. Bids were still included, however, which committees did not expect to have accepted but which were intended to put down a marker for the following year. There was of course no guarantee that bids excluded at the Department or Directorate level or classified as a lower order priority would not be reinstated by the chairman or raised at committee or chairmens' group level.

The close involvement of the Leader, Deputy Leader and Chairmen in the run up to the production of the bids, however, ensured that there was a general level of political support at the top level when they came forward for consideration. A similar process of rank ordering was carried out in identifying cuts, although the lists tended to be much shorter.

All budgets had to be cleared with the accountant assigned to each Council committee. These officials have a fair amount of power since they can make an issue of any item of the budget. Their role, however, is essentially to apply the rules of the game, to question, challenge and ensure that the estimated expenditure can be justified. The view of officers in the spending departments was that generally the Committee accountants were open to persuasion and that real disagreements were rare. 80 per cent of the budget would be cleared without issue and only perhaps 20 per cent would involve any dispute.

Once the bids left the Departments and were approved at Directorate level they went forward to the Treasurer, the Chief Executive and the Management team. It was clear by late November that the overall level of bids for capital expenditure was too high. The bids totalled over £5 million and the original "guidelines" from the Treasurer's department had been £1 million. At a meeting of the Leader, Deputy Leader, Chief Executive and Treasurer in early December it was decided that the level was totally unacceptable and chairmen and officers directed to review their bids. In the event they were reduced by over one-third. Some hard bargaining took place within the Management team and at member level before the new capital starts were finally agreed at just over £2 million. (3) Revenue bids proved far less controversial than capital ones. Most were incorporated into the base or approved as new growth. The remainder were included in the contingency funding and were therefore likely to go ahead.

The task of choosing from the bids was made easier after the Government announced its policy on the new grant system in December. The GREA allocations turned out to be considerably higher than had been anticipated and this allowed for a higher level of expenditure. The GREA was fixed at £16.483 million, an increase of 19 per cent over the 1985/6 GREA and the threshold was seven per cent above GREA at £17.68 million. Up to threshold the City lost £33,562 in grant for every £100,000 spent over GREA, beyond the threshold penalties rose to £82,081 for every £100,000 overspent. It was decided to spend up to threshold. To spend at GREA would have meant less loss of grant but this was not acceptable to the Leader, the Conservative group or the Opposition parties.

The final outcome of the budgetary process was a budget providing for expenditure of £17,675,000 or £1,192,000 above GREA. This rate-borne expenditure was to be financed as shown in Table 10.3.

Table 10.3

FINANCING OF RATE-FUND EXPENDITURE 1986/7

	£
Block Grant	9,364,189
Local Taxation Licenses	2,300
Contribution from balances	692,461
	10,058,950
	7,616,000
	17,674,950

The rate levied was an increase of 1.12 pence or 4.1 per cent over 1985/6. This was in line with the Leader's stated objective - back in June 1985 - to keep the rate down to the level of inflation. The budget was made up of £18,131,000 for Committee spending plus an unallocated contingency of £320,000. Interest on the use of cash balances reduced this sum by £522,000. Contributions to, and from other funds further reduced the requirements by £254,000 to give a final budgeted expenditure of £17,675,000 as shown in Table 10.3 above.

In terms of patterns of expenditure the Council planned for new revenue growth of £498,000 (£349,000 on revenue schemes and £149,000 the revenue effect of new capital schemes), and £500,000 as a Passenger Transport Contingency to cover the residual costs of operating the new bus company. The new growth was accounted for by a large number of small expenditures spread across the Council's Committees. The largest single item was £55,000 allocated for the Australian bicentenary celebrations.

Final Estimates were presented to the appropriate Committees during January and February. There were no amendments and the Committee's approval was a formality. The Policy and Resources Committee met on 13 February 1986 and a special meeting of the Council was held on 4 March at which a rate of 28 pence in the pound was recommended. The Labour Group proposed that the budget should be increased by £500,000 to create employment in the City and that extra expenditure should be financed by drawing on the General Reserve Fund. This proposal was defeated and the Council approved both the budget and the rate. The rate to be set by the County was not known at that time although it was expected to be high. In the event it was 169 pence in the pound, an increase of 14.6 per cent. This brought the total rate to 197 pence a net increase of 13 per cent over 1985/6. After domestic rate relief was subtracted for householders the rate levied was 178.5 pence, an aggregate increase for domestic ratepayers of 14.5 per cent.

Analysis and Review

The budgetary process and the financial policy of Portsmouth are a result of a variety of environmental, political, organisational and situational factors. The decline of Portsmouth's naval based economy in the 1960s and its large stock of poor housing necessitated major programmes of urban renewal and economic regeneration. The Council has invested heavily in the City's infrastructure and has prompted and encouraged the growth of commercial docks, tourism and "high-tech" employment. Simultaneously it has pursued a high profile policy of urban development with 26 GIAs. These economic and social priorities have required heavy investment and this has resulted in Portsmouth emerging as a "big spender" with a large capital debt and heavy debt charges.

The stability of political control since 1974 has enabled the Conservative Group consistently to pursue an entrepreneurial approach. Officers and members perceive the Authority as go ahead, vibrant and innovatory with the former likening it more to high spending Labour led councils than traditional Tory ones. A centralised party organisation with power concentrated in the Leader and the stability of the group membership has also been important in member/officer relationships. Although some officers perceive the relationship as a balanced partnership, most describe the Council as either member or Leader led.

Portsmouth exhibits strong coordination at both member and officer level, with the Policy and Resources Committee and the Management team providing for integration and coherence in Council policy and administration. There is a high degree of consensus on the Council's policies and its priorities even amongst some of the Labour Opposition. The values of the majority party members and senior officers are largely in tune with the general commitment to economic development, expansion and growth, the maintenance of services and a responsible attitude towards the rate. The Opposition is divided, weak and quiescent. Relationships with local business and the Chamber of Commerce are generally good.

It is this political stability, the experience of the leading members and the high degree of consensus on the policies of the City which has allowed the adjustment to the changing external environment to be achieved without undue pressure either from the Opposition or professionals within the Departments. The establishment of strong leadership and central mechanisms for coordinating and directing Council policy before 1979 has also aided the process of coping with fiscal stress in the 1980s.

Portsmouth's high level of spending has brought it into conflict with Central Government since 1979. The GREA system has been particularly disadvantageous compared to similar authorites and the Council has kept up a constant battle with the DoE to get the GREA changed. From 1981 onwards it has only avoided grant penalties by underspending and finding other ways of funding its activities. Portsmouth conforms very closely to Wolman's (1984) observation that fiscal stress produces novel responses including creative accountancy, drives for greater efficiency and the search for additional sources of revenue. The creation of new funds to equate rate contributions, the pooling of capital right to spend, contracting out, management reviews and an increase in charges have all been means of enabling the City to continue to maintain its services, finance its large capital programme and circumvent the Government's attempts to reduce its expenditure. In particular, it has used separate trading accounts to restrict expenditure charged to the general rate fund and it has used the surpluses which have accrued on these accounts to finance rate fund expenditure so as to avert a penal loss of grant. In 1984 it created a general reserve fund to help avoid grant loss affecting expenditure and reduce annual rate fluctuations. Since 1981/2 planned contributions from "other sources" to the rate fund have exceeded £5 million.

Portsmouth also fits Wolman's pattern of an authority which has been forced to review its expenditure patterns and the way in which it takes decisions about spending because of external Government pressure on resources. It has departed from a more traditional incremental budgetary strategy, when growth was the norm, to one in which base budgets and committed expenditure are reviewed annually and new growth, wherever possible, is matched by savings. The Council has sought to avoid either incrementalism or decrementalism by requiring all Departments to look at base expenditures annually. This has not, however, amounted to a thorough zero base approach. Portsmouth has never practised PPBS and has eschewed the idea of a corporate plan but it would appear that the fiscal pressures on the Authority have led to a more rational approach to budget making and control and rooting out of unnecessary and wasteful expenditure. The requirement that all new revenue and capital bids are accompanied by full costings and justifications and the vetting of all estimates by the Treasury accountants to ensure conformity with the general guidelines ensures a higher degree of integration in the budgetary process than in the past.

The relatively small size of the Authority and its limited range of activities, combined with the commonality of values amongst members and officers, have permitted this centralised, integrated process to evolve. However, some elements of incrementalism are still in evidence. Departments continue to be the main source of policy initiatives, they regularly put in bids for new or increased spending which they expect to get over time and the more they ask for the more they tend to get. "Expectations tend to drive budgets" (Schick 1983) and although officers and members have accepted that the days of permanent growth have gone, they are committed to an expansionary policy which is only mediated by Government policy, not stopped by it. Nevertheless Portsmouth's budget is resource rather than expenditure led and it is the Government grant with its associated penalty system which has become the dominant factor in the Council's budget equation, certainly since rate-capping. Although in the early stages of the budgetary process in 1986/7 it appeared to be expenditure led the actual level of the grant and the penalty system announced in December determined the final decision on what to spend. In the event the grant enabled a higher level of expenditure because of the 17 per cent increase over the previous year. It also enabled the Council to achieve the four objectives it had set for its budget:

(1) to keep expenditure down to the threshold in order to avoid penal loss of grant and to avoid rate-capping again;

(2) to keep moving forward, continuing with a fairly substantial capital programme and developing services;

(3) to have a rate increase no greater than inflation; and

(4) not to milk the reserves but to keep enough in reserves and balances for a rainy day.

It was the level of grant which triggered off adjustments in other elements of the budget equation. In 1986, however, the commitment to keep the rate down was also strong - first because it was an election year, second because a high County rate was anticipated and third because the Council wanted to stabilise the rate and avoid the wide fluctuations which had occurred between 1980 and 1985.

Portsmouth has coped with fiscal stress fairly sucessfully. In spite of rate-capping in 1985/6, it has pursued an expansive capital programme and has maintained its services without any significant decline in quality. It has done so by resorting to new methods of funding its activities and by increasing its own efficiency. Rate-capping in 1985/6 led it to adopt a penalty-avoidance strategy and to keep within the Government's new threshold, but it has never tried to get down to its GREA or to avoid some "claw-back" of grant because that would mean a politically unacceptable cut in its activities.

The future may well be different, however, because there are consequences of the policy which the Council has pursued and these may well result in more fiscal stress in the future. Capitalising to get expenditure down and using capital grants to finance revenue expenditure does result in higher revenue costs which have to be funded. High capital expenditure also depends on the Government's approval of right to spend. For the first time since the new capital expenditure controls were introduced in 1981/2, the Council does not have a large excess of right to spend. The excess was only £0.7 million in 1986/7 compared with £9 million in 1985/6. If and when this limit is reached then another important source of finance may be capped.

So the foreseeable future looks no more certain than in the past. Until the Government stabilises its own grant and capital expenditure control policy, the Council will continue to react each year to the external constraints and to be primarily resource led. Its scope for responding may be more constrained, however, as a result of the consequences of the responses in the past.

Notes

[1] Portsmouth embarked on a major General Improvement Area Programme during the 1970s. To date it has declared 26 GIAs covering over 14,000 properties. In 1984/5 alone it planned for 1,100 improvement grants amounting to nearly £3 million.

[2] The sources of revenue contributions identified by the Treasurer were the Housing Revenue Account, Docks Undertaking and a provisional figure of £500,000 was suggested as a realistic transfer.

[3] One of the most hard fought battles was over the bid for £25,000 for a new piano for the Guildhall. Other bids which were strongly contested related to GIAs and a neighbourhood centre, in all cases members were fighting for ward interests.

11. Redditch Borough Council

BRIAN RANCE, J. ROUSE, J. MCDONAGH AND J. WILKINSON

Introduction

The Borough of Redditch lies south of the West Midlands conurbation in the predominantly rural County of Herford and Worcester. With an area of 5,427 ha. and a population of 73,000 (1984) the Borough can be divided into two distinctive parts, a small rural area and the New Town which was designated in 1964. Prior to local government reorganisation the area constituted the Redditch Urban District in the County of Worcestershire, although in 1974 there was, unusually, no boundary change because it was felt that the area would undergo rapid growth as a result of the New Town designation. Indeed, the town has grown rapidly with a population growth rate of 63 per cent between 1971 and 1981 and a projected growth of 23 per cent in the 1981-91 decade. The difference between the official 1984 population of 73,200 and that used by the Department of Environment for block calculation of 70,800 is a source of considerable grievance to the Borough and of frequent but as yet unsuccessful, representation to the DoE. Compared with similar authorities, as defined by the Audit Commission, Redditch has a relatively young population and a higher than average birth rate. At 46 per cent of the housing stock, the population of council house dwellers is also above average.

On 1 April 1985 Redditch took transfer of the assets of the New Town Development Corporation via the Commission for New Towns. The transfer mainly involved Council housing and community related assets such as district centres, community rooms, etc. A certain amount of income generating assets such as factory premises were also transferred to offset the additional costs imposed on the Borough. The result has been that the transfer, as required by law, has not caused a major drain on resources, although it has increased the preponderance of council housing as the major source of income and expenditure in the authority. Expenditure on housing accounts for 68 per cent of total expenditure for 1985/6. The next largest item is Rate Rebates and Rate Collection, at 7 per cent of total spending. The other main services provided include: public and environmental services, planning and transportation, amenities, recreation and leisure, economic development and employment services. The main source of finance remains Central Government grants and subsidies which account for 45 per cent of a gross expenditure of £32.9 million although the proportion of specific grants, particularly housing grants associated with HIP submission, have increased over undifferentiated block grant. Block grant itself has been reduced progressively since 1981/2 and in 1986/7 a dramatic fall is anticipated. However, when these estimates are compared with the actual outcome then the situation does not appear so dire. Indeed, an additional £144,000 has already been allocated on top of the estimated block grant entitlement for 1986/7, though this was only as a result of recycling grant withheld from other local authorities.

In recent years Redditch has had an expenditure target above its GREA and has spent at target level, thus incurring no penalty. Next year, with the abolition of expenditure targets, estimated expenditure is well above GREA but below threshold and grant loss is anticipated for the first time. Increasingly, local sources of revenue have played a greater part in financing gross expenditure which has continued to increase every year since 1981/2. These sources are in part rate revenue, amounting to 8 per cent of gross expenditure and other local sources such as council house rents, fees and charges and interest repayments which together account for 47 per cent of total gross expenditure. The total rate levy for 1985/6 was 171.5 pence in the pound yielding a total income of approximately £18.7 million of which Redditch received £2.7 million, equivalent to a levy of 25p. in the pound. The remainder was paid to the County Council by way of the precept, together with a very small precept for Feckenham Parish Council.

The political history of Redditch since reorganisation has been one of a marginal council where control has changed hands between Conservative and Labour. After reorganisation, because the Ward boundaries were under review, the Council were required to hold whole Council elections at irregular intervals rather than the usual election of thirds. The council in 1974 was under Labour control but the Conservatives won the elections of 1976 and 1979. The new Ward boundaries were used for the first time in 1983 which saw the return of Labour control which has continued to the present time. The current Council consists of 29 members drawn from eleven Wards.

The Labour Group is currently firmly in control of the council (as Table 11.1 indicates) and is planning its policies into the medium term in the knowledge that election by thirds guarantees them a more secure future.

County Council elections were last held in 1985 when Redditch returned 6 Labour and 2 Conservative Councillors (with 4 of the 8 being Borough Councillors too) and the County remained firmly in Conservative hands. Redditch is represented at the National and European levels by Conservative MPs.

Table 11.1

POLITICAL CONTROL OF DISTRICT 1983-86

	Labour	Con.	Ind.	Alliance
1983	17	9	3	-
1984	19	9	1	-
1985	19	9	1	-
1986	20	7	1	1

It became apparent early in our study of the budgetary process of Redditch that 1985/6 was not a typical year. The Chief Executive Officer herself described it as an "interim phase", a unique experience representing a transition from and displacement of, the prevailing orthodoxy based upon departmentalism and professionalism towards the development of a "policy planning system" with its emphasis upon corporate strategy and planning. A number of internal and external influences and pressures help to explain both the desire for and the implementation of organisational change in the policymaking/budgetary process during 1985/6. The appointment of a new Chief Executive Officer in the early part of 1985 by a Council under Labour control since May 1983 after a decade in opposition was highly influential. The new CEO, an external appointment, was neither the traditional lawyer nor accountant but a Masters graduate in local government studies with a strong management background. She sees financial planning as part of the corporate planning process with the annual budget as the financial representation of the Council's **political** policies. She is committed to altering existing arrangements so as to reorientate the policy making and budgetary process away from departmentalism, which conceives the role of the authority as the administration of a series of essentially independent services with statutory requirements, towards a more corporate managerial approach involving financial planning and strategy in order to realise opportunities as defined by the controlling political group. Hence, there exists a commitment to strategic change by the senior executive who has sufficient authority to raise and press for structural review and reform. In this commitment she has been given considerable support by the leading members of the controlling Labour Group who desire a reorientation of Council policy in line with the Manifesto emphasis on economic development, jobs, housing and community provision and care. Both CEO and Leader, together with key members and officers, are developing cooperatively a coherent alternative policy planning system with implications for the budgetary process in 1985/6 and beyond.

The desire for strategic reorientation of the policy making/budgetary process has been given reinforcement by the external threat of anticipated increasing fiscal pressure. Until the present time Redditch has been able to keep within central government guidelines and has experienced no major fiscal stress. They have not been forced to consider significant cuts in the base budget in order to generate desired increments to expenditure in spite of the declining block grant. This is largely because they have been able to buy time by creative accounting schemes (see Appendix 1) and more recently, by drawing on reserves. It is now felt that both methods are largely exhausted and modest fiscal pressure is anticipated in 1986/7 and beyond. Given the Labour Council's desire to implement its Manifesto by selective increases in expenditure in the face of declining resources, a more thorough review of corporate strategy and policy is essential, with implications for the budgetary process. Hence, in the unique climate of 1985/6, change agents on both the members' and officers' side of Redditch Borough Council were exploring and re-evaluating the existing procedures of the policy making/budgetary process largely to avoid a potential crisis of performance.

Decision Making Structures and Processes

With the establishment of the Economic Development Committee by the incoming Labour administration in May 1983, there are five service committees (Amenities, Housing, Planning and Transportation, Public and Environmental Services) and one coordinating committee in Policy and Resources. The latter has a number of sub-committees including two of the Bains type (Finance and Personnel), three joint sub-committees (with the County Council, with the Commission for New Towns, and with the employees) and three ad hoc sub-committees (on computer development, appeals, and maladministration and complaints). The decisions of all committees are formally ratified by a monthly Council meeting. Debate in the Council chamber is ritualistically along Party lines and is rarely about local policy. The decisions taken by Committees are seldom debated by the whole Council and in only rare cases does the full Council refer back a committee decision. Council has been about ritual and ceremony rather than policy.

The role of the Policy and Resources Committee in relation to the other service committees is poorly defined in that fairly detailed issues can be brought before the committee. However, the committee does take an overview of all personnel and financial issues including the approval of the major financial documents and stages in the budgetary process. The Chief Executive Officer said that the P & R committee was not a policy committee of the Bains type but a financial and general purposes committee with most of its discussion on financial decisions. In the past it had certainly not brought issues together, examined policy strategy and priority, nor concerned itself with policy and performance review. Indeed, the CEO said that no committee had responsibility for performance review, although she saw this function as essential for effective policy making and its place within the organisation was an area of ongoing discussion. The Council Leader agreed that P & R is really a "finance" committee since policy is "a matter for the Party Group". He argued that "the idea of P & R as a coordinator is an officer orientated one" and is not central to the Labour Group vision of an improved policy planning system.

Each of the six committees normally has twelve members with eight currently being from the controlling Labour Group and four from the opposition. Hence all committees are securely controlled by the Labour Group though the opposition is not excluded from any committee. Each Councillor is on average a member of two committees. One exception to this is the Chair of P & R who sits on no other committees but chairs or is involved in all the sub-committees that report to P & R.

An analysis of the formal councillor hierarchy would appear to reveal
that control of policy making by the members is not centralised in a few
hands, in that only 12 of the 29 members are not either chairs or vice-
chairs of committees or members of P & R. These include six controlling
and six opposition party members. The composition of the Policy and
Resources Committee unusually does not include all committee chairs and
vice-chairs. The chairs of the relatively big spending Housing
Committee and Public and Environmental Services Committee are not
members. From the formal Councillor hierarchy then it would appear that
power and influence is widely shared amongst Councillors generally.

Within the controlling Labour Group the absence of a formal elite or
inner caucus may help to avoid problems of the back bench alienation and
revolt typical of larger more politically centralised local
authorities. However, because of the small size of the controlling
Labour Group there appears to be a greater reliance on informal
organisation than may be the case in larger authorities with formal
status hierarchy amongst members. With a Group of only 19 Labour
Councillors almost everyone is able to take part in discussions and
exert some influence. However, although there is on paper no formalised
elitist Party caucus it would appear that there is a well defined status
hierarchy operating among Labour members. During the current
transitional phase which has arisen since the appointment of the new
CEO, a 'Financial Planning Group', a special advisory group outside the
committee system composed of 'senior' Labour members and 'key' chief
officers, has been discussing the approach to forward policy planning
and the shape of the future policy planning system in Redditch. It is
apparent that senior members exert considerable influence within the
Labour Group. The Council Leader, the Deputy and Chair of P & R are
dominant figures in opinion formation and policy making within the
Group. The Leader in particular, with his vast experience and long
service in Redditch, is highly respected by members and officers
alike. Hence, we would conclude that certain processes between members
and officers make the councillor hierarchy somewhat more elitist than
would appear by observing the formal and public structures themselves.

Although formally represented on all committees, the Conservative
opposition are not involved in consultation and liaison with officers
nor involved in the Financial Planning Group's deliberations over the
future policy planning system. All contact between the officers and the
opposition is purely ad hoc and informal. Though the opposition is
often quite vocal in Committee it is largely impotent in influencing the
policy making/budgetary process.

Since regaining control in May 1983 on an ambitious Manifesto, the
Labour Group have been developing a number of explicit policy strategies
in such areas as economic development and employment, equal
opportunities, housing, community services, etc. The District Labour
Party hold annual policy conferences to determine these strategies and
the Manifesto content. However, it is apparent that it is the key
Labour Group Councillors in Redditch that have most influenced
outcomes because they also hold the key posts within the District
Party. It appears that the development of the overall political
strategies is largely the prerogative of the elected Group and in
particular the dominant figures in the group. Party discipline within

the Labour Group is assured and effective use of pre-committee and pre-Council meetings to sort out the Party line means that committee and Council meetings take the form of ritualistic combat, with decisions being taken within the Group and outside the formal committee arena. Thus Redditch currently enjoys strong and experienced political leadership presenting an increasingly clear and comprehensive set of policy strategies for the guidance of officers in the management of affairs of the local authority both in the short and medium term.

The officer structure of Redditch Borough Council is dominated by six departments of which there are four service departments (Amenities, Housing, Planning and Technical Services) and two coordinating departments (Chief Executives and Treasurers). Redditch had remained a relatively traditional authority where the main focus of policy making was with the strong professional departments. The only evidence of any clear inter-departmental 'corporate' structure was an officer management group on which all Chief Officers are represented. It has had until recently two sub-groups concerned with financial resources, the Revenue and Capital Groups (which are discussed more fully in the next section) and a wide variety of other sub-groups of a more ad hoc nature. The Chief Officer's Group (COG), as it is called, meets fortnightly and its discussions were largely confined to routine management matters with little time spent on Council strategy and review of service delivery and performance. The role of the Chief Officers in general had been largely defined in terms of professional advice to members and management of one or more service areas with little reference to wider more corporate responsibilities. In Redditch, although there is no strict congruence between committees and departments, the importance of the traditional Chief Officer/Committee Chair relationship has remained paramount in service provision. Overlying these traditional relationships, however, is a set of more centralised liaison between members and officers centring on the Chief Executive Officer and Leader of the Council.

The appointment of the new Chief Executive Officer early in 1985 was heavily influenced by the leading Labour members who themselves had only recently gained control. The new CEO is concerned to move Redditch away from traditional finance-led departmentalism towards a more structured and coordinated policy planning system where policy is initiated, executed and reviewed on the basis of clear statements of **political** policy strategy. "She likes firm guidelines", as the Leader put it and wishes to see the political message disseminated among council officers and translated, primarily by them but with member involvement, into medium term strategies and "annual policy action plans" for each main service/policy area. Officers would then have firm directives from members and could present alternatives accordingly. The budgetary process would reflect rather than determine policy priority in contrast to its role in the past. In pursuit of this more structured policy planning approach the CEO has appointed research and intelligence staff to assist strategy formation, an assistant to act as policy coordinator and has initiated a community review to obtain survey information so that policy can be grounded in a factual assessment of conditions in the Borough.

In developing the policy approach the CEO is answerable to the Leader of the Council for reporting on progress in the implementation of the political strategies. Whereas prior to her arrival there was no formal contact between the Chief Executive and the Leader, other than at briefings before Council meetings, there is now a regular weekly meeting. This involves a mutual exchange of information and review of progress and strategy. This formal dialogue has been supplemented in the current financial year by the officer-member working group, the Financial Planning Group. As already explained, this has involved 'key' members and officers discussing the structure of the policy planning process and particularly, the budgetary process to accompany it. Further, as part of the move towards more corporate policy making, changes in the objectives of the Chief Officer Group have been made to move it towards a more corporate group taking collective responsibility for management of the authority. The new terms of reference, agreed in early 1986, emphasise the role of policy planning. This is seen to involve interpretation and evaluation of Council's goals, translation of these goals into strategies and programmes of action, reviewing and monitoring progress towards implementation of Council policies and coordinating the deployment of resources to these ends. The structure of inter-departmental lower tier officer groups was also reviewed with the aim of devising a system which best helps COG achieve its objectives. New working groups are frequently ad hoc, more functional and issue based, generally chaired by Chief Officers. Examples include the audit profile working group, one on the DLO, and a user group on IT. Further, the Council meeting itself is now more concerned with policy with the Leader required by Standing Orders to give an annual policy statement at the beginning of the year and a review statement at its end. As we shall see in the next section, there have been a number of changes to the specifically budgetary decision making structures during 1985/6 as part of the transitional arrangements towards a more structured policy planning/budgetary system.

The Budgetary Process

As emphasised in the previous sections, the budgetary process in 1985/6 was not typical of what had preceded it: a number of new arrangements, some temporary, were introduced to bring about a transition to a more structured policy planning/budgetary process. This section will first outline the traditional budgetary process and then identify the changes implemented in 1985/6.

The Traditional Process

A common perception by the Council Leader, the CEO and other Chief Officers, including the Borough Treasurer, was the dominance of finance in the traditional budgetary process of Redditch. The budget was primarily concerned with management and financial control i.e. with managing on-going activities by programming the use of resources to carry out approved activities efficiently and controlling spending. Lacking was any emphasis on strategic planning i.e. the establishment and specification of objectives and choosing between alternatives to best meet the Council's objectives.

It was also commonly agreed that the financial angle had been too important in the past. The Labour Leader described the traditional approach as "a stultifying experience which ossified rather than allowed for change". In part the dominance of finance resulted from the attitude of the previous low spending Conservative administration who tended to emphasise financial control and partly to the previous CEO's willingness to delegate matters to the Treasurer's Department, enabling them to play the pivotal role.

The centrality of finance was largely maintained by the existence of two inter-departmental working groups, the Capital Group and Revenue Group, whose primary function was the coordination of the budgetary process and determination of the budgetary timescale. The groups, involving lower tier officers as well as chief officers, were concerned with resources and not substantive policy which remained the prerogative of the individual departments. Formally responsible to COG we were informed that the decisions of the two groups were rarely debated, let alone changed, by the management team. Although originally designed by the Treasurer's Department as an incipient approach to corporatism, the Treasurer claimed that, particularly with respect to the revenue process, the individual departments have not been willing to play the game, continuing to behave departmentally and preferring the more direct link with their own committee chairmen. Indeed, he stressed the close contact between committee chairs and chief officers because this substituted for the lack of an overall corporate strategy and the consequent importance of personality in resource allocation. There is evidence that the Capital Group operated more successfully, primarily because the capital allocation process involves only two departments to any great extent, Housing and Technical Services and therefore, more straightforward bargaining.

One of the main functions of the Capital and Revenue Groups was to lay down the budgetary timescale for the year. In this timescale the capital process preceeded the revenue process. By mid May in a financial year service departments were required to complete the two distinct aspects of the capital programme:

1) updating the approved programme so as to take account of change in costs, development periods, etc;

2) the introduction of new schemes or the increase of existing projects in the programme.

These were then considered by the Capital Group at the end of May and a draft capital programme drawn up and sent to the service committees in June/July with the revenue consequences of capital spending detailed against each scheme. At this time the HIP submission is being prepared and the two processes are closely coordinated.

According to the Treasurer the revenue process is a continuous one, with a set timetable and a quarterly review, which affects all departments and committees. Following the above capital process, which included the identification of the revenue consequences of capital spending, the revenue process began with a base budget review in September/October. On the basis of information provided by the Treasurer on the present level of service provision, the resources used and likely over or under spending, each committee was given an opportunity to examine the service it provided to ensure it was still "relevant and provided at the correct level". Each Committee was also expected to highlight those areas of its responsibilities where it was not meeting "need".

Meanwhile the P & R Committee of September considered the level of revenue spending for the following financial year implied from previous

Council decisions and the likely level of resources available to finance that expenditure. On the basis of this P & R, under strong guidance from the Treasurer, made recommendations to Council on the desired level of overall spending in line with anticipated resources, particularly grant.

In December the 'bids' for additional resources were examined by each Committee. It was intended that the bids should arise from both the comments at previous committee meetings, especially during the base budget review and also from officers' recommendations. Each committee was then required to examine the need for each bid and to prioritise. The December committees were also required to consider the revised Estimates for the current year and the following year's original Estimates excluding the bids.

The Policy and Resources Committee, following the service committee meetings, considered the Estimates and bids in total against the Council's budget strategy as determined in October. If necessary, spending committees were requested to reduce/cut expenditure to comply with resources available. By February, with housing revenue, block grant and balances known, final decisions were made by the committees and Council received, via P & R, information on the capital programme, the estimates plus bids, the housing rent levels, fees and charges, the size of the contingency fund and the required rate.

Both members and officers agreed that the above process had not been successful in the sense that financial considerations rather than policy ones had been paramount. In particular, the base budget review "didn't produce anything", largely because it failed to raise questions of policy strategy since this was not articulated. Base budget review often meant base budget approval since, given the resources available and their enhancement by creative accounting schemes, it was feasible to continue current activities and finance modest bids. The system threfore tended to perpetuate the status quo and sanctify past decisions and practices without subjecting them to scrutiny and review. Unevaluated inertia was the outcome.

The 1985/6 Budgetary Process

The process of budgetary decision making in 1985/6 involved significant changes from previous years. The resulting process was not fully planned prior to the 1985/6 financial year but in part evolved incrementally in that year, often as a response to unforeseen events. The proposed shape of the new system and its rationale was discussed formally throughout 1985 and 1986 in the Financial Planning Group and was a major item on the agendas of the COG. The objective was to devise procedures for the coordination of the 1985/6 budgetary process in the context of a policy planning system. Debate about these procedures rarely surfaced at the committees and was very much confined to key members and officers.

The increased awareness of the climate of financial stringency was an additional influence on the direction of events in the proposals for and developments in the budgetary process. In the 1984/5 cycle a quarterly financial review system was initiated to provide more information on the savings that were generated during the year and the resulting additional income available. In the first six months of 1985/6, for example, cumulative salary savings of £110,000 were identified. This process had encouraged the controlling Labour Group to eliminate the general contingency fund in 1985/6 and rely on savings occurring during the year to cover "unknown and unquantified expenditure". In fact significant sums were allocated from anticipated savings early in the 1985/6 financial year. In order that requests for additional resources are considered in line with known resources, it was decided that in 1986/7 such requests for non-urgent items should only go to the P & R committee at which the quarterly reviews were received.

The chronology of the 1985/6 budgetary process was broadly similar to that of earlier years and at least initially, the Revenue and Capital Groups continued in operation. There were, however, a number of significant changes, particularly in the revenue process. First, the whole process was to be guided by policy strategy statements derived by officers from the objectives of the Labour Party as contained in the Manifesto. These would include strategies on economic development, amenities and community development, homes, equal opportunities, information technology, neighbourhood provision, promotion and publicity. Strategy statements were originally intended to be available by September 1985 so that they could form the basis for policy review and the bids process. As it turned out only the Amenities, Housing and Economic Development strategies were available on time.

Secondly, the September base budget review was suspended since, as agreed by the District Auditor, it was not of value. It was argued that without policy strategies it could not take place effectively as an objective review of aims and implications of policy. For 1986/7 the base budget was accepted and attention devoted to instituting the new policy making process. The suspension of the base budget review was attacked by the Conservatives since they claimed that the base contained "extravagances". In response the Chair of P & R argued for the suspension as a temporary measure in order to move towards "a more productive and visible" policy review exercise in future years.

Thirdly, given the anticipated damaging effects of government grant allocation, it was decided that the P & R committee should review the revenue bids for additional expenditure corporately. This would be prior to receipt of information on grant and to the deliberations of the individual service committees. A special Bids Sub-Committee of P & R was created in September 1985 composed of committee chairs and two opposition members. According to the Leader the Bids Sub-Committee was intended to encourage "across the board bargaining" and a more corporate view of the use of the growth increment than the previous departmental/committee approach. A first task was to agree "priority categories" into which service committees could order their own bids. The categories were formulated by COG, accepted by the sub-committee, and were as follows:

1) Bids in support of mandatory statutory requirements;

2) Bids to maintain existing standards of service and to include provision for town growth;

3) Bids which would result in savings or increased efficiency over the next two years;

4) Bids in support of major strategies;

5) Bids which do not fall into any one of the other categories.

The original intention had been for the Bids sub-committee, on the basis of advice from COG, to weed out the bids at its 2nd December meeting. However, this original intention was not fully achieved since participants continued to behave departmentally and failed to reach a corporate view of prioritisation. As a result, all the Bids sub-committee could do was to argue about priority categories into which the COG had eventually placed and prioritised the committee bids. The sub-committee resolved that "the bids as now provisionally categorised by the sub-committee and including suggested additions be referred to the service committees for them to determine the Priority Categories of their bids and to determine their own priorities within each category".

In the delayed cycle of meetings which took place in January each service committee considered its bids, including certain items included by the Bids sub-committee, with suggested groupings in the priority categories. Committees generally seemed to accept the categories and priorities suggested by the Bids sub-committee though they were occasionally observed to move bids between categories on the basis of their relative desirability rather than their objective positions in the categories.

With the revenue bids of service committees prioritised, a special Joint Meeting of Housing and Policy and Resources met on 5 February to recommend the priority order of the bids submitted by committees "irrespective of category or service", to consider rent levels and the capital programme. The bids were prioritised within each category and were then placed in ordinal priority from 1 to 98. Following the collation of all the relevant financial information on RSG, on the capital programme, on fees and charges, contingency and reserves, the March rate setting Council meeting determined the cut off point for the revenue bids.

During 1985/6 the Revenue and Capital Groups continued in existence for at least part of the year. The Revenue Group was disbanded during the early part of the financial process since its main role of coordinating the base budget review was not required. The Capital Group has also been disbanded. During 1985/6 the capital process followed the traditional procedures more closely than the revenue process. However, two procedural changes were made in early 1986 reflecting the more active role in the capital allocation process to be played by the chief officer management team. First, the Capital Group was disbanded and for the future the capital programme would be considered by the whole COG in terms of policy strategy, with a HIP working group to deal more specifically with housing. Hence, working groups dominated by finance and the Treasury view are replaced in favour of a policy orientation. Second, a new style of capital programme which, according to the joint officers' statement, "will more clearly demonstrate the Council's policies subject to resources becoming available" has been accepted. In future the capital programme is to be presented in two parts, viz:

1) the Active Programme - representing those schemes which will be undertaken during the various financial years and to which resources have been allocated, and

2) the Planned Programme - representing those schemes which members would wish to undertake as and when sufficient resources are available.

As the CEO put it, this change is an attempt to make "the capital programme more policy orientated". It "should enable schemes to be readily identifiable and brought into the Active Programme when either slippage occurs or additional financing is available".

The financial year 1985/6 was recognised by both members and officers as an interim period. The new policy planning system was not fully established, nor fully worked out and had not always operated according to intention. Strategy statements had been delayed with the result that in the bids process those with a strategy reference were at an advantage. The Revenue and Capital Groups had been abandoned into the financial year without very much rationalisation. The COG had been unable to instil a corporate approach on the bids procedure and delay had crept into the original timescale due to tardiness on grant and subsidy advice from the DoE. The Treasurer's Department had felt concerned by the changes taking place since their traditional role of departmental liaison would have less purpose in a more corporate approach. The new role for the Treasurer's Department would be to advise COG on whether the resources for programmes could be found.

In addition to the uncertainty generated by the procedural changes in 1985/6 there was also considerable financial uncertainty. In an interview early in the financial year the Leader said he did not know whether decisions for 1986/7 would be "a crunch year" in terms of the decision of choosing between spending over target, significant cuts in services, or large rate increases, or whether this might be postponed for another year or two. At the end of the process the Treasurer stated to the full Council meeting that the budget for 1986/7 had been "the most difficult I have put together" because of the different assumptions that could be made at the various stages in the process and the changes in significant items of information. For example, early in December 1985 the P & R committee received a report outlining the factors used in the calculation of block grant estimating Redditch's GRE at £3,896,000 which would have yielded £76,000 more grant at the then anticipated expenditure levels than the actual GRE figures produced. This uncertainty continued until the very end of the financial process when Redditch received notification of a payback of £115,000 from grant recycling. It was decided to add these funds to the reserves because the notification came too late to allow major alterations to expenditures or rate levels. Such funds might cushion future rate rises if there were to be further cuts in central grant, while uncertainty on clawback levels for previous years would remain until out-turns became known.

Conclusion

The experience of Redditch in 1985/6 is of an authority attempting to deal with circumstances of uncertainty and increasing financial stringency. Apendix 11.1 indicates the sort of manoeuvres necessary. They are attempting to move from a traditional financially orientated policy making/budgetary process towards a policy planning system where explicit policy strategies and action plans derived from members' objectives guide officers in a corporate pursuit of political goals.

Apendix 11.1 CREATIVE ACCOUNTING

Redditch has employed a number of creative accounting techniques to offset fiscal pressure. These have not been confined to the Labour administration: in 1980 the controlling Conservative Group financed the new Town Hall largely by a deferred purchase scheme amounting to some £4.3 million to be repaid over 20 years. The Labour Group's priorities have meant that creative accounting operations for capital expenditure have been largely directed at helping meet the Manifesto commitment to reverse the decline in the housing programme and build at least 100 houses per year. The main operations used for this purpose have been:

1) An advanced payments scheme involving payment of a capital sum to a company enabling the local authority to increase its use of capital receipt augmentation powers as the advance payment is deemed to be prescribed capital expenditure rather than individual contract payments. Such a scheme was entered into just before the start of the 1985/6 financial year to allow funding of one housing development from 1985/6 to 1986/7.

2) Sale of council mortgage portfolio. Between 1982 and the start of 1985/6 about £1.1 million of the mortgage portfolio was sold to generate capital receipts. During 1985/6 a further £350,000 was sold leaving a portfolio of around £800,000. Consideration of the sale of a higher proportion, if not all, of the remaining portfolio and the possibility of linking the sale with a barter scheme was made by the officers in the Treasurer's Department but was prevented by DoE announcements. This left the financing of the next major housing scheme problematic at the start of 1986/7.

3) In order to exclude expenditure from the definition of prescribed expenditure, Redditch Council has leased all vehicles, equipment and computers before 1985/6. In 1985/6 the Council entered into a lease for the sum of £600,000 for the provision of central heating plant in respect of the housing programme.

A number of schemes were used on the revenue account but these raised relatively minor amounts. For example, Redditch previously paid the full amount due on a concessionary travel scheme on 1 April although the scheme runs from 1 July. By deciding to pay for only that part of the financial year Redditch made a one-off 'saving' of a quarter's expenditure (£60,000). However, when the County Council advanced the date for its precept rate this caused Redditch lost interest on balances of £40,000.

Hence creative accounting schemes of ever increasing inventiveness have been used in Redditch and these have helped ease the pressure on resources. However, their scope in the future is likely to be less.

PART II SCOTLAND

12. Tayside Regional Council

JOHN BERRIDGE AND IAN CLARK

Description of Area

Tayside, third largest Scottish Region in area and fourth largest in population, reaches from the Firth of Tay in the south to the Grampian mountains in the north and from the east coast to the borders of Strathclyde and Central Regions in the West. Dundee and Perth are the largest of the few urban centres and overall 82 per cent of the population lives on only 2 per cent of the total land area, which varies from rich farmland (Tayside has 27 per cent of the best agricultural land in Scotland) to remote and sparsely inhabited mountain areas.

Dundee, Scotland's fourth largest city and Tayside's administrative capital, has 46 per cent of the population and provides just under half of the Councillors. Once renowned for jute, jam and journalism, it has retained Keiller's confectionary and D.C.Thomson's publishing empire, although the jute industry has diversified into related areas and there is now a wide spread of light and heavy industries including an important electronics sector. A considerable oil-related industry has developed, augmenting the harbour's normal commercial activity.

Stretching westwards along the north bank of the River Tay are the berry farms which constitute one of the most important soft-fruit areas in the world, with livestock, arable and hill farming further North. On the East coast the fishing industry, although diminished is still active - particularly in Arbroath, home of the famous "Smokies".

Unemployment varies from 9.8 per cent in Perth to 17.9 per cent in Arbroath; this has been reflected in the designation of parts of

Tayside as an area of special development and parts of Dundee and Arbroath as the Tayside Enterprise Zone. The local Councils have been promoting tourism - perhaps the most important growth area as an employment creator - since Tayside's geographic position as the "crossroads of Scotland" for road and rail makes it an excellent touring centre for North-East Scotland, and there is a range of outdoor recreational activities probably unparalleled in the United Kingdom. Attention is now being given to Dundee's architectural heritage and the Dundee-built R.R.S. "Discovery" has been brought home and moored opposite the "Unicorn", the oldest surviving "wooden-wall" frigate, as the start of an ambitious waterfront project to improve employment prospects and attract tourists.

The Political Background

Tayside contains five Parliamentary constituencies, three District Councils and comprises nearly half the European Parliamentary constituency of North-East Scotland. Politically, it has been atypical of Scotland as a whole because of its substantial Conservative representation, although taking Parliamentary, Regional and District levels into consideration it exemplifies the diversity of Scottish politicals rather well.

Table 12.1

PARTY STRENGTHS IN TAYSIDE; REGIONAL COUNCIL ELECTION RESULTS: PERCENTAGE SHARE OF THE VOTE AND SEATS WON

	1974		1978		1982		1986	
CON	44.9%	22	42.7%	25	36.8%	27	28.4%	14
LAB	32.5%	15	34.4%	15	25.3%	12*	29.7%	20
LIB**	1.7%	0	1.6%	0	5.2%	0	10.8%	1
IND	19.9%	9	3.4%	6	4.6%	2	2.7%	2
SNP	-	-	16.2%	0	20.5%	5*	27.9%	9
OTHER	-	-	-	-	-	-	0.3%	0

  * 1 SNP defected to Labour, therefore party strengths LAB 13, SNP 4
 ** For 1982 read Liberal/SDP, 1986 Alliance.

NB: The Scottish local government electoral term is four years, with all Councillors retiring simultaneously, and District and Regional elections alternating.

The last Parliamentary boundary revisions had hardly any effect on the two Dundee seats, both Labour-held since their creation in 1945 until Gordon Wilson won Dundee East for the SNP in 1974. (1) The new landward seats are all Conservative, as are 37 per cent of the District and until the 1986 elections, 33 per cent of the Regional seats. Moreover, (Table 12.1), until 1986 the Tories gained no extra seats at each Regional election. The European Parliament seat has been Conservative since its establishment.

These statistics are somewhat misleading. Table 12.1 also shows that the Conservative percentage of the vote has **declined** at each Regional election and they lost two of their three Parliamentary seats (regarded as amongst the safest in Scotland) to the SNP in 1974; although they regained them and subsequently won the three new seats, only North Tayside can now be considered safe. Locally, too, their support has declined; from control of all four Councils in 1977, the Tories lost their tenuous hold on the City of Dundee in 1977 and Angus to the SNP. They lost overall control in Perth and Kinross in 1984 and the Region itself in 1986. [2] Politics in Tayside is thus a four-party system (five-party at the local level, since Independents are still active in some areas) which in the main exhibits a third-party-vote syndrome; where the Alliance vote is weak the SNP is strong, and vice versa.

The Formal Organisational Structure

The formal organisational structure in Tayside Region was basically on a Policy Committee model, with a Policy and Resources (P & R) Committee as the instrument of co-ordination and management. During our 1985/6 study there were seventeen Departments working to thirteen main Committees.

Committees and departments can be divided into two main categories – public service provision (the Service group) and the Central group, some of which provided services to other Departments while others had a co-ordinating, monitoring and to some extent controlling role. The categories are not mutually exclusive and there were some hybrids. Two of the Central Departments, the Chief Executive's and Finance, played a direct and crucial role in the budgetary process.

The Chief Executive's Department was represented at all meetings. It advised on policy, provided legal and other central services and was responsible for ensuring that all officers and Committees who should have been consulted received the relevant reports. All policy proposals and Committee inputs and outputs had to go through the Department, emerging if necessary with supplementary documentation and/or comments from the Chief Executive. There was no separate Director of Administration; the post had been merged with that of the Chief Executive in 1982.

The status of the Finance Department has grown considerably since its reorganisation four years ago, which was aimed at reducing the independence of the Departmental baronies and strengthening the central co-ordination of Council policies by appointing Assistant Directors of Finance, each to be responsible for a group of Departments. These Assistant Directors worked with the Departmental Chiefs and senior administrators on all financial matters, so the Department always had an overall view of the Region's finances during the budgetary process, which made its contributions to P & R Committee meetings especially important.

The formal cycle of meetings covered five to six weeks, with business passing in full public view through the Committee system to the P & R Committee before it went to the Council but in practice most of the important budgetary decisions were taken in private, in Sub-Committees (closed sessions, until recent legislation required them to be held in public), in the Conservative Group or by some informal body like M7 (see below). Consequently, most formal Committee and Council meetings did little more than act as a rubber stamp, although they were certainly the arena for democratic debate and the only place where Opposition councillors could be seen to be publicly active.

The Informal Structure

There was also an informal cycle and an informal structure. We identified three main groupings of Senior Officers - the Chief Officers' Management Team (COMT), the Policy Co-ordination Group (PCG) and the "Group of 4" (G4) - and one group comprising Central Senior Officers and leading Administration politicians. This group was mainly concerned with the revenue budget, while the PCG and G4 did most of the work on the capital budget.

All Chief Officers were members of the COMT and all those we interviewed were quite emphatic that it was not, and was not meant to be, a corporate management body. The Chief Executive himself made no such claim for it; he wanted his Chief Officers to meet regularly to discuss current issues and he also saw the COMT as a useful opportunity for newly appointed or promoted officers to meet their opposite numbers. Assessment of the Team varied; a common opinion was that the Chief Executive chaired it very well but otherwise comments ranged from the mildly appreciative ("It's a good opportunity to meet and talk to other Chief Officers") to slightly dismissive ("It's a bit of a talking shop").

The PCG (the Chief Executive and his Depute, the Directors and Senior Deputes of Finance and Planning, the Senior Depute of Architectural Services and the Regional Quantity Surveyor) normally met fortnightly. The PCG's original purpose was to co-ordinate preparation of the financial plan; one of its members told us that it had recently started to look at long term revenue problems, although the financial plan and the capital budget were still its main concern.

G4 was an ad hoc Sub-Committee of the PCG, consisting of the Depute Chief Executive, the Senior Deputes of Finance and Planning and the Regional Quantity Surveyor. It fleshed out and worked on the capital budget, and developed aspects of financial planning discussed by the PCG.

Objective assessment of the PCG and G4 was rather difficult, mainly because outside the members' immediate colleagues, few people seemed to have heard of either, although capital-intensive Departments knew about the PCG. There was much less elected member involvement in capital than in revenue budgeting, so all this was powerful fuel for conspiracy theories. But we concluded that the PCG and G4 **were** more or less what they were made out to be, with G4 in particular doing most of the work on the capital budget, as a sort of Praesidium for the PCG.

It is necessary to consider the capital budget briefly if we are to evaluate the role of the PCG and G4: after this we shall be referring exclusively to the revenue budget, from which the capital budget differs qualitatively.

The capital budget was related to the five-year financial plan and the block allocations on which it was based were consents to spend and **not** grants. There was much more flexibility insofar as some virement and anticipation of the next year's allocation was allowed, and in contradistinction to the revenue budget the Scottish Office positively preferred to see the allocations spent - consents were only pared if Departments constantly underspent, so the concept of "cutback management" did not appear to apply in the same way to capital spending. Consequently the capital budget work was "expert-intensive" and it was only rarely that matters needed anything more than formal resolution by a Committee.

Besides the capital budget, the officers in the PCG had the revenue estimates and other work to handle, so they had little time or effort to spare for attempts to extend their authority further. In any case, however influential officer groups may be, policy initiation needs delegation or participation by politicians; so to reach the heart of the decision-making structure we needed to consider the group which was constantly identified during interviews as having the greatest influence on the budget. It consisted of the Conveners and Vice-Conveners of P & R and Finance, the Chief Executive and the Director of Finance and his Senior Depute. These seven men were behind virtually every major decision concerned with the 1986/7 revenue budget, so for want of a name we dubbed them "The Magnificent Seven" (M7).

M7 combined the professional financial, legal and administrative knowledge and skills of the officers with the political nous of the four leading politicians, two of whom were particularly important. We did not consider it to be a Star Chamber model because such unsavoury connotations were not apparent and perhaps completely absent; it did not seem to be resented, nor regarded as unfair or authoritarian by other officers. Undoubtedly its success in not provoking adverse reaction was partly because the mutual respect between its professional and elected members enabled them to work easily and well together, with neither side trespassing on the other's preserves and partly because of the personality factors we shall discuss below.

Ian Mackie, the P & R Convener, had also been Leader of the Administration and Tory Group Leader from the first day of the Region's existence and Leader on the old Dundee City Council prior to that, so he was a shrewd politician of long experience who carried a great deal of political clout, respected by both colleagues and political opponents for his integrity. His diligence in reading and annotating the paperwork was near-legendary; no detail escaped him, he certainly put in more time than anyone else and his careful consideration of the agenda before every meeting minimised opposition. His acceptance of Government financing policy stemmed from party loyalty rather than conviction - he had been quite happy to preside over the Council in times of incremental growth. These factors, combined with his party's majority and strong Group loyalty, enabled him to convert decisions taken at M7 meetings into Tory Group and Regional Council decisions.

The Finance Convener, Sir Alan Smith, came into Local Government a lot later than Ian Mackie. A successful businessman with his own international company, he brought with him a greater financial awareness than most politicians and the ability to keep an overall objective in view without getting lost in detail. Sir Alan did his job competently and thoroughly, although unlike his Group Leader, he did not live for local politics and could close the door on it when he went home. He saw local government largely in administrative

terms and although he rarely showed it, he was somewhat impatient with
politicking if it interfered with the business of running the Council.
He found the concept of judging efficiency in terms of input costs
familiar and acceptable from his business experience, quite apart from
any reasons of political loyalty. In every respect he was the complete
counterweight to Ian Mackie.

As the Tory Whip Norman Jamieson (the P & R Vice-Convener) provided a
soothing buffer for any Group grumbling and discontent, acted as the
progress-chaser and trouble-shooter, nudged people into action when
necessary and delivered unwelcome messages with delicacy. He was a
quiet man with a courteous manner which was well suited to explaining
the consequences of hard decisions but which could have been a
disadvantage for anyone that had to make them. "When I see him avoiding
me on the stairs", said one Convener, "I know Ian has decided on
something I won't like and Norrie's got to tell me." His job was not a
particularly pleasant one but it was necessary; the two Conveners would
have found that the burden of having to give a series of individual
explanations in defence of M7's decisions would have considerably
increased the coefficient of friction.

M7's three officer members also had the task of translating its
decisions into formal procedures and persuading their Service colleagues
to administer, usually with restricted resources, policies which
everyone knew they had helped to formulate. It said a good deal for
these officers and their Departments that everybody we interviewed spoke
well of not only their professionalism but also their courtesy and
helpfulness. There was no doubt that their friendly and tactful
approach was a major factor in oiling the wheels of the Regional
machinery in very difficult circumstances.

It is doubtful whether the budgetary system (described below and
outlined in Figure 12.1) could have worked without this mixture of the
necessary political and professional expertise allied to a set of
personalities which dovetailed so neatly for the task in hand. It will
be interesting to see whether the new Labour Administration attempts to
operate the same system and, if so, how successful they will be.

The Revenue Budget Process

When Tayside was created in 1974 the work of the Finance Department was
little more than book-keeping and the budget was demand-led. The
process has been deliberately changed since then to cope more
effectively with the problems of a firmly resource-led budget. In 1986
the political members of M7 had a long term aim to meet the government
guideline and the threat of grant penalties dominated the process from
the start. (3)

We identified four stages which showed the main elements of and
participants in the revenue budget process. First, M7 made an
estimate of the Government guideline and from this, calculated the
percentage reduction in total expenditure necessary to meet it. In
view of the complexity of the other three stages it may seem odd to
take this one separately but M7 formulated their rough financial
objectives at that time without consulting anyone else. Although M7
members were unaware of the individual Departments' views of their own
budgets and had only sketchy ideas of the scope for growth within the

limitations imposed by the Government guideline, the decisions they made at this stage, while not irrevocable, tended to set the scene for the detailed work that was done during the rest of the year.

Secondly, Departments conducted the RE (Revenue Estimates) exercise to identify the potential cuts which would reduce their estimates by the necessary percentage and to give notice of additional expenditure items which they thought desirable. It was emphasised in the Chief Executive's memorandum which accompanied the RE forms that this exercise was not council policy – it merely investigated the implications of a percentage cut in services. Nevertheless, it was an extremely important exercise for M7, as the returns gave them the data they needed to set initial guidelines for each Department. Items listed as potential cuts by Departments were taken into account, although partially offset by growth items thought desirable and many of the most important decisions were made at this stage.

Thirdly, the Departments built up Base Budgets (1985/6 outturn budgets adjusted to November 1986 prices) and completed PB (Provisional Budget) forms on which they made prioritised bids for the reinstatement of cuts provisionally selected during the RE stage and for the acceptance of additional growth items. Most of the Chief Officers we interviewed perceived their "real" work on the estimates starting either here, or at the preceding meetings with M7 to discuss the RE returns. One said the RE stage was "a theoretical exercise – a dry run"; which is not how M7 members would have described it, or we would evaluate it.

By that time the Government guideline would have probably been published. M7 considered the rating and political implications of accepting or rejecting the PB bids, earmarked most of them one way or the other and passed on the proposals to the Tory Group, where each bid was considered for acceptance or rejection. The Finance Convener, acting on the advice of his Senior Officials, subsequently made provision for inflation and decided whether to use balances. Finally, the completed Budget and proposed Rates went (via P & R) to the Special Finance Committee and Council Meetings for ratification.

We were not allowed to attend the Tory Group meeting, so we cannot report factually on what took place. However, there were only three conceivable outcomes. The Group could have rejected the proposals and substituted others but this would have meant revising three months work in one meeting without the benefit of expert advice from officials and this possibility was so unlikely that we think it can safely be rejected. Secondly, the Group could have amended the proposals substantially or in detail, in which case the same point would have applied to a greater or lesser extent; or it could have agreed to them. In any event, this Group Meeting represented the final effective decision on the bids, since the Tory majority would have ensured safe passage through P & R, Finance Committee and Council. If the Group had decided to change the proposals then it could validly be argued that the whole process was subject to some sort of democratic debate and decision; but if in fact the Group ratified the proposals, the decisions would have effectively been taken by M7 and the Tory Group itself would have acted as a rubber-stamp. Given Ian Mackie's influence and our impressions gathered over the year, we think it is most unlikely that the Group would have ignored his advice; although it has to be said that we were assured by some Group members and even

SUB-COMMITTEES, COMMITTEES, FULL COUNCIL   OTHER BODIES   DEPARTMENTS

M7

May: Estimated govt. guideline & discussed rough budget objectives → June: CE & Dir of Fin initiated RE exercise to assess effects of % cut needed to hit guideline

July: Depts worked on RE forms

M7

2nd week Sept: Bilateral meetings with CO's/Conveners to discuss RE returns. Political considerations by the 4 politicians in M7 ← Aug: RE forms returned to Finance

Sept 19th: P&R authorised P&R & Finance Conveners to set initial guidelines for Departments

Oct.4th: Depts told to draw up Base Budgets in accordance with guidelines & complete PB forms

(ADFs worked Depts on — with most Base Budgets)

Nov 18th: P&R Sub-Committee's 1st consultations with NDR's

Nov 22nd: Base Budgets & PB forms to be returned to Finance, by which time Government guideline usually known

M7

Dec 3rd/4th: 2nd series of bilateral meetings with CO's/Conveners. Base Budgets & implications of retaining or excluding PB bids considered

Dec 19th: P&R fixed provisional upper spending limits for TRC & allocated overall sums to Depts

Finance prepared Budget Book (all Base Budgets) and report itemising PB bids for all Cllrs.

Jan 13/14th: Service Committees considered Base Budgets; chose PB bids for inclusion

162

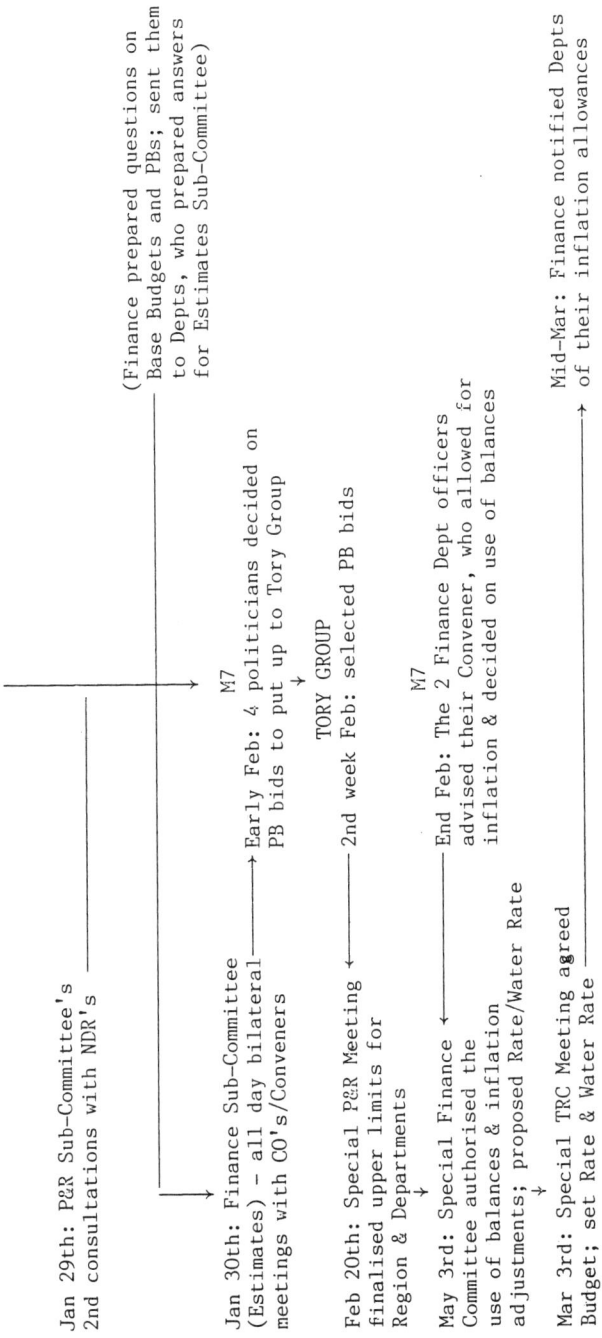

Jan 29th: P&R Sub-Committee's 2nd consultations with NDR's

(Finance prepared questions on Base Budgets and PBs; sent them to Depts, who prepared answers for Estimates Sub-Committee)

Jan 30th: Finance Sub-Committee (Estimates) - all day bilateral meetings with CO's/Conveners

Early Feb: 4 politicians decided on PB bids to put up to Tory Group

M7

TORY GROUP

2nd week Feb: selected PB bids

Feb 20th: Special P&R Meeting finalised upper limits for Region & Departments

M7

End Feb: The 2 Finance Dept officers advised their Convener, who allowed for inflation & decided on use of balances

May 3rd: Special Finance Committee authorised the use of balances & inflation adjustments; proposed Rate/Water Rate

Mid-Mar: Finance notified Depts of their inflation allowances

Mar 3rd: Special TRC Meeting agreed Budget; set Rate & Water Rate

Figure 12.1   The Revenue Budget Process

163

Ian Mackie himself that he did not always get his own way.

We should emphasise that we do not think the behind the scenes activity of M7 was in any way sinister - indeed, it is difficult to see how such a complex process could have been carried through without some small group of people getting their heads down in private; constructing the budget for a large local authority must be like trying to play bridge with cards that have been cut into jigsaw pieces. The confidentiality of the process up until the 19 December P & R Meeting was more likely to have been the result of Ian Mackie's extreme caution (somebody used the phrase "near-phobia").

External Influences

There were a number of bodies which might have been expected to have some effect on the budget. Non-domestic ratepayers (NDR's), were probably the most important of these, because they had a statutory right to be consulted. The consultations started with prepared statements from the NDR's, leading into a discussion in which they complained about the cost of given services, comparing them with other authorities. The all-Conservative Special P & R Sub-Committee and their officials answered criticisms but made few concessions. It was not apparent to us that the NDR's had any significant effect on the budget; their main concern was to keep the rates down, which was Tory strategy anyway. The impact of other community pressure groups was negligible or non-existent.

The local Conservative and SNP Associations were not formally consulted, and the Alliance had no seats on the Council. Only the local Labour Party seemed to liaise with its Councillors, some of whom attended Management Committee meetings to report on current issues and answer questions from the grass-roots membership. The budget as a whole was not discussed, although specific points relating to improvements in individual services may have been raised.

Opposition parties had no chance of outvoting the Tories but could publicise measures of their choice by forcing divisions in Committees and Council, thereby bringing such matters to the notice of the press and subsequently the electorate. Very occasionally this has happened on important issues but on the budget we were unable to detect any effective influence by the Opposition.

The widely-read local newspaper, the *Dundee Courier*, reported Council and Committee meetings fully (but of course it was unable to report Sub-Committee meetings), so the Conservatives were anxious not to appear in a bad light. Reports of bad pavements tended to produce Council workmen fairly quickly; however, extensive reporting of the biggest local controversy, school closures, did not affect the Administration's policy one iota. Ian Mackie was extremely suspicious of the media as a vehicle through which Councillors could "make mischief", although the paper had a policy of avoiding controversial reporting.

Conclusions - Managing The Cuts In Tayside

Budgeting under cutback management took up an enormous amount of time. There were three main undesirable effects on Departments. First, their day to day work suffers; from the Chief Officer down, a disproportionate amount of effort has to be spent on devising ways to keep the Department viable. Secondly, there is not enough time for fundamental reviews of their work; Tayside has briefly considered zero-based budgeting but we detected a lack of enthusiasm amongst officials and of understanding amongst Councillors and in the end there was a somewhat half-hearted decision to try it out in the Planning Department and parts of Education and Social Work Departments *"if those Departments will co-operate"* (our italics). That is not an indication of the bloody-mindedness of the Departments, but a realistic recognition by Central Departments that although they had the expertise they had not the time to lay on a ZBB exercise in a Department, whilst the unfortunate Department had neither. Lastly, there is not enough time for long term planning; it is a costly and time consuming job and staff cannot be spared to do it. We spent some time discussing with the Chief Executive and other officers the potential benefits of an overall review team; there seemed to be quite a lot of agreement that some sort of more general review **ought** to be done, but that nobody had time to do it and that the necessary finance was unavailable.

The point was frequently made to us that 90 per cent of the time spent on the budget is "at the margin". As one senior officer from a Central Department said to us, "items argued about during the budget process are only the tip of the iceberg - nobody looks at the whole thing". Apart from the relevance of this remark to the absence of "base" budget review and of financial planning, there are other implications.

First, virtually nobody gives the Base Budget any consideration; they are all concerned with fighting against cuts or desperately trying to inject a little more growth into a particular service. "Only proposed cuts or proposed insertions are looked at closely now; few people are going to argue about programmes and services that are already accepted as being in the Base Budget." Ergo, services already in are not examined and questioned while anything that is not in, however virtuous, has to face a series of stiff hurdles - unless of course it is a new statutory requirement. Secondly, it follows that there is scope for manipulation of the Base Budget. If it is not examined, not even the eagle eyes of Finance will be likely to detect insertions and deletions. We were told of one Convener who had in fact "swapped" an item he was keen on but which should have faced the bid procedure, with an item from the Base Budget; the result was that it did not have to face competitive consideration at all. Thirdly, far too much senior management time is wasted "on the tip of the iceberg". We do not need to labour this point; seven of Tayside's most valuable members and officers were forced to spend a good deal of their time in effect considering peripheral cuts and bids.

There was evidence of a change in the criteria by which Departmental management's approach to its work is judged: a senior Conservative view was that Chief Officers and Departmental staff who saw themselves as (say) educationalists, social workers or transport specialists first and Regional Council managers second, belonged to the "old school". This view showed a clear preference for a more detached "managerial" approach from the senior Departmental staff whose first loyalty, it was implied, should be to the Region.

165

There was insufficient evidence to suggest that a definite policy existed deliberately to appoint managers rather than specialists when Chief Officer vacancies arose but there was little doubt that the most influential Councillors would prefer to do so, because the specialists' professional concern made them less flexible than managers. In the long run this could be one of the most profound results of the period of financial stringency, because it would shift the emphasis of local authority service management away from expertise in the specialist service area and towards a Whitehall system of "expertise" in administration - a shift from specialism to the generalism which has been attacked in virtually every report on the Civil Service. In those circumstances, local government officers would soon become accustomed to more central control (internal as well as external) and to the need to exhibit more managerial than specialist zeal if they were to advance in their jobs.

The tight curb on the recruitment of new staff is furthering this tendency; it makes good financial sense to appoint as low down the scale as is commensurate with efficiency and the "generation gap" between the "old school" professionals and junior officers, accustomed to a generalist theory of administration, is likely to grow as a result. On the other hand the fact that most job specifications still demand professional rather than managerial qualifications and the lack of proper facilities for training local government officers qua local government officers, is likely to work in the other direction.

There was a surprising lack of liaison in places where one might have expected to find it either convenient or necessary. There was no machinery for liaison between Tayside and the three District Councils, either formal or informal; this was true even when all three Districts were Conservative. In 1974/5 there was "talk of a Liaison Committee" but the proposed representation was to be weighted strongly in the Region's favour and the indignant Districts declined to participate on those terms. From time to time District Chief Executives or possibly Directors of Finance may telephone their Regional peers on a particular matter but that seems to be all, apart from the minimal District Councillor representation on the Economic Development Committee. There was also virtually no liaison between political groups on the Council and the parties which had supported them and helped to get them elected. We have very little evidence on party activists' reaction to this fact, which one might have thought could be a cause of considerable friction.

Notes

(1) When Gordon Wilson won Dundee East his majority rested heavily on Labour defectors and Tory tactical voters, but he worked diligently as a constituency MP and built up a personal following in the city which enabled him to survive the three subsequent General Elections. It is extremely doubtful if there is support for an independent Scotland in his constituency but in electoral if not philosophical terms it must now be regarded as a strong SNP seat. In Dundee West, Labour resisted successive SNP challenges in the 1974 and 1979 elections and it was not until 1983 that the Tories returned to their traditional position of runners-up there.

(2) Further evidence of the Tory decline came from across the Tay, where the Alliance won North-East Fife District and pressed the Tories very hard in Parliamentary elections. Not so long ago the loss of any of those Districts would have been unthinkable.

(3) Three years ago the Scottish Office changed its method of apportioning grant penalty, thereby confining penalties to authorities which spent in excess of their guidelines. Before then grant penalty had not been a major factor in M7's calculations, and they did not anticipate it reaching such punitive levels. However, the amount of penalty that Tayside incurred as a result of the change meant that in subsequent years, meeting the Government guideline became a priority because of the penalty implications if they budgeted over the guideline.

13. Banff and Buchan District Council

MICHAEL DYER AND JOHN SEWEL

Socio-Political Background

Banff and Buchan District, situated on the north-east shoulder of Scotland, is one of five lower tier authorities in the Grampian Region. The area of the district is 152,634 hectares with an estimated population in June 1984 of 83,216. Traditionally, the most salient social division was between the fishing culture of the coastal burghs like Peterhead, Fraserburgh and Macduff together with their associated villages and the agricultural hinterland centred on the settlements of Turriff, Aberchirder and Fyvie. Within the fishing villages fundamentalist religious sects thrive. The Exclusive Brethren, whose members eschew all forms of political activity, are particularly strong.

Peterhead, with a population of 18,100 is the largest settlement in the District, while Banff, population 4,040 is the administrative centre. It is situated some 50 miles north of Aberdeen. The main traditional industries have been agriculture, fishing, food processing, textiles and light engineering. However, in recent years there have been major employment reductions in engineering and food processing. Over the past 15 years the industrial structure of some parts of the District have been transformed by the impact of North Sea Oil. Oil related development is the main reason for an increase in the District's population of 12.3 per cent between 1971 and 1984. Virtually all the oil related growth is concentrated in Peterhead, with its two oil service bases and the immediate surrounding area. Over approximately the same period Peterhead developed as Scotland's premier fishing port. Relative prosperity has not been distributed evenly over the district. Fraserburgh, 15 miles along the coast from

Peterhead, has witnessed major job losses in food processing, and engineering with minimal off-setting gains. In January 1986 an unemployment rate of 12.5 per cent in Fraserburgh compares with the district rate of 9.3 per cent.

The area off the Banff and Buchan District is coterminous with that of the parliamentary constituency of the same name. The present constituency, being a product of the most recent parliamentary redistribution, was first contested in 1983 when the Conservative candidate, Albert McQuarrie was returned. Prior to 1983 the area of the present district was partly in East Aberdeenshire and partly in the Banffshire parliamentary constituencies. Throughout the post-1945 period until 1974 both constituencies returned members representing the Unionist/Conservative interest. By the early 1970s a major political division had become established between the fishing villages and burghs which had become increasingly Nationalist and the agricultural communities which remained Conservative. The two general elections of 1974 saw the SNP victorious in both Banffshire and East Aberdeenshire. In 1979 both constituencies were recaptured by the Conservatives and in 1983 the new seat remained a Conservative/SNP marginal.

Prior to local government re-organisation in 1975, what is now Banff and Buchan was administered in part by Aberdeen County Council and in part by Banff County Council. Many of the settlements, some of which had populations of just a few thousand, enjoyed the distinctive Scottish local government status of small burghs with their own town councils. They not only had responsibility for housing and local planning but also appointed the burgh representatives to the county councils. Re-organisation swept away the old system in its entirety and replaced it by a two-tier structure of directly elected Districts and Regions.

As a society of primary producers, Banff-Buchan has a relatively high proportion of small-scale self-employed businessmen and artisans together with small numbers of skilled workers and persons with professional qualifications. A nineteenth century petit bourgeois mentality is pervasive and dominates the values of local political life. In terms of local government there is a generally negative attitude towards the need for public provision, antipathy towards policies involving anything that smacks of redistribution and an emphasis on retrenchment rather than reform. Where public provision is made it is frequently accompanied by a strong infusion of voluntarism. Attempts to secure new public facilities often start through the taking up of public subscriptions and the public is often expected to play a part in administering the facility once it is provided.

The Politics of Local Government

Prior to re-organisation, local government in the area traditionally operated on a 'non-political' basis, to use the popular expression, with candidates standing without any label at all. (We shall refer to them as 'independents'). Occasionally, the Labour Party in the small Burghs fielded candidates under a party label. These attempts at introducing partisanship, where the burghs formed at-large constituencies, ran up against the refusal of the electorate to 'vote the ticket'. Municipal politics in the burghs has been described as being dominated by the ideology of retrenchment, expressed through low tax, low expenditure and high rents policies. (Bealey and Sewel 1981; Dyer 1973 and 1979).

The first Region and District elections in 1974 were contested by candidates openly representing the Conservative, SNP and Labour Parties together with some independents. Since 1974 Regional elections have been contested on a party basis but this has been much less marked in the District elections. The rise of the SNP has challenged the former ethos of the politics of independence with important consequences for the operation of the council itself. By 1980 all four seats in Peterhead were held by the SNP and in 1984 the acquisition of an extra ward in Fraserburgh gave the party five of the eighteen seats. After the 1984 election the council comprised 5 SNP, 1 Conservative and 12 independents.

The SNP refused to accept the politics of consensus and operated as a 'group' within the council, forming an opposition to what they considered to be right-wing leadership. Increasing partisanship has not been welcomed by existing independents. As one remarked:

"I was on Aberdeen County Council for 40 years. There were no politics at all on the county council, completely non-political. I don't like politics, no time for it. You can get a bit of a consensus of an opinion when no politics."

The creation of the SNP 'group' forced the remaining councillors to take defensive action. A minimal degree of organisation was necessary in order to prevent the SNP exercising control through the use of its block vote and the picking up of votes through debate:

The SNP told us in the first place that they were a group. They always vote as a block. The rest of the council isn't a party, they don't vote as a block. (independent councillor)

The politics of the council has been dominated by the need to freeze out the SNP while maintaining the politics of independence. An informal, non-SNP majority exists in opposition to the SNP but without constituting an organised group: a development which would compromise the desire to avoid party politicisation. The Majority consists of 10 "independents spelt with a 'I'" who take their cue from the Convener and Vice-Convener, both of whom are farmers.

Two other independents who stand outside the Majority are thought to be Liberals but unlike the SNP, they are incorporated into the dominant ethos of the council. A recent addition to the council has been a young, southern Englishwoman, the wife of a helicopter pilot, who is the only formal Conservative on the Council, having been returned against Labour opposition. The Convener and Vice-Convener, who define their job as 'giving a lead', enjoy considerable authority within the Majority. Effectively, the two leaders make the major decisions and the Majority follow their lead, with or without prior personal consultation. It is the Convener and Vice-Convener who take the initiative in sorting out committee convener and vice-convenerships after the elections.

Since 1984 a dispute within the SNP over the selection of a parliamentary candidate has resulted in one of their most senior councillors leaving the party to become a Liberal (he had previously been group leader) and another has become disaffected over his failure to secure the parliamentary nomination. The disintegration of the 'group' may well modify the political organisation of the council, (and indeed the SNP councillor for Fraserburgh has become the vice-convener of the Leisure and Recreation committee) but during the course of our fieldwork it had yet to do so.

So far, the main line of cleavage within the council has been identified as that between the Majority's consensual politics of independence and the aggresive partisanship of the SNP. However, other lines of cleavage do exist; between burgh and landward representatives as well as between the representatives of different burghs. The concentration of SNP representation in the burgh of Peterhead means that the lines of cleavage are super-imposed so as to enhance the isolation of the Nationalists. The way in which different lines of cleavage isolate the SNP can be shown through two examples. A rural councillor explained the different attitudes between burgh and rural communities towards public provision.

> In Peterhead and Fraserburgh the bowling greens are financed completely by the council but in the rural areas it's left to the community. In the burghs there are more facilities. The townsfolk will do nothing themselves, Peterhead especially, they will do nothing and have everything. In the rural areas people are more self-sufficient and have more of a social conscience. I'm getting very annoyed with the money going into the burghs. It would be alright if the townsfolk tried to help a wee bitee.

> (independent councillor)

A second example shows how on one occasion a major council house modernisation and improvement programme due to take place in Peterhead was very nearly sabotaged at the last moment by the intervention of a councillor from another burgh. This occurred despite the fact that the council had previously accepted that the houses in question were in need of urgent, comprehensive treatment and that it had included the programme in its housing plan. The basis of the opposition was that the level of expenditure required was too great an amount to be allocated to one burgh and that regardless of housing need the money ought to be spread around. Significantly, at the meeting when the opposition was victorious, the Convener and Vice-Convener of the Council were not giving their colleagues consistent advice. Without a firm lead from the leaders of the Majority, the anti-Peterhead, anti-SNP and pro-pork barrel values triumphed. The rationality of professional advice counted for nothing. It was only at a subsequent meeting, once the Majority leadership asserted their unified authority, that the programme was re-instated.

Council Organisation and Budget-Making

(i) Organisation

In common with virtually all other local authorities in Scotland, Banff and Buchan adopted the management and committee structures recommended in the Paterson Report. Formally, the conventional wisdom of the corporate approach was accepted. A Chief Executive was appointed together with a Management Team and the council established a Policy

171

and Resources Committee. The content of the corporate approach, however, with its explicit statement of objectives and the identification of policy options was at odds with the implicit consensualism of the politics of independence. The Chief Executive was very soon declared redundant and his office abolished. Consequently there is now no official with responsibility for co-ordinating the activities of the council or in overall charge. Instead, the convention has been adopted whereby the Director of Finance offers financial advice to the Director of Law and Administration and the Director of Law and Administration offers advice on law and administration to the Director of Finance.

The Policy and Resources Committee has survived but as corporate objectives are not made explicit, its policy formulation role is virtually nil. In matters of finance it is totally subordinate to the Finance Committee. A sign of the enfeebled status of Policy and Resources is that its convener is not the Convener of the Council (the leader of the informal Majority) but one of the Indpendents outside the Majority who is thought to be a Liberal.

Somewhat surprisingly, the Finance Committee is also chaired by the other independent who is thought to be a Liberal. The reason is that although Finance is recognised as important, its activities are not contentious because, apart from members of the SNP group, there is agreement amongst councillors as to the primacy of retrenchment. Thus, competence rather than partisanship could dictate the choice of Finance Convener. The current occupant is, indeed, articulate, able and fully committed to the objective of exerting the strongest possible control over expenditure. He sees as one of his major achievements the virtual abolition of the practice of officials seeking approval for supplementary expenditure during the course of the financial year.

If the Policy and Resources Committee is unimportant and Finance uncontentious, then Planning is seen as being both important and contentious but not in a party sense. Significantly, the Convener of the Council is also the Convener of the Planning Committee: perhaps a unique arrangement. The wish of the councillors to maintain the widest area within which they can exercise their discretionary powers by treating applications 'on their merits' has from time to time led to conflict with officials who have been more concerned to produce policy statements and plans. It is also of value for small businessmen and farmers to serve on the Planning Committee to keep themselves informed of what is going on in the commercial world: as one dissident councillor remarked,

> I've always been on Planning. You have a terrible job in Banff Buchan getting a house built in a rural area, it's ridiculous. You would miss a fair bit if not on Planning. We had a bit of trouble with the planners. They think a house is bad for tourism, what nonsense. Our planners think to build in the rural area is wrong. A nice bungalow in the countryside is good for tourism. They are always going on about the need to keep agricultural land. There's no shortage of agricultural land, we're overproducing food.

> (independent councillor)

The re-organisation of local government brought some changes to municipal politics in Banff Buchan, some purely formal and others short-lived but the value of retrenchment not only survives but has been reinforced. Retrenchment is such a widely shared value, among officials and councillors alike that only rarely does it have to be made explicit. The widely shared objective of controlling expenditure means that in preparing the budget the council and its officers work to the unstated assumption that the Government's expenditure guideline should not be exceeded. Banff Buchan's 1983/4, 1984/5 outturns and 1985/6 Estimates have all been within the guideline figure. Over the same period only 5 other authorities out of 53 Scottish district councils had a similar record. Of the other 5, Gordon and Kincardine Deeside are also within the Grampian Region. A determination to keep within guidelines does not necessarily imply an acceptance of the guideline system. Hostility towards the guidelines was strongly expressed when at an early stage in the budgetary process it seemed that the authority would not be able to come within the guideline despite rigorous austerity. The reason for the acceptance of the guideline figure is determination to avoid the grant penalty. The idea that every £ of expenditure above guideline will cost the ratepayer more than a £ is so offensive to the value of retrenchment that it is never seriously contemplated:

> The guidelines are very important, we try to keep it within the guidelines. We cut all we can but we cannot as yet get within guidelines. We are one of the lowest rating authorities in Britain, we try and save all the way, it's ridiculous that we are called overspenders. We are by no means extravagant, we are a saving council. From the county days there was room for curtailment, they were a bit too free with money in Peterhead but now we are cut too much. We are cut to the bone, we have managed but no more. It's always in our mind to protect the ratepayer. To keep the rate down; no money is spent foolishly in Banff Buchan. Now we are being punished for being too thrifty.

(independent councillor)

Attitudes towards the budget are not made explicit by the councillors but phrases such as 'good housekeeping' and the need to get 'value for money' form part of the received wisdom on financial matters. The main concern of most councillors is less with the services provided than with the ultimate rate poundage and the avoidance of penalties. Although a low rate is desirable, there is also reluctance to invite wildly fluctuating rate levels, so that until recently the council has built up substantial surpluses against 'a rainy day', when 'a pound in your pocket is a useful thing to have'. Examples of councillor values are expressed below:

> Nothing in government local or national is free. The ratepayer and taxpayer must meet the cost of all services ... and it is surely the councillor's responsibility to consider the effect on those who pay the bills. I offer nothing less than total dedication to the task of providing maximum personal service and giving value for money.

(Election Address, 1984)

Finance - Continuation of the rigorous budget control. I have almost eliminated the practice of supplementary lists e.g. the additional items of expenditure not included in the original budget.

(Election Address, 1984)

The objectives of the council to sum it up are to buy the bare necessities for the least amount of money. Not sure why - perhaps the farming influence: the thrifty Buchan tradition.

(Councillor Interview)

The attitude of the SNP is not made explicit in that they do not produce their own budget or challenge the rate proposed by the Majority. In the past, the Nationalists have limited their opposition to arguing for lower rent levels but as we shall see, government moves to limit the degree of rate support to the housing revenue account has removed even that option. The former leader of 'the group', however, did indicate that if the SNP were in control that rates would increase to provide more services. Outside the council there are no strong lobbies for the expansion of services. The public service unions exert almost no influence on this authority.

The commitment to provide services at the lowest possible cost, together with the relative weakness of the public sector unions, may account for the council's decision, unlike most Scottish local authorities, to examine seriously the case for privatisation. The council responded to an enquiry from a company in the south of England which had successfully negotiated contracts with some English local authorities for operating the refuse collection service. The initial costing exercise carried out by the company indicated that the council would save approximately £160,000 a year. However, the exercise was based on refuse collection within the burghs, leaving the service in the most sparsely populated and therefore most costly landward areas uncosted. Privatisation was rejected because of the fear that, on a District basis, it would either be more costly or result in a lower level of service:

It was going to be more expensive and a poorer service. In a couple of years we would have had no men and no vehicles and be at their mercy.

(independent councillor)

The council's consideration of privatisation was devoid of any ideological overtones about the relative values of private or public provision. The decision to investigate privatisation and its eventual rejection were both totally compatible with the politics of independence and its emphasis on retrenchment and "good housekeeping".

So far, attention has been focussed on the values and organisation of the council because it is only against such a context that what may appear as a routine and uneventful budgetary process can be understood. The final pieces of background for an understanding of the 1986/7 budget are provided by the council's expenditure record, in terms of both the housing revenue account and the general revenue budget, over the three years 1983/4, 1984/5 and 1985/6.

It has already been pointed out that over those three years Banff and Buchan District council was one of only six district councils, out of a total of 53, which had kept within their current expenditure guideline. Table 13.1 compares Banff and Buchan's net expenditure per head of population with the overall Scottish Districts figure, in terms of both total expenditure per head of population (before taking account of grants and balances) and net rateborne expenditure per head.

Table 13.1

BANFF AND BUCHAN DISTRICT COUNCIL NET EXPENDITURE 1983/4 - 1985/6

	Total Expenditure per head of population		Net Rateborne Expenditure per head of population		Rate Poundage
	Banff/Buchan	Scotland	Banff/Buchan	Scotland	Banff/Buchan
1983/84 (actual)	£62.65	£124.37	£22.52	£77.21	12p
1984/85 (actual)	£74.67	£134.80	£28.89	£78.57	13p
1985/86 (actual)	£79.22	£138.47	£46.97	£95.74	8.5p (revaluation)

Any attempt to rank Banff and Buchan's performance against that of all other Scottish Districts is complicated by the fact that in the Highland, Dumfries and Galloway, and Borders Regions the regional councils provide a limited range of services which elsewhere are provided by district councils. For the purposes of the present ranking exercise, a district council in one of the three regions where the region has district responsibilities, is only taken as having an expenditure level below Banff and Buchan's when the combined figure for the district's own expenditure per head and that incurred by the region on district services is lower than Banff and Buchan's. When a ranking exercise is carried out on this basis, the position of Banff and Buchan can be summarised as follows:

1983/84	Total Expenditure Per Head -	2 district councils had lower levels than Banff and Buchan's, both of these authorities were within Grampian Region.
	Net Rateborne Expenditure Per Head -	3 district councils had lower levels than Banff and Buchan's, and all 3 were in Grampian Region.

1984/85	Total Expenditure Per Head -	5 district councils had lower levels than Banff and Buchan, of which 3 were in Grampian Region.
	Net Rateborne Expenditure Per Head -	3 district councils had lower levels than Banff and Buchan, and all three were in Grampian Region.
1985/86	Total Expenditure Per Head -	3 district councils had lower levels than Banff and Buchan and all three were in Grampian Region.
	Net Rateborne Expenditure Per Head -	6 district councils had lower levels than Banff and Buchan, of which three were in the Grampian Region.

When Banff and Buchan's expenditure record is examined, what emerges is a council which has been outstandingly successful in consistently maintaining low spending levels. Indeed, only the three other rural district councils in the Grampian Region - Gordon, Kincardine Deeside and Moray - emerge as rival champions of retrenchment.

Housing finance has been the area where the difference between the SNP and the rest of the council has been most explicit. Within the council a story is told of the Convener of the council being stuck in a snow drift on his way to a rent-setting meeting and of this concern only giving way to a wry smile when he realised that if he was stuck so were the SNP councillors. The district council has followed the policy line of its predecessor authorities in having a relatively high rent level and a low rate of fund contribution. The power now possessed by the Secretary of State for Scotland to impose a maximum amount by which individual housing authorities are allowed to subsidise the housing revenue account from the rate fund, has effectively removed rent setting as a divisive local issue.

Within the council the sale of council houses is seen predominantly as a financial rather than an ideological issue. Although there is some disquiet that the sale of council housing is having an adverse effect on the ability of the council to meet housing need, the dominant reaction is that only through the sale of houses will the council be in a position to continue its capital programme. In Scotland, unlike England, all the net receipts from the sale of council houses enhance a housing authority's net capital allocation. The net allocation is the gross allocation decided by the Scottish Office minus the amount of income that the Scottish Office considers the authority should be able to raise during the course of the financial year through the sale of houses.

(iii) The 1986-7 Budget

The task of producing the budget lies mostly with the Director of Finance. As the former Chamberlain of Fraserburgh Burgh Council, he is well-grounded in the local political culture and well aware of the constraints within which he has to work. This is all to the good as he has to operate with few explicit instructions from councillors - he has to anticipate their reactions. The existence of known but inexplicit values permeates the whole process.

The first stage in preparing the 1986/7 budget began in August 1985, when work started on compiling an outline budget, as part of the statutory consultation with non-domestic ratepayers. At that stage the outline budget was nothing more than the previous year's figures plus an inflation allowance of 5 per cent. The outline budget was produced without any councillor involvement and was presented to the Policy and Resources Committee on 26 September. The consultation with the non-domestic ratepayers (in effect, Aberdeen Chamber of Commerce, Peterhead Feuar's Managers, Arnots and British Home Stores) took place on 28 November. At the meeting the Director of Finance was able to indicate a possible rate poundage of 12.7p. The non-domestic ratepayers expressed themselves as well satisfied with the consultation.

The second stage, the formulation of a draft budget, began in October and was completed by the end of November. For this exercise, the Director of Finance with the various departments worked from the base of the 1984/5 actual expenditure figures. The aim was to build up on a ledger line basis an expenditure figure for every service.

First, the 1984/5 figure was repriced to 1985/6 with plus and minus adjustments made to take account of exceptional items. The figure was then adjusted in the light of new expenditure commitments undertaken since the 1985/6 budget, essentially pay awards and the full year expenditure implications of committee decisions taken during the course of the year. At this stage the opportunity existed, under the non-committed heading, for service directors to make bids for new expenditure. The known values of the council, reinforced by the Director of Finance, had the effect of militating against directors making bids which involve any significant expansion of service provision. The final adjustment was an anticipated inflation factor for 1986/7. By mid-December the completed draft budget was sent to the service departments for their comments.

By the time the draft budget went to the departments, the Finance Department had already taken the draft budget against the expenditure guidelines and had also taken into account the maximum rate fund contribution to the housing revenue account allowed by the Secretary of State. At that stage the indications were that the budget was some £295,000 (6 per cent) over guidelines and the Director of Finance asked the service directors to begin the process of identifying non-critical areas for savings. The incentive for the service directors to volunteer savings at this stage was that if the guideline figure was reached the councillors would be satisfied but if not, the councillors would intervene and make decisions in light of their own priorities.

The third stage, on 9 January 1986, was a meeting of the Management Team (all the chief officers: Administration, Finance, Planning, Environmental Health, Leisure and Recreation, Housing and Technical Services). There the draft budget was discussed in terms of the guidelines and possible rate poundage. Although councillors had still not been involved in the budget-making process, the Director of Finance emphasised the need to meet guidelines and asked for sacrifices "there and then" to the tune of £295,000. After the meeting of the Management

Team, a further £140,000 in cuts still remained to be found in order to get within the guideline. The Management Team took the view that the savings could only come from two departments - Environmental Health and Leisure and Recreation. The directors of those departments were told to prepare lists identifying savings ranging from £70,000 to £140,000 and to indicate the consequences for their service. The proposed cuts had to be put forward within the constraint of avoiding any major policy changes. Within a few days, Environmental Health had identified £48,000 of possible savings and Leisure and Recreation £141,000.

The fourth stage, which for the first time involved councillors has many similarities with the Cabinet's Star Chamber procedure. On 13 January the Director of Finance reported to the "Big Three" - the Convener and Vice-Convener of the council and the Convener of Finance - the results of the Management Team meeting of 9 January. Although this meeting was informal and therefore secret, it was of critical importance as it was where the major decisions regarding the budget were effectively agreed between councillors and officials. The non-involvement of the convener of the Policy and Resources Committee in the Star Chamber exercise highlighted the difference between the formal structure and the actual process of decision-making.

The Director of Finance pointed out that the draft budget without any revisions was £295,000 over guideline and that it was likely that such an excess would incur penalties of £508,000. The Director of Finance also presented the "Big Three" with a document indicating the cuts that had been agreed by the Management Team. The task of the "Big Three" was to decide whether to accept the proposals of their officials and to find the further cuts necessary to bring the budget within guideline. In preparation for the meeting, the departmental directors, in consultation with their respective committee conveners, had been requested to submit a list of possible cuts, in addition to those already identified, in descending order of priority. Environmental Health and Planning were at something of an advantage in that their conveners were also members of the Star Chamber.

The response of the Convener of Finance to the Management Team's report was to encourage his colleagues to find sufficient savings to push the rate below 10p but the leaders of the Majority, the Convener and Vice-Convener of the council, fearful that a reduction below guideline would result in an even lower guideline figure for the following year, indicated that they would be satisfied if the guideline was achieved. The majority view prevailed, as the Director of Finance had anticipated at the very beginning of the budget process. Having decided on their strategy the "Big Three" then proceeded to interview over a space of three hours the conveners and directors of each committee. The various stages at which cuts were identified and in part restored, are shown in Table 13.2. The decisions of the 13 January meeting formed the basis of the amended draft budget.

The first time the budget had entered the formal council process, (excluding stage 1), occurred on 20 January when the amended draft budget was presented to the District Council and was sent to be considered by committees during the following cycle of meetings. During the cycle of committee meetings it was still open to individual committees to adjust their intra-departmental allocations within the overall total ascribed to them. No attempt was made to do so. The final consultation with the non-domestic ratepayers was held on

3 February, who were also informed of the proposed rate poundage. It was well received.

Table 13.2

THE CUTS

	Agreed by Management Team 9th January	Restored by Big Three	New Cuts 13th Jan	Nett Cuts
Leisure & Recreation	£92,380	£6,930	£105,190	£190,540
Environmental Health	£15,695	-	£ 47,650	£ 63,345
Planning	£ 5,250	-	£ 17,925	£ 23,175
Aden Country Park	£ 8,400	-	-	£ 8,400
Administration	£20,420	-	£ 950	£ 21,370
Central Services	£ 2,120	-	-	£ 2,120
	£144,265	£6,930	£171,715	£309,050

The culmination of the whole budget process took place in a series of meetings on 13 February. The budget estimates were presented by the Director of Finance to the Finance Committee at 10.10 a.m.. A prepared statement by the Convener of Finance was circulated but not read out. The budget estimates together with a rate poundage of 10.7p were approved at 10.15 a.m.. No counter proposals were made. At 10.16 a.m. the Policy and Resources Committee convened and by 10.17 a.m. had endorsed the decisions of the Finance Committee. Finally, at 10.18 a.m. the Full Council met and in two minutes had accepted the budget, the rate and the five year capital programme.

(iv) Conclusions

No doubt Banff and Buchan District councillors share many of the ideals that informed Alderman Roberts and his colleagues on Grantham Town council, which in modern times have been translated into the conduct of national policy. It would, however, be a mistake to describe the low spending, low rating authority as Thatcherite because it is non-ideological (e.g. its attitude towards the privatisation of cleansing and council house sales), non-dogmatic (issues are treated on their merits) and consensual (non-members of the Majority, including an SNP councillor, have become office holders). Like the father its conservatism is traditional, whereas the daughter's is radical and partisan.

As a traditional authority it also rejects the reforms of the 1970s whose barely hidden agenda was designed to turn local government into an instrument of social change with its emphasis on managerialism, the definition of priorities and the subordination of expenditure decisions in various committees to the corporate goal. Instead, Banff and Buchan dismantled the chief executive and his office, rendered

179

the Policy and Resources Committee vestigial, leaving the Finance Committee as the clearing house it had been in the old authorities, concerned with controlling the level of overall expenditure but not concerned with departmental priorities or priorities across departments.

In common with many forms of traditional rule, it is not necessary in Banff and Buchan to debate the central thrust of the line to be pursued in the budget, the focus of the authority's activity. Budget-making is an essentially routine matter and can be left to the discretion of the Director of Finance and his depute because they know the values of the council and the parameters within which they must work. These parameters have become even more circumscribed of late by guidelines and government policy towards rate fund contributions to the housing account which, linked to a pathological fear of penalties, have the power of command. Councillors are only involved at a late stage in the preparation of the budget and most of them have no direct input at all. The process is consensual and non-controversial, leaving the councillors free to subvert the activities of the planning department and to allocate council houses, which are both controversial and more rewarding.

Superficially, such authorities can appear to be dominated by officials for, as we have described, budget-making is very much in their hands. Such a conclusion is quite erroneous. The values of the budget are those of the councillors beyond all shadow of a doubt and we might venture to suggest, of the majority of the electorate. It would not be possible, for example, for a high spending, high rating Director of Finance to slip his proposals through the Star Chamber. The political leadership of the Convener and Vice-Convener of the Council (supported in the budget by the Convener of Finance) is able, effective and dominating and would pass muster in any company of council leaders.

Ironically, the council-official relationship over budgeting in Banff and Buchan is very close to that advocated by the Wheatley Report, which was anxious to draw a firm distinction between the role of councillors as the setters of objectives and the role of officials as implementers and was critical of too much member involvement in the details of administration. Perhaps we could further suggest that the implicit objectives of the council, "To buy the bare necessities for the least amount of money", constituted as precise a corporate objective as one can ever establish and that the budgetary process, in true corporate fashion, subordinated other values to that end. Indeed, one might argue that Banff and Buchan is more truly corporate than much bigger authorities where full-blown chief executives and their offices spawn voluminous corporate plans, vacuously promulgating worthy and amorphous objectives that can justify any ad-hocery arrived at through good old-fashioned politicking. It is in Banff and Buchan, by contrast, that we see the triumph of substance (the realisation of objectives) if not the appearance (the formal structure and processes) of Reform.

Note

The research on which this chapter is based was supported by the University of Aberdeen Development Trust as well as by the Leverhulme Trust. The authors acknowledge their gratitude to both bodies for their support.

14. Stirling District Council

JACQUELINE CHARLTON AND CLIVE MARTLEW

As with all local authority budgetary processes, that of Stirling District Council is constantly evolving. The process is never finalised or perfected but is being adjusted constantly day by day, month by month, year by year. This evolution occurs along unpredictable paths and is influenced by both internal and external factors. Recent years have seen major changes in the way the budget is compiled. The process has responded to the external pressures of generally scarcer resources and the specific actions of central government in relation to Stirling. It has responded to the internal pressures arising from a change of political control in 1980 and from the arrival and then departure of a Chief Executive with strong views about how the budget should be put together and managed. It is thus difficult to view the year under specific investigation as "typical". The evolution of the process instituted in the early 1980s will, it is clear, continue for a number of years to come. It is therefore particularly important to briefly examine the fiscal and management history of the authority in order to understand the particular process undertaken during the period September 1985 to February 1986 for the 1986/7 budgetary year.

The period before the compilation of the budget for 1986/7 began was characterised by three factors. First, the introduction and modification of two new approaches to budgeting. After the Labour Party took control of the Council in 1980, leading elected members pushed for the introduction of Zero Base Budgeting in place of the existing 'bottom up' incremental approach. In practice a modified form of ZBB was used from 1981/2 to 1983/4 which took the existing level of service as the zero base. In this modified ZBB process, ranking of decision packages above this base was undertaken by officials. The result was that the period immediately after 1980 saw large increases in spending and rates. ZBB, such as it was, facilitated this, led to an improvement in services and greatly improved councillors' awareness of budgetary issues.

After 1983/4 the practice of taking existing spending as the base and considering bid packages for extra resources above this ceased under the pressure of central government "selective action" and rate capping. However, certain aspects connected with the aims and results sections of decision packages were retained and built upon. In the 1984/5 budget the concept of Action Plans and Performance Budgets emerged.

This was the brainchild of a new Chief Executive who did not like the idea of budgets comprising little more than a mass of figures which portrayed an accountant's picture of the authority but which were of little use to anyone else. The budget was therefore based on Action Plans for each of the more than 90 activities the Council undertook. The idea was that the resulting "Performance Budgets" should clearly demonstrate:

(a) the results than an activity would achieve;

(b) who would benefit, in what way and to what extent;

(c) how those benefits would be secured;

(d) what indicators would be used to assess whether or not the results sought were achieved efficiently; and

(e) what specific target levels of performance would be set by reference to those indicators.

In this way, it was intended that elected members would have clearly indicated to them the range of choices available, the cost of each activity they chose to undertake, the results that were being sought and the criteria that would be used to assess performance. The aggregate document for the whole authority extended to some 600 odd pages and this certainly proved excessive for most elected members. In addition, Performance Reports were produced for each activity which looked back and assessed whether the standards set in Action Plans had been achieved. These formed the basis of the revision of Action Plans and Performance Budgets for the next year.

The scrutiny of these Action Plans was delegated to a group comprising the Chair of the Policy Committee, the Treasurer, the Majority Group Leader, the Council Convener and the Conservative Finance Spokesman. This Budget Scrutiny Group required Directors and Chairs of Committees to present their case and undergo some fairly stiff cross examination. This approach was further developed in the following year (the process for 1985/6).

The second characteristic factor of the period before the compilation of the 1986/7 budget was political brinkmanship between the Council and the Scottish Office. This occured as the Labour Council after 1980 tried to raise its base spending and this brought it up against the current expenditure guidelines set for each authority by the Scottish Office. In 1981 the Scottish Office initiated action to reduce the authority's Rate Support Grant by £1.25 million because its budget was deeded "excessive and unreasonable". This cut was eventually negotiated back to £700,000. In 1982/3 a reduction of £1.5 million was proposed but in this case the authority cut its rate poundage from 44p to 40p and made savings of over £800,000 to avoid the penalty. In 1983/4 Stirling District was 'rate capped' and compelled to reduce its poundage from the proposed level of 40p to 38p. This represented a partial success for the Council in that it managed to reduce the reduction from 3p by negotiation. Spending was maintained with the shortfall in income being met from balances.

The Budget for 1984/5 was above the authority's guideline and it lost £500,000 in Rate Support Grant "clawed back" by the Scottish Office. The 1985/6 Budget was a 'guideline budget' and no attempt was made at confrontation on that issue. However, the Council budgeted for a Rate Fund Contribution to Housing Revenue Account above the statutory limit imposed by the Scottish Office. This led ultimately to a public inquiry and to the issue of an order of Specific Performance by the Court of Session. This led to a rate cut of 1.6p to 20.4p.

The third characteristic of the pre 1986/7 period arose from this friction between the Authority and the Scottish Office. This was the increasingly common requirement towards the end of this period to rework the budget during the financial year in order to cope with the consequences of Government action. This eroded the time available to construct the next year's budget.

Over the period since 1980 this need to re-budget during the financial year had required the use of various devices to limit expenditure such as shelving staff increases (1981), across the board percentage reductions in budgets (1981), selective reductions in particular costs (1982 and subsequently) and "unallocated" percentage cuts across the board (1985).

Although Stirling District had been developing its budgeting processes since 1980 it was clear at the end of the 1985/6 cycle that problems remained with the Performance Budget procedure. Members wanted to start the budget earlier rather than have a last minute rush, although the need to re-budget made it difficult to introduce a more rational timescale. Lack of consideration had meant some elements in the budget were not properly resourced. When officers submitted Action Plans they were in effect stating what they would like to do and there was a perception among many senior officers that the system allowed some departments to "talk up" their budget provisions. In many cases the actual budget provision made on the basis of these plans was inadequate due to economies, cuts etc., which had had to be made or simply because plans had not been costed properly. This inadequacy did not lead to a revision of the Action Plans however. They had become bids for resources rather than a mechanism of management control as originally intended.

Finally, there was a lack of strategy: the Performance Budgets only looked at the current year. Only the Labour Manifesto, which had been adopted as a council policy document, looked beyond one year. There was no attempt to look at shifts in priorities which might be desireable or necessary in the longer term and certainly no attempt to relate this to central government plans. This was seen as a weakness by the departing Chief Executive and in framing the 1986/7 budget the new Chief Executive incorporated a section in the documentation to show 1987/8 costs arising from 1986/7 expenditure.

183

Budget for 1986/7

In the summer of 1985 the Chief Executive left for another authority. The new Chief Executive brought with him a different conception of how the revenue budget process should work placing much less emphasis on the 'words budget' as expressed in the Action Plans. The new emphasis was to apply a "cash limit" discipline to all parts of the budgetary exercise and to highlight continuously the financial implications of decisions as they were taken. There was a marked change in the overall approach as a result. Action Plans were prepared on the same format as for 1985/6 but they did not receive the same attention as they did in the past. Consequently it was decided not to completely re-write Action Plans for 1986/7 before the budget process began. Only specific measurable things were changed and the figure updated. (They will be re-drafted at the end of the process and based on the budget). Nevertheless, officers and members continued to maintain that the Action Plans formed an important part of the exercise for service committees, although at the time compilation of the figures was of relatively more importance to officers than the redrafting of Action Plans. In practice the authority's attention was focussed on marginal adjustments to base expenditure and the budget scrutiny exercise reverted to a more incremental style tempered by a three-pronged analytical process involving:

1. A detailed investigation of the costing of the base budget of all activity areas. This process was led by the Assistant Chief Executive (Review) and carried out in conjunction with the managers concerned.

2. The carrying out of a corporate issues analysis in certain key areas. It was argued by the Chief Executive and accepted by the members, that important areas of expenditure such as the Economic Strategy, the training, marketing and property plans and the "Going Local" Strategy, should be subject to separate scrutiny in order to establish in true base budget fashion whether expenditure was required and how much expenditure should go into particular activities. For the 1986/7 financial year, therefore, a global amount was set aside to cover each of these activities and it was decided that during the course of the financial year the committee and performance review system would be used to determine actual allocations to these heads. In this sense the 1986/7 budget process did not end with the setting of the rate.

3. The Budget Scrutiny Group exercise, which itself examined the proposed bids and economies from each activity manager in a detailed, line by line analysis.

Budget Strategy

In the 1985/6 budget cycle, councillors had initiated the process with general guidance as to the assumptions to be made about the finance available. For 1986/7 the Labour Group gave general guidance at a meeting with the Chief Executive and Director of Finance in the late summer. The "budget principles" which were established were as follows:

Consolidation of the Council's previous commitments

Continuation of previous commitments for the full year

Extension of services through bids for resources that were necessary to allow previous commitments to function fully (e.g. maintenance services for new works and staffing for new Leisure and Recreation projects).

The Chief Executive then interpreted these principles in more managerial terms. He initiated the budget cycle with a memorandum issued on 26 August 1985 which stated that in drawing up budgets, officers "should bear in mind the general wish of the Majority group that the budget for 1986/7 should consolidate as far as possible the initiatives of the Council in the past year". Officers were asked to budget realistically for current levels of service and to ensure that adequate resources were built into estimates to cover the full costs of commitments taken on during the year. Having done this, they were then asked to identify the economies which would be necessary to take them back to the position of a standstill budget figure. It was intended that the Budget Scrutiny Group would thereby be in a position to appreciate the options open to them if they were going to head for a standstill budget in overall terms.

From this point the budget process can be characterised as consisting of 4 processes:

- a managerial process which built and reviewed the base budget

- a politico-administrative process in the form of the Budget Scrutiny Group

- a strategic political process in which the majority party group and local Labour Party set strategy and examined detailed budget issues

- a technical stage in which the financing of the budget within the limitations imposed by central government was devised.

The Management Process: Costing the Base Budget

In his memo of 26 August, the Chief Executive issued a timetable for the budgeting process and gave this to Heads of Departments and councillors. This memo described the background to the budget exercise for 1986/7 as being 'extremely tight' and pointed out that "hard decisions will have to be made about competing priorities". The next stage was the issue, again by the Chief Executive but following discussions with his Director of Finance, of the financial guidelines for the 1986/7 budget, on the basis of which the individual departments would then prepare their Action and Resources plans for the coming year. The main guideline given to departments for the coming year was that they had to plan for a "standstill budget". This meant that they had to budget using the figures from the final revised budget for 1985/6. This entire exercise was undertaken at current (i.e. November 1985) prices. The Finance Department undertook repricing calculations once the budget was approved. The 'standstill' guideline did not imply, however, that the existing budget would simply be rolled over. It did mean that managers had to offset any bids they made for extra resources with economies.

The drawing up of the budgets was decentralised within departments to the managers of the individual activities. For example, Leisure and Recreation is divided into 21 activity centres with managers responsible for budgeting for those activities falling within their remit. Thus, three of the activity centres fall within the remit of the Chief Librarian, who was therefore responsible for drawing up the Action and Resource plans for them. At this stage, councillors collectively were not involved at all. Although some officers stated that budgets were prepared "without any political guidance", in fact they were required by the Chief Executive's guidance to consult with the Chair and Vice-Chair of their committees in drawing up draft Action and Resource Plans. Members, although aware that the budgetary process was underway without their specific involvement, did not indicate any rejection of this officer-led approach to early stages in the budgetary exercise.

The process of drafting resource plans was managed by the Assistant Chief Executive (Review) in consultation with the Finance Department. The Finance Department at this stage played a co-ordinating role in ensuring that all managers understood what they were to do and that they all worked within the given guidelines. A finance officer therefore was assigned to each activity manager, and in the period September to November sat down with him to help with the drawing up of the budget for his activity areas. Additionally, the finance officer's role was to brief the manager on the likely responses of the Budget Scrutiny Group (see below) to the proposals which he was presenting and to make sure that the manager prepared himself with sufficient information about the previous year's proposals, to be able to answer the in-depth questioning which he would meet. The Finance Officer also carried out this exercise with the Director of the service under consideration and expected him to ensure that his managers were well prepared to defend the budgets which they were presenting. The Finance Department regarded this pre-BSG exercise as being particularly useful as it helped identify savings and clarified bids. In particular, it allowed them to examine the current year's 'spend to date' in order to highlight activities where the budget was likely to be underspent and hence identify areas for potential savings in 1986/7. Many such adjustments were made bilaterally between finance and services departments in the pre-BSG exercise without taking them to the BSG itself. As a result of this process the BSG was provided with greater scope for accepting bids for extra resources and the Chief Executive argued that it allowed the BSG to "concentrate upon those major areas of expenditure over which they had total policy discretion".

For each Action Plan the manager had to specify separately:

(a) Increases in the cost of current levels of service due to either full year costs of part year commitments or other reasons.

(b) Decreases in the cost of current level of Service due to either a continuation of reductions imposed in the previous year (if these could be achieved) or other reasons.

(c) Bids for additional resources either because of a policy commitment of the Council or other reason.

(d) Economies which could be identified by curtailing or altering a method of service delivery.

All of these additions, deductions, bids and economies, which arose from the officer meetings, led to the production of a 'Monitoring Schedule' which was then submitted to the Budget Scrutiny Group for consideration.

The Politico-Administrative Process: Budget Scrutiny Group

This officer-based exercise completed, the next stage of the process was to evaluate the estimates produced by the departments. This evaluation exercise was undertaken by the Budget Scrutiny Group comprising the Chair of the Policy Committee, Treasurer, Majority Group Leader, the Council Convener and the Conservative Finance Spokesman. Additionally, the Chairs of the individual service committees were invited to attend when their service was under discussion. Also in attendance at the Scrutiny Group meetings were the Chief Executive and his Depute, the Director of Finance and the finance officer responsible for the individual briefings within departments. This forum acted as a 'star chamber' in examining the budgets of each department.

A preliminary meeting of the group was held to decide what documentation and information should be made available for discussion at BSG meetings. Officers tried to persuade the councillors that they should keep paper to the minimum. However, the councillors felt that what was being proposed by officers would be inadequate and insisted on having additional information. They wanted to go through the revised 1985/6 budget line by line to build up the budget for 1986/7. In fact the amount of written information provided to councillors on the BSG was simply too much to cope with and attention focussed almost exclusively on a small proportion of it. The documents ultimately provided are as listed in Appendix 14.1.

The Budget Scrutiny Group began its meetings on 3 December (much later than councillors and officers had wanted). The Group began its deliberations with a debate on whether general and cross departmental issues should be discussed immediately, or postponed until all the budgets had been assessed. Although a number of councillors expressed the view that the "issues" should be discussed prior to the in-depth discussion of individual departmental budgets since they would appear again and again during questioning, the Chief Executive and his Depute argued forcibly for postponing the discussion of general issues until after the departmental budgets had been discussed. The latter view prevailed, and therefore the Group began by looking at the individual services. What this meant of course was that decisions on many individual items had to be deferred pending policy decisions on the general issues.

The Budget Scrutiny Group examined the monitoring summary sheet for each activity to identify how underspends in the 1985/6 financial year could lead to savings in 1986/7. Then for the same activity they examined the bids and economies sheet. Action Plans and Performance Reports were referred to service committees for discussion in the next cycle. Thus, although councillors were in in possession of a great array of information this proved to be too voluminous and attention was focussed on that small proportion of the documents that were essentially only figures. The narrative background papers appeared to be simply too much to cope with. When background information was required councillors generally turned to the officials present for guidance.

In general terms, each service took one full-day session to complete. Service Directors varied considerably in the approach which they adopted to presentation of their cases. Although in most cases Service Directors brought the individual activity managers with them to defend their activity area, in one case (Housing) the Director conducted the whole defence of his department's prepared budget himself. Directors and Managers showed considerable differences in the ways in which they presented their cases. Some were extremely well prepared and had clearly tried to provide themselves with quite detailed information covering all the possible lines of questioning which they might encounter. Others were not so well prepared and often produced a poor defence of their position. Some Directors took an active and supportive role in defence of their managers, otherw were more inclined to leave the defence to the manager.

The general pattern was that the Group went through the bids and economies sheets on a line by line basis. In some cases councillors themselves suggested new ideas for bids and economies as a result of BSG discussions. For example, councillors asked for a bid from the Environmental Health Department for extra resources on street cleansing and suggested that it might be financed by seeking advertising for refuse bins. This reflected the fact that in a tourist oriented area like Stirling, "street cleaning is an issue".

The councillors on the Budget Scrutiny Group were all members with quite extensive local government experience and although initially questioning tended to be dominated by one to two members, as the cycle of meetings progressed, all members increasingly took an active part in the process. Usually, meetings were chaired by the Chair of the Policy Committee of the council. He saw his role as that of relatively impartial chairman, although from time to time he engaged managers and directors in detailed questioning. Often his rather diffident attitude and seeming unwillingness to make firm proposals led the Budget Scrutiny Group to postpone a decision, or to leave in the budget items which clearly could have been cut. In practice the leader of the majority Labour group opted out of the process, rarely being present. He perceived it as an activity that only made marginal adjustments. He felt it was fragmented and "manipulated by officers" who "had already set the agenda". However, most members seemed content with the way the exercise was conducted and relationships between members of the committee were, it was agreed by all concerned, very cordial. The Conservative finance spokesman was given every opportunity to speak. Interestingly, there was at this stage little conflict between the ideas of the Labour and Conservative members, although the Conservative finance spokesman argued that the best way to compile a budget was to begin by setting a limit on resources and make departments work within it while the Labour Councillors argued that the size of the budget should be primarily determined by need.

The Chief Executive saw his role as that of counsel and expert. Thus, he often pointed out what the consequences of a particular decision would be, so influencing the decision eventually made. Additionally, he examined witnesses, (i.e. Directors and managers) on points not already raised by members but which he felt should be explored. His Depute provided back up to this function. The finance officers responsible for individual departmental briefings often intervened during questioning to prompt the Director or manager by reminding him of the discussions which they had had and suggesting to the particular manager what a figure or item might mean.

The Budget Scrutiny exercise, was expected to be completed before Christmas. In fact it went on until the end of January. A number of reasons for this are apparent. First, the level of detail in which the BGS became involved made the process extremely time-consuming. Councillors were regularly involved in twenty or thirty minute discussions on items as small as £25, such as the purchase of small itmes of equipment. Secondly, the documentation was extremely complex and in some cases (such as spreadsheets) difficult to read. One councillor was compelled to use a magnifying glass at times. Partly because of this, attention in practice focussed on the Bids and Economies sheets and their supporting reports. Action Plans and Performance Reports were virtually ignored at this stage and the lower priority given to the 'words budget' meant the final document for 1986/7 was all figures. This complexity and lack of narrative led the Leader of the Labour Group to complain that the result was that only officers had a full knowledge of the Council's services (in Stirling, Committee chairs change every two years creating problems of continuity).

The BSG process also became protracted because decisions on many of the bids and economies coming before it were deferred. Councillors were generally reluctant to make many decisions until a very late stage in the cycle. The early BSG meetings were largely an exercise in deciding which items were 'unacceptable' with the rest being left for further consideration when the totals resulting from the first run through were available. In many cases deferral was to allow further consideration by groups of officials particularly where these issues were cross-departmental (for example, the provision of publishing, printing and publicity). In some of these cases the BSG agreed that bids had not been properly worked out and set aside a cash limited figure pending production of a coherent policy (for example, a bid from the Economic Development section was allocated funds subject to production of an Economic Development Strategy). In other cases decisions were deferred for political reasons such as the need for 'clearance' from the majority group. (For example, several decisions were delayed pending political decisions on the Council's decentralisation policy and a decision on whether to impose a charge for uplifting commercial refuse was deferred for consideration by the Labour Group as it was considered to be a highly political issue). In other cases inter-organisational issues had to be resolved (for example, in the case of one joint Regional/District project, a decision on a proposal to delete a staff post was deferred until the attitude of the Regional Council to its share of the cost became clear). Finally, some decisions were deferred simply in the hope that more

189

money would become available. In this sense the decisions of the BSG were clearly influenced by the unpredictability of the authority's financial environment, especially the scale of grant penalties for overspending guidelines. This later translated itself into a situation where several bids were designated as "1st of August items": that is they would be activated if money was still available after grant clawback. This problem of unpredictability became particularly clear in the Scrutiny Group's discussion of items funded by Urban Aid (see below).

In total, £750,000 of bids (excluding inflation) offset by equivalent economies had been identified by activity managers. By the New Year £173,000 worth of bids had been accepted and £563,000 had been deferred and these returned to BSG for reconsideration during January. It was only after the middle of January that final decisions were made on the deferred items and this occurred once the majority group had sorted out its attitude to the key strategic issues of rents and current expenditure guidelines (see below). Many of the deferred items re-emerged on an 'Action List' of 117 items presented to the BSG for discussion on 23 January.

The BSG exercise itself was essentially incremental budgeting. Most of its work focussed on rolling over the 1985/6 budget to 1986/7 by first examining the revised budget for 1985/6 and then making volume adjustments by accepting bids and economies. One of the difficulties this threw up was that in some cases the figures put forward by activity managers were simply a revaluation of those for 1985/6 and did not properly reflect changes in council policy or administrative practice from one year to the next (despite the Chief Executive's instruction on 26 August). For example, when the BSG discussed the Housing Revenue budget a good deal of attention was directed at a £30,000 increase in the allowance for voids (empty properties). The size of this increase concerned councillors of all parties. However, after considerable debate it emerged that the Housing Department had simply rolled forward the 1985/6 voids allowance without taking into account the authority's new housing allocations system which was supposed to reduce voids. The matter was ultimately deferred for further study by the Directors of Housing and Finance. In another case a large underspend for 1985/6 was identified on printing and stationery costs for another service because of a roll-over of the previous year's estimates which had included a large 'one-off' order for headed note-paper.

Finally, it is often said that in local government officers engage in various forms of budget tactics in order to defend or enhance their service. The BSG inquisitorial style was clearly intended to prevent and identify any such manoevres. In our observations of the BSG only rarely did anything which might be interpreted as 'a ploy' emerge. One director was, at one stage, accused by councillors of only offering high priority items as economies, in the knowledge that it would be difficult to accept them. On another occasion a Director caused consternation when his bid for an extra member of staff was rejected by asking if he could come back with the same proposal if it could be financed within the existing budget. Councillors were naturally concerned that he might have savings available about which they had not been informed.

The Strategic Political Process: Rent and Rates

The BSG process resolved itself into a very detailed study of the bids and economies put forward by activity managers. The large scale issues such as rent levels, rate levels and the policy of the Council in relation to current expenditure guidelines "emerged" from a rather hazy parallel process in which local politicians had a primary role and of which officials (with perhaps the partial exception of the Chief Executive) were largely ignorant.

The Labour Group is composed of all Labour councillors, including those from the Budget Scrutiny Group, plus three representatives from the local Labour Party who attend meetings, participate in discussions but who do not vote. In practice, discussion of the budget at these meetings tended to be dominated by the members of the BSG who were clearly by this stage well versed in its intricacies. In particular, the Labour Party representatives, unless skilled in financial matters, can make little input. The only exception to this dominance by BSG members was where the interests of a particular committee chair were at stake, in which case the Department concerned would often be defended.

The role of the Labour Group was two-fold in practice. In the first place it settled strategic issues related to rents, rate fund contributions to housing revenue account and current expenditure guidelines. Secondly, in the light of its strategic decisions it participated in decisions on individual items of expenditure. In neither case could we identify any significant political cleavage on the policy to adopt, nor could we identify any case where a BSG recommendation was rejected.

In relation to the first of these categories the limit placed by the Scottish Office on the authority's rate fund contribution to Housing Revenue Account was reduced from £2.026 million in 1985/6 to £1.272 million in 1986/7 - a reduction of £754,000 or 37 per cent. In 1985/6 the authority had initially defied the limit imposed by budgeting for a higher rate fund contribution, until it was forced to comply by the Court of Session, when it imposed an additional £2 a week rent increase and reduced its rate by 1.6p to 20.4p. By December of 1985 however, it was clear that for 1986/7 the Council would comply with the limit set and would increase rents although the actual size of the rent increase was not decided upon until early February when other factors such as the extent to which external maintenance of council houses should be capitalised were also decided (see below).

The majority group's attitude to the current expenditure guideline was not firmed up until mid-January although the guidelines themselves had been announced in early October. Stirling's current expenditure guideline was increased by 3.8 per cent from the 1985/6 figure compared to an average 5.3 per cent for all Scottish District Councils. It was only in January that councillors were in possession of all the information which would allow them to see the rating consequences of sticking to the rate fund contribution figure and accepting all the budget bids. The Labour group decided to go beyond the guideline (in the event by 8 per cent) and this "emerged" to officers at the end of January.

The decision to fix a budget so far above the guideline figure had implications for the authority's rate support grant. The Scottish

Office has in recent years reduced Scottish authorities' needs element on a progressively harsh sliding scale should their spending exceed their guideline figures. The scale of such penalties is known to an authority when finalising its budget but Stirling anticipated that on spending 8 per cent above guideline it would receive virtually no Needs Element at all (in fact £23,000 was the estimate compared to £838,000 in 1985/6). As the authority receives no Resources Element and no Housing Support Grant, its services will be virtually entirely financed by locally generated income during 1986/7.

Once the decision to go beyond the guideline had been made there was a rapid resolution of many of the outstanding budget issues facing the authority. In essence the 'hard' economies considered but deferred by the BSG were mostly dropped and bids totalling £590,000 were accepted. This resolution came about partly through the BSG and partly through the Labour Group in consultation with the local Labour Party. On 23 January a meeting of the BSG was held which considered the outstanding bids and economies which had been consolidated into a single document. Some of the issues raised here were, however, further deferred pending major policy decisions on for example "Going Local", (the Council's decentralisation initiative), on the authority's Economic Strategy, or were designated as "1st August items". This meeting of the BSG also discussed those budget items which were up for urban aid funding. The authority did not know at that stage which of its bids for urban aid the Scottish Office would accept and so it could not accurately estimate what resources it would require. As approval would not come until some (unspecified) time during 1986/7 it was not possible to set a start date and hence estimate the cost. Given such utter uncertainty the BSG set aside one third of the total that would be required if all submitted projects were approved. This was a completely arbitrary decision and illustrates just how provisional many budget estimates are in practice.

At three meetings of the Labour Group on 28 January, 6 February and 11 February, decisions on specific bids and economies within the BSG exercise were taken. Some items continued to be deferred, however. The involvement in the Labour Group in resolving the deferred items varied from service to service. In the case of Housing all the BSG items and recommendations went to the Labour Group and then to Housing Committee. This happened because of the political importance of the Housing service but also because the Labour Group leader, who was also chair of the Housing Committee, thought that insufficient guidance had been given by officers to the BSG on the implications of its decisions on Housing. He was also unhappy with the level of discussion of the Housing budget within the department and with councillors and said that "the Director prepared it from above". Bringing the whole budget back to the Labour Group was obviously a way of ensuring more complete political input. In the case of other services specific items went back to the Labour Group but not whole budgets. In fact decisions on specific items were being made right up until the deadline date of 11 February with councillors trying to match expenditure proposals to the resources available.

The Technical Process

Towards the end of the budget cycle a further stage in its construction began. This involved primarily the Finance department and concerned such things as inflation, charges, balances and what might be termed "accounting tactics".

Inflation

As has been mentioned, all resource plans were drawn up at current (i.e. November 1985) prices. Once the budget process was complete the Finance Department revalued the figures to outturn prices for 1986/7. In doing so it assumed that wages would increase by an average of 7 per cent as a result of the local government pay negotiations and as the settlement date is in July that this would increase the authority's salary costs by 5.25 per cent (75 per cent of 7 per cent). Other costs were estimated as being likely to increase by 5 per cent on average, although within this there were some exceptions. For example, car allowances for staff were not increased at all, nor were costs for purchase of oil, while electricity costs were increased by 4 per cent.

Charges

During the autumn a decision was taken by the Labour Group on the percentage increase in charges. Its application to each service was essentially the responsibility of the Finance Department. A general policy was established that charges would increase in line with inflation (an average of 5 per cent) and this was applied centrally by the Finance Department to all activities. Thus a department seeking an increase of less than this amount had to present its case as a bid for extra resources to the Budget Scrutiny Group. For 1986/7 the overall estimate of income was, however, less than for 1985/6 as the authority had experienced a substantial fall in income that year because of the bad summer weather. A good summer in 1986/7 could therefore lead to higher than estimated income and hence a reduction in net expenditure.

Balances

The authority's position before 1980 was to maintain relatively high balances. However, the period from 1980 had placed considerable strain on this policy. The 1985/6 budget had had to recover a £640,000 deficit and but for the windfall rate income arising from higher than anticipated valuations after the 1985 property revaluations, a substantial deficit would also have had to be carried into 1986/7. In the event a small surplus of £65,000 was carried forward and a total working balance of £360,863 was built into the 1986/7 budget (3.6 per cent). According to those officials we interviewed the size of the balance was entirely a "technical judgement based on prudence" and not determined by political factors in any way, although the amount obviously had the approval - albeit tacit - of the majority group.

'Accounting tactics'

When the Council had established the broad direction of its policy through the BSG and Labour Group, the Finance Department then devised various ways in which this could be carried through at least cost to the authority. This had two meanings in this context. In its normal sense, it meant that the Department tried to minimise expenditure and maximise income. There was another sense in which it was used however in that the Department also ensured that expenditure was maximised within the rate fund contribution limits, guidelines and capital expenditure consents set by the Scottish Office. For 1986/7 the authority adopted a number of devices to achieve this.

First, the authority's HRA capital allocation was about £800,000 more than it had anticipated. In 1985/6 it had been £4.8 million and this was increased to £5.6 million for 1986/7 by the Scottish Office. This allowed the capitalisation of £740,000 of major works in the external maintenance programme (EMP) contracts. Only £300,000 of the EMP was left in housing revenue budget. (These sums reflected the Council's quantity surveyor's estimate of the proportions of capital items contained in any EMP works). Thus, although the authority's limit on rate fund contributions to HRA had been cut by £754,000, capitalisation of EMP relieved a considerable burden on the housing revenue account and allowed the authority to proceed with EMP at a level near to that planned while keeping the rent increase at "only" 12 per cent. It was stated to us that the Council would not have increased rents by more than this, in which case it would have lost a considerable proportion of the EMP if capitalisation had not been an option. At a different level the Council also capitalised certain other costs. For example, the salary of a new landscape architect post and of Development officers for the Housing Department were to be paid for from the capital budget.

Secondly, the Finance Department also revised the loan charge figures in order to further reduce the burden on the HRA. This was done by rescheduling some capital repayments so that debt was repaid over a longer period. This reduced annual loan charges on HRA by £500,000, and created room for improvements in the service.

Thirdly, as in 1985/6, a "vacancy adjustment" has been applied to the budget of the whole District. This was a mechanism by which the authority kept its budget nearer to the current expenditure guideline. The authority adjusted its expenditure on staffing downwards by 3.2 per cent to take account of the fact that a proportion of posts would be vacant for part of the financial year. The adjustment in other words would bring the budget more into line with actual behaviour. The effect in 1986/7 was to take £252,715 out of the budget (slightly less than for 1985/6). An additional staffing adjustment was made in the 1986/7 budget for the first time. Provision for advertising of vacancies, for interview expenses and for travel was taken out of the budget as it was argued that the period during which posts were vacant would provide the revenue for these items.

Furthermore, considerable effort was taken to ensure that bids or economies put forward at BSG did not worsen the authority's financial position. For example, the Housing Service proposed to make an economy by recharging the Environmental Health Department for assistance it provided with cleansing in a joint District/Region scheme which was part funded through urban aid. This, had it been accepted, would have reduced the charge to the HRA but would have placed the expenditure within guidelines thereby increasing the authority's "overspend" (and grant penalty) and would have reduced the charge to the Regional Council by taking the cost outside the joint arrangements. As one councillor said, this was "not the cleverest of options".

The chronology of the decisions on such tactical adjustments is difficult to trace. In making decisions on individual bids and economies the authority by implication also had to devise mechanisms for funding them within the limits set but such procedures only became finalised at a late stage in the process - late January to early February.

Consultations with Non-domestic Ratepayers

During the final week of February 1986 consultations, as required by law, were held with local non-domestic ratepayers in the 'District Forum'. At this meeting the Chamber of Commerce criticised the Council for not trying to stay within Government spending guidelines and thus qualify for RSG of £892,000. The Forum were presented with all the bids and economies put forward to the BSG and were informed by the council that if all bids were accepted the expenditure of the authority would rise by 20 per cent and the rates by 4p in the pound - although it was clear by this time that this would not be the ultimate outcome. Consequently there was considerable criticism from local business that they had been presented with "an unrealistic budget", and the Chamber of Commerce spokesman complained that "the Council would do better to give people a better guide initially rather than produce a pile of papers a foot high that are not going to mean anything." (Stirling Observer, 26/2/86). The Council of course faces the dilemma that if it presents only its final decisions on the options it will be accused of presenting a fait accompli and not taking the consultations seriously.

At the end of the process the Council fixed its net revenue expenditure at £9.96 million for 1986/7 compared to the revised budget of £9.43 million for 1985/6 - an increase of 5 per cent. The rate was fixed at 22 pence - an increase of 8 per cent from 1985/6. This increase took account of the likely grant clawback for exceeding the current expenditure guideline. Rents were increased by an average 12.4 per cent to comply with the rate fund contribution limit.

Conclusion

The authority has moved from a situation prior to 1981/2 when budget preparation and presentation was led mainly by the Finance Department in conjunction with spending departments, through a period from 1981/2 to 1983/4 when it was led by members and spending departments with assistance from Finance, to the period 1984/5 to date when it is led by the Executive department in co-operation with Finance and in conjunction with spending departments.

They had moved overnight from a relatively non-political atmosphere prior to 1980 to a highly political one and a period of adjustment was required. The council has come almost full circle, from one which whilst never accepting guidelines tried to recognise their existence, to one which flatly opposed them, to one which still opposes them but is beginning to recognise that if improvements in services are to be secured, some cost reductions must be found to finance them. Despite this, however, in the last 2 years there have been a number of high priority services introduced - e.g. the Futureworld programme which envisages regenerating the area round the castle and the top of the town as a tourist attraction, economic and community development teams, marketing and publicity teams and women's service, and substantial improvements in the Housing Service, all of which have been funded in the main, from internal resources such as departmental reorganisations and cost reduction.

A study of the events described here will also indicate that the term "budget process" implying as it does the logical progression of one activity developing from one stage of creation to the next, is misleading. In fact there are several "budget processes" in Stirling District Council going on side by side and often connected only in a vague sense which many of those involved do not fully understand.

To begin with there is the budget process of the activity managers who must construct their resource plans, hold consultations on them, work through them with the Finance Department and the Assistant CEO (Review) and present them to their service Director. They and their Service Directors then become involved in the BSG process, at which point the political world meets the official world. While these activities are progressing yet another process is unfolding among politicians and the local party with attention focussed here on those issues such as rent levels and 'guideline policy' which are fundamental to the overall budget outcome. Finally, there is the process of 'technical' adjustment through which solutions are suggested to some of the dilemmas which have emerged from the three preceding processes.

It is also important to recognise that these budget processes are constantly evolving and changing. The process for 1986/7 is a mere snapshot. We have attempted to put it into the context of the processes for previous years in order to show how such evolution occurs and how managerial, political and technical considerations interact over time. In some ways the process that unfolded inbuilding the 1986/7 budget was a transitional one. In particular, the status and purpose of Action Plans and Performance Reports was in question. Their future was being rethought and new elements of Performance Review were being developed as a direct result of the budget process. Councillors of all parties with an interest in budgeting, as well as officials, wish to see the system improve and are committed to seeing that this happens. Councillors in particular who have invested a great deal of time in coming to grips with the complex processes of local authority budgeting are unlikely to wish to see this investment come to nothing.

Appendix 14.1   DOCUMENTATION PRESENTED TO THE BUDGET SCRUTINY GROUP

(1) Performance Reports 1984/5

(2) Action Plans 1986/7

(3) Monitoring Reports (budget control statements which showed actual against estimated expenditure and variances on a subjective basis for the first 7 months of the financial year).

(4) The proposed budget for 1986/7 in computer printout form showing increases/decreases, bids, adjustments and economies. These were produced by the Finance Department and were effectively a record of the various changes made to the 1985/6 budget to arrive at the 1986/7 budget.

(5) Financial Guidelines showing how the original 1985/6 budget had been adjusted or was proposed to be adjusted to arrive at the 1986/7 budget. It was in other words a repricing of the 1985/6 estimates to roll them forward to 1986/7, including full year costs and other changes which did not represent a change in volume. It then detailed bids for additional resources and any economies identified to finance these in order to come back to the 1985/6 repriced 'full year' cash figure.

(6) Monitoring Summary Sheet. This emerged from the exercise led by the Assistant Chief Executive (Review). It summarised the main issues highlighted in the Monitoring Reports by showing the main underspends in the first 6 months of the financial year. Where such underspends occurred it flagged those areas where possible savings could be made in the 1986/7 budget. So against each item was a proposed adjustment. In essence these sheets showed the adjustments necessary to the 'base budget' (the 1985/6 estimates) to maintain existing levels of service. They also showed up the thoroughness with which some managers monitored spend. Some came to BSG well briefed on underspends and their causes while others were vague and had not prepared proposed remedies.

(7) Bids and Economies: identified bids for additional resources to improve the service and economies which would reduce service levels on a line by line bases. That is, they were variations to the constant volume base set out in the monitoring summary sheets.

(8) Finally, an 'Issues' paper was produced by the Assistant Chief Executive (Review) covering a range of general issues applicable to all services and certain political issues and 'one-off' matters that required special treatment. It had a particularly important role in highlighting longer term problems. These included:

–   The treatment of monitoring and provision for overtime.

–   Approval for expenditure on attendances at conferences and training.

197

- How to deal with 'surplus' labour generated by changes in service delivery (given the Council's no redundancy policy).

- Vehicle replacement policy and the Council's inability to keep up a proper programme of replacement within its capital allocation.

- Capital expenditure: the lack of an approved capital budget meant that at this stage managers could not estimate for consequential revenue costs.

- Certain other items such as member services and new technology expenditure were also proving difficult to estimate for as members had not set a clear policy.

- Lease/rental expenditure: the possibility of capitalising leases/ rentals was highlighted so that payments could be charged as loan charges and hence fall outside the current expenditure guideline. The Chief Executive (Review) estimated "several thousand pounds" could probably be treated in this way.

- "Vacancy Adjustment" and recruitment costs. In the past the budget had been reduced to take account of unfilled posts and this allocated pro-rata to each activity whether or not a vacancy was likely to arise. This had proved unrealistic and the paper called for a rethink of how this was approached. Managers were also required to offset any recruitment costs arising from filling a post by leaving it vacant for a time.

- Repair and Maintenance: many budget items for this were really 'contingency items' but it was proposed to leave them in because of their importance. The paper suggested centralising responsibility for maintenance (except council housing) in the Property Group of the Development Directorate.

- Postages: budgets had to be adjusted to take account of reduction in 2nd Class post rate.

- Marketing: highlighted the duplication and lack of control exercised over budgets for promotions, publicity, exhibitions, advertising, campaigns, etc.

- Sales, fees and charges: the paper pointed out that some managers treated these items differently.

- Purchase of furniture, fittings and equipment: the Halls and Centres budget for this was underspent after 6 months and the paper raised the possibility of reducing either the current budget or future provision. This could apply to other items also.

- Futureworld: consultants had done considerable work on this activity in the past. A question arose about whether future provision for consultants should be seen as a 'bid' or as maintenance of ongoing activities.

- Typewriter maintenance: this had been centralised but items in departmental budgets for this had not yet been identified and transferred to Management Services.

- Contingency Budget: to reduce the level of contingency items to a realistic level a central contingency budget was proposed from which certain types of unpredictable or occasional spending could be financed.

Investigations were to be undertaken into telephone costs, car allowances, centralised purchasing, charging of departments for work study/O & M and equity of provision to staff of training, conferences, clothing, uniforms, etc.

PART III WALES

15. Ceredigion District Council

DENNIS BALSOM

The over-riding feature of local government in Ceredigion is its
non-partisan character. This attribute affects all its processes and
deliberations and deeply permeates the political culture of the whole
area. Ceredigion remains one of the few genuine non-party authorities
and as such, serves as an 'ideal-type' to illustrate a particular
Welsh stereotype, familiar in caricature but nowadays, perhaps, more
rare in practice. To those involved and indeed for many of their
electors, this absence of party represents a higher order of politics.
The excesses of intense partisan rivalry, the nonsenses engendered
by bitter competition are removed and in their place come rational
argument, genuine debate and 'true' democracy. Other, less noticed
casualties, however, include party leadership, discipline, purpose,
unity, shared values and expectations. Writing in 1973, prior to
reorganisation, P.J.Madgwick noted of Cardiganshire, that:

> ...in the non-partisan situation, the elector looks to local
> government for personal services rather than the solution of major
> social problems. In accordance with this tradition the local
> councillor is seen not as a protagonist in a political conflict
> but rather as an intermediary protecting and promoting the
> interests of his constituents. (Madgwick 1973, p.180)

Madgwick anticipated that, with reorganisation, this traditional
style of politics would pass. To some extent, at the new county level
this has happened. Within Ceredigion (the former Cardiganshire)
traditional custom and practice persist.

Physical and Socio-Economic Environment

Ceredigion is a rural district on the West coast of Wales. It has a population of approximately 61,700, a land area of 179,000 hectares and thus a population density of 0.3 per hectare. The principal factors affecting population are migration, both outward in respect of rural depopulation and inward, particularly of those seeking retirement and others wishing to find an alternative 'life style'. 18.2 per cent of the population is aged 65 and over and approximately 65 per cent of the population is Welsh speaking.

Prior to local government reorganisation, the area that is now Ceredigion D.C. was constituted as Cardiganshire County Council. There has been no substantial boundary revision but the District Council had largely to assume the role and powers of the former boroughs, urban districts and rural districts, other functions being maintained at the new County level. Some evidence of these more diverse entities survives in local rivalries. Ceredigion now falls within the administrative county of Dyfed, along with the other Districts of Presceli, South Pembroke, Carmarthen, Llanelli and Dinefwr.

Ceredigion's principal industries remain agriculture and tourism, although there are major public sector employers such as two University Colleges, hospitals, a Royal Aircraft Establishment unit, local government itself and sizeable local offices of the Welsh Office, the Inland Revenue, etc. Unemployment is very high in the south of the district, 25 per cent in the area centred upon Cardigan and Lampeter. In the North, the area around Aberystwyth, the rate is 12 per cent.

The area is not prosperous, a weak commercial and industrial sector depresses the total rateable value to £5,164,000 and the product of a 1p rate is thus approximately £50,000. Ceredigion is also highly dependent upon grant aid. Of an expenditure of £3.88 million, grants constituted some £2.86 million, more than two-thirds. As such, income from rates forms a small part of the council's revenue, a mere 6 per cent of total expenditure.

Political Composition

As already noted, since reorganisation Ceredigion has been a non-partisan authority, as was Cardiganshire before it. The last round of elections in 1983 produced a Council of 28 Independents, 11 Alliance members (mostly Liberals), 2 Labour and 2 Plaid Cymru members. In this context, 'Independents' are genuinely independent and not surrogate Conservatives or Ratepayers. Members of all parties are found amongst councillors, indeed the 1983 Conservative Parliamentary candidate sits as an Independent on the Council but an independent ethos prevails and also characterises the behaviour of even nominally partisan councillors. The 43 councillors are elected from 35 wards, many with small rural electorates of less than 500. It is thus easily possible for the local councillor to know well every family in his ward, especially so after many years of being returned for the same district. In such circumstances, to be opposed at an election implies disrespect and if so challenged, the incumbent may well retire. Should such a challenge come from those seeking to politicise local government, however, it will inevitably be seen off by an appeal to the higher democratic values of the independent ethos. Many councillors have been members for many years and there are a high number of uncontested candidacies. This provides a good deal of stability in both representation and in the overall character of the Council (see Table 15.1). Not withstanding these factors, turn out in local elections remains high and immediately following reorganisation in 1973 exceeded 93 per cent. High turnout is undoubtedly partly a result of the low number of contested elections. The average age of councillors is high at around 65, and the members from the county districts are often hill farmers. There is little evidence of any caucussing; indeed every effort is made to avoid the charge of being party political. Leadership of the Council and the principal Committee chairmanships are distributed in rotation by seniority. Some care is given to balancing posts between representatives of the main geographical areas; Aberystwyth, Lampeter, Tregaron and Cardigan. Members espouse their particular local interests and officers are always keen to involve the local member on any specific local issue. This can, in effect, amount to a considerable position of influence for the local member regarding, say, planning applications or the siting of new Council housing projects.

Table 15.1

ELECTION RESULTS SINCE REORGANISATION

	Turn-Out %	Independents	Labour	Liberals (Alliance)	Plaid Cymru
1973	93.9	30	4	9	–
1976*	60.0	30	3	7	2
1979	81.2	30	4	7	2
1983		28	2	11	2

* one vacancy

The absence of party politics affects the structure of local politics in Ceredigion as well as determining its style. Councillors speak for their communities and respect the rights of their colleagues to do likewise. Such conventions make it difficult for a common sense of purpose to emerge and perpetuate attachment to locality. In this sense, the identities of the former boroughs and districts persist and remain perhaps stronger than any emergent sense of common identity. Only in the urban areas is there any tradition of party competition and even there, the non-party ethos is not entirely absent. Political recruitment and the relationship between elected and electors is based upon acquaintance. Once elected, even party councillors act as independents with no evidence of whipping or caucussing. Such concerted action as might emerge will combine the common concerns of a group of councillors from a particular district, or from similar wards, such as council estates, rather than around any sense of party loyalty or discipline. Again Madgwick's observation from 1973 remains relevant:

the intervention of party in recruitment and in the organisation of business would diminish the role of the councillor as an individual concerned for a 'parish', which is the Cardiganshire ideal. (1973, p.187)

In such circumstances, the collective sense of the authority is better represented by the officers of the Council than by the members themselves. Similarly the rotation of Chairmanships of both the Council and the principal service committees prevents individual senior councillors assuming particular responsibilities and acquiring a wider, collective sense of responsibility to the party, at least, if not to the community itself. In its absence, again it is the officers who, alone, have a clear sense of collective policy and direction.

All this is not to suggest that councillors are impotent or totally without influence. Indeed, freedom from party considerations considerably enhances the role of a 'backbench' member, who, by rote, in due course, will acquire chairmanships and senior positions. Their prepresentative function is not prejudiced by party affiliation, nor are their dealings with officers. An intervention on a policy issue thus becomes the personal advocacy of a local interest rather than an ideologically hidebound confrontation over policy. It is the Chief Officer within a particular policy area who aggregates demands rather than a party committee chairman, thus removing any dimension of programme making, electoral mandate or record of policy implementation from the electoral contest. Such considerations play a significant part in budgeting and will be discussed further below.

Although party loyalties may be shunned by individual councillors, there is an undoubted set of shared values which generally sustains a broad consensus within the authority. Foremost of such mores is perhaps that mentioned already, respect for the right of others to promote and defend their locality. On a broader level, however, the values of rural Wales provide cohesion. Most councillors are of a similar age generation, the majority are Welsh speaking, many are farmers or closely allied to the rural tradition of Ceredigion. A broad cultural consensus provides, perhaps, the cohesion that elsewhere would be provided by party. Furthermore, such cultural values are important in the appointment of Chief Officers and other staff. Professional and technical competence is clearly allied to cultural compatibility in the upper echelons of the authority. What is more, there exists in rural Wales a highly educated, professional middle class to fill such posts, whilst still sharing the cultural outlook of the traditional community.

Internal Organisation and Committee Structure

Following reorganisation, Ceredigion adopted in large measure the recommendations of the Bains Report. The authority is headed by a Chief Executive and is divided into five Directorates; Administration, Finance, Planning, Technical Services and Housing and Public Health. The Chief Executive and the five Directors constitute the 'management team' but this is an informal rather than an official internal committee. The authority does not have one central administrative headquarters: the Directors of Administration, Finance and the Chief Executive are located in Aberystwyth. The Director of Technical Services is located elsewhere in Aberystwyth, whilst the Directors of Planning and Public Health and Housing have offices in Aberaeron, some sixteen miles away. Council meetings are also held in Aberaeron which is approximately the mid point on the coast and is central to the district as a whole.

The committees are organised upon a largely functional basis with co-ordination and strategy being determined by a Policy and Resources Committee. The service committees are Amenities and Leisure, Housing Services, Planning and Development and Environmental Health, Licensing and Public Works. The Policy and Resources committee has three sub-committees: Finance, Land and Personnel. Work is structured around a six week cycle culminating in a full meeting of Council. In line with other District Councils in Wales, any necessary consultations or negotiations with the Welsh Office tend to be through the Welsh Association of District Councils (WADC) rather than bilateral. Several members of the Council and several officers are active on the various committees and panels of the WADC.

Again the non-partisan character of the authority affects the way in which committees function. The absence of permanent chairmen has been noted but also significant is the right of any member to attend any committee meeting. In this way local interests can always be safeguarded and a particular policy direction cannot be determined by the formal committee members alone. As there is no centralised headquarters building or offices, travelling to council and committee meetings also serves the function of enabling members to contact officers informally on neutral ground concerning local matters.

The 1985/6 Budgetary Cycle

The budgetary cycle leading to the annual rate settlement provides, perhaps, one of the few regular items of Committee business. The cycle commences with the announcement by the Welsh Office, in July, of its broad targets for the coming year. Notice of the Welsh Office guideline is incorporated in the directions from the Director of Finance to the various Departments for inclusion in the preparation of their draft Estimates. In a small community like Ceredigion, Finance Department officers assist in the preparation of Estimates but are not formally seconded to Departments. The cycle of presentation of Estimates to various Committees of Council began in November with the Estimates for Central Administration Departments. Once accepted by the Finance Sub-Committee, items under this head could then be reallocated to their various functional committees. These service Committees met in January to review Estimates for their own policy areas.

In nearly all instances, the draft Estimates were accepted without dissent or even comment. Usually the Director of Finance would introduce the item, detailing the Welsh Office guidelines, make a few general remarks concerning likely targets for wages, salaries and inflation but not deal in substance with the specific detail of the estimates. Likewise the Chief Officer responsible for the policy area under review rarely made any comment other than in the most general terms. Even where it was apparent that the growth envisaged in the Estimate was in excess of that likely to be permissible within the total budget, there was little comment. To a marked degree, the Estimates presented were not only the work of the officers concerned but genuinely 'their' budgets rather than those of the Committees. Because individual committees do not have particular policy goals, there is little sense of competing for a budget to meet particular objectives. Of course, Chief Officers doubtless have policy ambitions but these will be determined by their own definitions of managerial, professional and technical necessity. The bounds of such professional ambitions were inevitably broadly defined within the management team, thus the estimates brought to the service committee represent a fairly specific draft budget, agreed in principle by the Chief Executive and Director of Finance. Input from elected representatives appears to have been largely restricted to individual members, not necessarily of the relevant Committee, advancing claims for particular schemes and projects to be undertaken. Such representations are made throughout the year and naturally many will be queued for funds in the next financial year. Where these could not be included as 'policy' items, they were entered in the estimates as 'special' items but fully included, at this stage, for aggregate purposes. The draft budget then, including additional items of special concern, allows for a degree of flexibility pending the final availability of funds.

These processes were common to the submission of all Estimates to their relevant service committees, bar one: the Housing Services Committee. In respect of Housing, the service committee was required to take a decision regarding rent levels, rather than merely endorse the Estimates and pass them on to the Finance Sub-Committee. In this context perhaps the single genuine debate of the whole budgetary cycle occurred. The debate over rent levels was not overtly party political but between members representing predominantly council house estates (many of whom also sit as party councillors) and others less directly involved. The background was largely determined by the Welsh Office's decision to reduce housing subsidy for 1986/7 by the equivalent of 65p per dwelling. This adjustment alone would have required a rent increase of 4 per cent to make good. A second factor concerned the maintenance of a working balance in the Housing revenue account, the Director of Finance recommending a balance of £200,000. The committee was presented with these facts and 'offered' several options ranging from a 4 per cent rise, the minimum which would also completely deplete the balances, to a 10 per cent increase, the amount required to generate a balance of £200,000. Committee papers had been circulated a few days in advance and a good many members were present for this item. There was, however, no attempt to lead by the Chairman who appeared unbriefed as to the specifics of this particular item. The debate continued for some time and hinged essentially on the psychological barrier of raising rents by more than £1 per week, (6 per cent), as against the need to protect balances and not endanger the general rate account in future years. The Director of Finance's option 3, a 7 per cent rise, which would result in carrying over a balance of £106,000, was moved from the floor and carried by 18 votes to 11. At no point was the obvious connection between Welsh Office policy and the subsequent rent increase made. No one was defending a policy, a programme or a Government; no one was attacking a policy, a programme or a Government. A genuine decision was taken by the Council, the prior discussion had been lively and free of ideological dogma but the debate was essentially ill-informed, the voting spontaneous and without a good deal of prior thought and discussion; the members had merely that data which officers chose to give them and the options they had also determined. Undoubtedly a sensible and sound decision was taken, on this matter as on many others but the decision-making process appears to involve a number of highly random factors, not least the actions of the 'free-spirits' amongst the Independents and is highly susceptible to strong leadership by the Council's senior officials.

The officers always defend themselves against any such charge by reference to the fact that the support of no councillor can be taken for granted, it is not a party whip alone who needs to be persuaded of the merits of any case but a majority of 43 independent-minded members - the higher-order democracy argument. The antithesis, of course, is that, by the same argument, opposition to officer domination also needs to win the support of a majority of independent-minded members rather than merely a party caucus. It must be stated, with great emphasis, that no criticism of the officers is implied here. Indeed, for a small authority, there is every suggestion that Ceredigion has an extremely dedicated, professional and competent management team. The point is that 'good government' should not be largely dependent upon the vagaries of personnel appointments and the maintenance of high-calibre officials. Elected representatives cannot opt out of the serious financial management of the authority, no matter how complex such matters have become. The single most valuable aid to councillors in such circumstances would be the leadership, unity and purpose of party groupings on the Council and the pressing sense of responsibility engendered by being held to electoral account.

With the decision on council rents achieved, the remaining sequence of the budgetary cycle proceeded relatively uneventfully. The various Estimates, once approved by the relevant service committees, were aggregated for submission to the Finance Sub-Committee in order that a recommendation for a new rate levy could be made to Policy and Resources and hence to the full Council. The Finance Sub-Committee met on 5 February at 10.15 a.m. to consider an agenda of 20 items, item 19 being consideration of the draft Estimates for 1985/7 and item 20 A.O.B.. The Estimates item was reached at 3.45 p.m., a break having been taken where, as usual, members and officers lunch together. By then only four members remained in the chamber; the Chairman, Vice-Chairman and two others. The Director of Finance reported that the aggregated committee Estimates showed a 13 per cent growth in projected expenditure, whilst real cost inflation was 5.5 per cent. The Welsh Office allowance for inflation was only 3.4 per cent and the target growth figure was only 5 per cent in total. The projected budget of the Environmental Health, Licensing and Public Works Committee was up 14 per cent, Planning and Development up 8 per cent, Amenities and Leisure up 9 per cent, Finance up 19 per cent and Housing Services down 22 per cent, a total projected expenditure of £4,516,705. Through the system of Welsh Office targets and penalties for failure to meet targets, in order to meet such a proposed level of expenditure, rates would have had to be raised by 105.5 per cent, from 18p to 37p in the pound.

Such a course of action was considered by the officers to be untenable, therefore a package of further proposals was presented by the Director of Finance. The officers' actions were clearly endorsed by the (few) councillors left present, not necessarily on grounds of political expediency or acceptance of Government policy but by a primary motivation to maximise block grant and not fall foul of the grant penalty system. The Welsh Office block grant would be maximised at an expenditure level of £3,885,000. A strategy of efficiency measures, reduction in services and reduction of balances had therefore been drawn up by the management team prior to the Finance Sub-Committee meeting to meet this optimum level (see Table 15.2). The degree of leadership given by the officers is not only demonstrated

Table 15.2
EXPENDITURE PATTERNS AND RATE OPTIONS
(extracted from a document presented to the Finance Sub-Committee)

	Revised Estimates 1985/6	Estimate 1986/7	Options 1	2	3
Net expenditure	3806580	4446705	4446705	4446705	4446705
Sewage & Water Guarantees		70000			
Total	3806580	4516705	4446705	4446705	4446705
Fund transactions: To General Purposes	50000				
From General Purposes	-167380		-250000	-300000	-350000
Renewal & Repairs			-42950	-42950	-42950
Housing Revenue					
Eisteddfodau Fund					
Capital Fund	-100000		-70000	-70000	-70000
Sewage & Water Guarantee Fund	100000		70000	70000	70000
Total Expenditure	3689200	4516705	4153755	4103755	4053755
Required Savings			-268755	-218755	-168755
	3689200	4516705	3885000	3885000	3885000
Less Block Grant	-2665000	-2675680	-2861000	-2861000	-2861000
	1005370	1841025	1024000	1024000	1024000
Adjustment of Balances	-106270	0	-122200	-72100	-22000
Total	899100	1841025	901800	951900	1002000
1p Rate Produce	49950	50100	50100	50100	50100
Rate for District Council Purposes	18	37	18	19	20
% Increase in District Rate Levy		105.5%	0%	5.5%	11%

by the absence of most members from this meeting but also by the position taken up by the Chairman. He had been briefed 24 hours earlier by the Director of Finance but was more than willing to allow the Director effectively to dominate the meeting. No particular judgement is implied here. The Director of Finance has a considerable reputation in local government financial matters and indeed leads for the WADC in negotiations with the Welsh Office on financial matters. Doubtless his advice was sound and well-founded but the political responsibility for such decisions was almost wholly abrogated.

Fund transactions, switching of balances and depletion of reserves achieved the necessary reduction of expenditure. A profit recorded by the Direct Labour Organisation of £50,000 was switched from the Housing Revenue Account to the general rate fund, this profit having accrued from the DLO's tenders won in competition with the private sector. This left between £268,755 and £168,755 to be found through cuts and savings, the exact amount being dependent, of course, upon the level of rate the committee wished to recommend. Almost inevitably the middle course was chosen, the prepared option 2 and again the officers were able to produce a schedule of proposed cuts sufficient to achieve the required savings and already approved by the management team. These savings included the deletion of some 'special' items from the estimates, transfer of other expenditures to the capital budget and delay in purchasing vehicles but the package was primarily dependent upon a saving of £98,000 in salaries being made. This saving in administrative costs would be achieved by freezing posts and in delaying the appointment of replacements. The savings package was totally initiated by the officers and there was no evidence of political priorities being determined in any other way than a general perception, by the officers, of what the Council would wish to see happen. The Finance Sub-Committee therefore drafted a recommendation to the Policy and Resources Committee that the rate for 1986/7 be set at 19p in the pound, a 5.5% increase over the previous year.

The following day, the statutory meeting with representatives of Commercial and industrial ratepayers was held. All Chambers of Trade in the district and the National Federation of the Self Employed had been invited. In the event, five people were present. The background to the draft budget was explained and the proposed increases declared. Minor representations were made by those present, the NFSE delegate making perhaps the only substantive and highly political appeal but recognising all the while 'that nothing could be done this year'. The meeting presented a fait accompli to those outside interests who, in turn, indulged in a limited amount of role playing, the greatest point of contention being the recently announced proposed level of expenditure by the County Council. This, taken together with Ceredigion's proposed budget, gave an 18.05 per cent increase in domestic rates to 201.4p and 16.3 per cent to commercial and industrial ratepayers at 219.9p, plus whatever precept was imposed by the relevant community councils. The affairs of the County Council were clearly beyond the remit of Ceredigion but the District Council did postpone its formal rate making Council meeting pending late negotiations between the Welsh Office and the Welsh counties regarding grant aid. In the even the Dyfed increase was held to 14.4 per cent and the rate levy for Ceredigion residents to 196.3p plus the community council precept, on average 5p.

Following the statutory commercial ratepayers consultation, the draft rate proposals were submitted to the Policy and Resources Committee. Details of the package were approved, the DLO was congratulated on its performance, as too, were the Director of Finance and his staff. The committee Estimates, and associated package of proposals and cuts, were accepted virtually without comment save for some bewildered admiration of the Director of Finance's 'creative accounting' procedures. The Director of Finance gave notice that balances could not be raided in perpetuity but that sufficient reserves had accrued to allow broadly similar strategies to be maintained for two further years. He advised against such a course however, on the ground that upon final depletion there would then be an excessively large shortfall of revenue over expenditure, necessitating a dramatic rate increase. The Director suggested that members might like to note the desirability of avoiding such erratic action. A senior councillor, much involved in WADC work, endorsed the Director's comments and proposed that a performance review body be created

> ...to review the work of the Programme Committees; to review the effectiveness of all the Council's work and standards and levels of service provided; to identify the need for new service and to keep under review the necessity of existing services.

This matter had not been raised in collusion with the Director of Finance but had been a particular 'hobby horse' of the member concerned for many years. There followed some discussion as to how this body might be operationalised, general support was lukewarm and a distaste for further committees and a greater workload was evident. The recent outside investigations of the Audit Commission into some of the Council's activities were referred to and their general level of approval of the Council's good housekeeping was cited as evidence of there being little need for too formal a review structure. Finally, it was concluded that the Performance review would be undertaken by the Policy and Resources Committee, meeting in special sessions, for a trial period of one year. Subsequent discussions revealed many to be sceptical of the potential of such a body. Although not articulated as such, this must inevitably be the case when it has no firm mandate from the Council, the Chairman or even its membership, other than a blanket moral obligation to secure value for money for the public and to maintain the professional standards advocated by the officers.

The formal rate making session of the Council was postponed seven days until 12 March, because of last minute renegotiation of the County precept but when convened the proposed levy was passed almost without comment. Throughout the final stages of the budgetary cycle, many members had muttered remarks concerning the forthcoming elections and how this might ameliorate their position and ease their discomfort at the actions they were being forced to take. They were of course referring to a forthcoming general election and the possibility of a change of government, rather than to their own pending re-election in May 1987.

Conclusion

The greatest likely contrast between local government practice in Ceredigion with that in many other localities, is its very heavy dependence upon Government funds. Its remote, rural location exacerbates the weakness of its revenue base whilst in turn creating demands upon its resources. The long coastline and associated protection works, as well as provision for a highly seasonal tourist market, serve as examples of demands that go beyond those of most modestly sized authorities. The non-partisan character of the authority is all-pervasive and this too is perhaps appropriate for an area with no real manufacturing base, no commuters and no tradition of class politics. Ceredigion is archetypically rural Welsh, proud and covetous of its traditions. Its political culture is community based, communities which are long established, many with stable if ageing populations. Inter-personal relations remain important and act as a mechanism of community and cultural defence in safeguarding the old order as well as demonstrating a solidarity to the world. Political parties, being founded on difference, have no apparent place. Local government and the Council act as a forum for the community, and their spokesmen. "...for many Councillors the motivations and rewards are those of community service and a prestigious hobby". (Madgwick 1973, p.182).

The growing complexity of local government finance, the deeper involvement of central government in the management of local authorities, the growing uniformity of service standards and provision have all, perhaps, created conditions with which such small but genuinely representative authorities, will have difficulty in coping. The high calibre of the staff attracted to work for Ceredigion has already been noted and in many cases clear cultural aspirations are being served as well as those dictated by any professional calling. Ceredigion remains relatively well run and managed because in many respects it remains central to the community as a whole. The authority is no mere bureaucracy or appendage to the local economy but very much part of society at large. As a major employer in the area, the local authority has a presence far greater than its budget would suggest and perhaps enjoys a degree of deference unusual nowadays. As the community remains largely homogeneous, so too does the Council and its officers. Custom and practice remain the guiding principles rather than any party programme. In such a way the community acts and stands together but also inevitably, in a rapidly changing political world, sometimes alone.

16. Mid-Glamorgan County Council

PAUL GRIFFITHS

The objective is to provide an analysis of the budgetary process of Mid-Glamorgan County Council as it created the budget for 1986/7. It is necessary to select criteria in which to locate that analysis. Budgetary processes may have their stress placed on the following criteria:

- 'Control Orientation' or 'Policy Orientation' (Schick, 1966)

- 'Incremental' or 'Strategic' (Greenwood, 1983)

- 'Rational' or 'Political' (Wildavsky, 1966)

Where Control Orientation is stressed the main purpose of the budget is to establish and maintain limits on the organisation's expenditure. The budget is presented as a list of resource inputs which can be used as means of continuous budgetary control. Every budget has a control orientation, the interest is in the extent to which it is supplemented with a Policy Orientation - a mechanism for employing the budget as a vehicle for the policy choice of employing resources for alternative ends.

Incremental budgetary processes are typified by the assumption that policy choice is limited to a narrow margin of activity and to a short time scale. A Strategic budgetary process considers a time scale greater than just the next financial year and creates a relatively wide margin of choice.

A Rational budgetary process is based on the assumption that the choice of allocating resources can be fully resolved by comparing the quantitative measures of marginal costs and benefits of alternative activities. A Political budgetary process stresses that whilst choice may be informed by analysis, it also requires the resolution of competing values.

There is a temptation to create a neat dichotomy through such conceptual analysis: political, incremental, control orientated – negative; rational, strategic, policy orientated - positive. The world is more complex. Necessarily each criteria appears in some part of each budgetary process, but with different stresses. Moreover each organisation will create some unique matrix of the various criteria.

In summary, this case study of Mid-Glamorgan will describe an intended budgetary process of remarkable ambition – policy orientated, strategic and rational. It will also describe how the intention became thwarted by events through processes which were political, incremental and control orientated.

The Context

The 1974 reorganisation left Mid-Glamorgan with a distinctive geography. Nationally the reorganisation absorbed the county borough urban centres into their counties. In Glamorgan the deep conservatism of vested interests ensured that the county boroughs maintained their status: Swansea became the basis for West-Glamorgan, Cardiff the basis for South-Glamorgan. This left Mid-Glamorgan as a primarily urban county with no urban centre. It has no town with a population of over 40,000. Its administrative centre remains in Cardiff in the neighbouring county of South Glamorgan.

The County is of two distinct parts. To the North there are the valleys typified by the Rhondda. Half of the 536,000 population live in these dense Victorian settlements. Their rapid creation resulted from the former employment of 140,000 men in 230 collieries. Now there are fewer than 10,000 men working in 14 collieries and the immediate future is still bleaker. The valley's population is rapidly ageing and declining. It suffers disproportionately from the County's high rate of unemployment of 19 per cent. In contrast, in the South of the County there is the emerging 'M4 Corridor'. In this area the economy grew and diversified in the 1970's to include new manufacturing units for Ford and Sony, a High Technology/Science Park and several out-of-town retailing sites. The growth of population in the South more than compensates for the decline in the North.

Politically the County has been dominated by the Labour Party continuously since 1919. That domination is now as complete as ever. Currently, Labour has 68 of the 83 seats. Plaid Cymru has 6 seats, Independent 5, Liberal 2, Communist 1, Conservative 1. The Opposition on the Council is numerically small, disparate and with no policy agenda of its own.

The Welsh political culture has never easily tolerated internal dissent and opposition. It thrives on the creation of external symbolic dragons - the English, the Tories, the Church of England, Twickenham. Thereupon it demands a consensus imposed by the authority of internal elites. Dissent is regarded with disdain Neil Kinnock learned his style of leadership in the South Wales valleys. The impact of this culture on Mid-Glamorgan County Council is clear. The Opposition Parties are hardly regarded as legitimate. Debate is confined to the

Labour Group. In the unlikely and rare event of debate spilling over into Committee, the Council has been so organised to ensure that all substantive agendas are given to sub-committees and that opposition members are excluded from sub-committees. In addition the positive cultural values given to authority and leadership discourage any public debate within the Labour Group itself. In many English urban centres a dominant Labour Party lives by faction, particularly as the participation of middle class professionals has created various ideological debates. Small town Mid-Glamorgan has few middle class professionals. In the Mid-Glamorgan Labour Group there are no significant factions that one can identify as left and right, young or old. The relationships between the council leadership, other councillors and Labour Party members are ones of deference and patronage. With no acceptable means of challenge and succession, the leadership is elderly. It has been compared to the Kremlin, but that is now an unfair comparison. Intra-party disputes in so far as they do emerge are based in the main on geographical ward-based interests and committee loyalties.

Relationships between officers and members are close but highly centralised to those of committee chairmen and departmental directors. The shared aim of these relationships is the protection of departmental interests. There has been no 'corporate revolution' in Mid-Glamorgan. Coordinating institutions of 'County Clerk and Coordinator', 'Management Team' and 'General Purposes Committee' do exist but whenever their role is discussed the primacy of service based organisation is adamantly stressed. Members have identified departmental hierarchy with centralised political control and perceive cross-departmental institutions as officer evasions of that control.

Background to the 1986/7 Budget

Before reporting the process of determining the 1986/7 budget an analysis will be provided of the main themes of previous budgets, with reference to both aggregate and allocative trends.

In 1985/6 Revenue Expenditure was estimated at £220.7 million. In real terms this has been a virtually constant figure since 1980. In comparative terms this figure of total expenditure is high. In 1982/3 it represented £399 per head of population, comparing with an English county average of £349 and a Welsh county average of £377. The Welsh Office believes that Mid-Glamorgan's expenditure is high in absolute terms. In 1984/5 the County's expenditure was 6.5 per cent over GRE and 4.1 per cent over 'Target'. In 1985/6 expenditure was 0.8 per cent over 'Target'. The targets set by the Welsh Office were more predictable than those set by the Department of Environment being determined by a set formula that gives a weighting of 60 per cent to GRE and 40 per cent to the past two years' actual expenditure. Nevertheless the Welsh Office's own statistics for the determination of GRE point to Mid-Glamorgan's high need for expenditure. In the GRE Assessment the Welsh Office employs 35 indices. Only 5 of these indices do not award Mid-Glamorgan the highest need to spend in Wales and those 5 are calculated with reference to a sparse population, road mileage and coastal length - they are the rural factors. It is to the chagrin of Mid-Glamorgan that these few rural factors are heavily weighted, reflecting the electoral interests of the present Welsh Office incumbents and the disproportionate rural representation

216

on the Welsh Counties Committee. In 1985/6 67 per cent of Mid-Glamorgan's revenue expenditure was financed by the Welsh Office Block Grant. This figure has fallen in recent years; in 1978/9 the Grant contribution was 73 per cent. Nevertheless in comparison with English local authorities it is a very high figure and the rate of decrease has been low. Part of the explanation for this contrast lies in the fact that rateable values are low in Mid-Glamorgan, as they are in Wales generally.

The allocation of expenditure to the various county services lies at the core of this study. Table 16.1 provides some of the historical background to this allocation.

Table 16.1

CHANGES IN SERVICE COSTS 1974/5 - 1984/5

Service	Estimates 1985/6 £'000	% of Total 1984/5	% of Total 1974/£
Education	140,292	63.5	69.5
Social Services	27,767	12.5	10.2
Highways and Transportation	18,591	8.4	8.4
Precept of Police Authority	14,378	6.5	5.1
Fire	7,425	3.4	3.0
Planning	1,402	0.6	1.0
Economic Development & Employment	1,094	0.5	0.04
Contingency	4,640		
Other	5,125		
TOTAL	220,714		

In the above data the annual costs of capital expenditure are absorbed into the figure for each service. The expenditure for 1985/6 can be represented in the following way:

Current Expenditure	£182m.
Annual Cost of Capital Expenditure	£23m.
Precepts to other Authorities	£16m.

Mid-Glamorgan has an established policy of financing, whenever possible, all its capital expenditure from current revenue. The Group Leadership has had a long term commitment to this policy. In the case of the Leader, he claims that the commitment goes back to 1937 when he pioneered an internal Capital Fund for the Penybont Rural District Council. Mid-Glamorgan has established an internal Capital Fund to organise the transfer of revenue into capital finance. In 1985/6 the Council, against the advice of the Treasurer and the Group Leader, broke this policy in order to limit the rate increase. For the £17 million capital expenditure it agreed to borrow £3 million. One member described this borrowing as a clear example of devious 'creative accounting'!

The most significant trend in the allocation of expenditure over the last decade has been the decrease in the allocation to education which is associated with the decrease in school population which is currently taking place at the rate of one per cent p.a.. The main beneficiary of this trend has been social services which has had an increasing proportion of the Authority's expenditure. The other services to gain increasing proportions of expenditure are the fire service and economic development. There has been an increasing proportion on police expenditure but this is the decision of the South Wales Police Authority, which covers the three Glamorgans. In Wales it has not been possible, as it is in England, to compare an Authority's budgetary allocation with the individual service Targets announced by Central Government for each Authority. The Welsh Office has declared that to set such service targets would undermine the proper role of each Authority in determining its priorities.

The Changing Environment for 1986/7

The Treasurer forecast an internal rate of inflation for the Authority for the coming year of 7.3 per cent. This figure was based on the wage settlements for manual workers and teachers, net changes in increments, changing superannuation regulations and a policy of limiting borrowing to £1 million. The financing of capital expenditure became a major issue in the budgetary process. It was exacerbated late in the process by the generosity of the Welsh Office in increasing by 30 per cent the County's allocation for capital expenditure from £17 million to £22 million. Fortunately at this late stage the Treasurer found that the debate on borrowing need not be re-opened if some Polytechnic buildings were sold and grants were forthcoming from the European Regional Development Fund.

The other factors known early in the budget process are related to the Welsh Office policy on Rate Support Grant announced on 25 July, 1985. 67 per cent of relevant expenditure was to continue to be met by grant. Relevant expenditure was increased by 5 per cent. As in England the target system was modified. In the words of the Secretary of State for Wales it was to be replaced by a "tough new system which will encourage authorities to restrain their expenditure". The important figure in this new arrangement is that of 'Threshold'. Expenditure above this figure will result in grant loss in a way that will insure that a one per cent increase in expenditure results in a five per cent increase in rate precepts. The Threshold figure is directly related to GREA, being 10 per cent above a newly defined, and diminished, GREA. For Mid-Glamorgan the Threshold was defined as £230 million, which compared with the Authority's assessment of £237 million as the cost of maintaining services. The net effect of these arrangements was the prediction that a 'standstill budget' would lead to a 14 per cent rate increase, a £2 million (one per cent) cut would lead to 10 per cent rate increase, a £5 million (two per cent) cut would lead to a 5 per cent rate increase. It is interesting to compare these calculations by the County Treasurer with the press release of the Secretary of State in which it is stated that "the allowance for the growth in both spending and grant is broadly in line with inflation. This being so, if rates next year rise on average by more than inflation this can only be due to excessive and unacceptable growth in expenditure" (Welsh Office, 25.7.85).

Zero-Base Budgeting

In the first two months of 1985 the Management Team discussed and reappraised its budgetary process. The Treasurer perceived two problems with the existing approach. First, there was no 'fundamental' review of the allocation between departments and therefore budgetary developments had been too 'incremental'. Secondly, budgetary allocations had taken insufficient note of their service implications. The Management Team decided to form a 'Budget Advisory Group' (BAG) of chosen officers with the brief of introducing a system of 'Zero Base Budgeting'. This unfortunate phrase has caused much misunderstanding in Mid-Glamorgan and elsewhere. In the pioneering ZBB attempts in the State of Georgia, the base was assumed to be 85 per cent of current expenditure. Mid-Glamorgan took the same baseline but several participants were concerned that this was not the real thing as the base was not zero.

The seven member Budget Advisory Group consisted in the main of second and third tier officers who did not necessarily represent major spending interests and who, in the nature of this Authority, were distanced from member relationships. The creation of BAG was purely an officer initiative. When, after the event, leading members were informed of its existence, they acknowledged it and asked for direct reporting of its work.

BAG was set a remarkably ambitious set of objectives and timescale:

MARCH   - Formation of BAG.

APRIL   - Request for all Departments to submit a statement of their priorities at a 15 per cent margin of current expenditure.

MAY   - Receipt of Departmental Statements. BAG interviews Departmental Teams.

JUNE   - BAG analyses departmental priorities at the 15 per cent margin and reports a recommendation for expenditure allocation at 95 per cent of current expenditure. This recommendation to be reviewed and agreed by the Management Team and General Purposes Committee.

JULY   - BAG continues analysis of Departmental priorities.

AUGUST   - BAG recommends expenditure allocations at the following proportions of current expenditure: 100.5%, 100%, 99.5%, 99%. 98.5%, 98%.

AUGUST   - Management Team and General Purpose Committee review and agree the second BAG Report.

SEPTEMBER   - In the light of RSG announcement General Purposes to agree aggregate expenditure level and in the light of the BAG Report to agree departmental allocations - the 'budget strategy'. Recommended budget strategy agreed by Full Council.

219

OCT/NOV   – Departments to prepare detailed estimates in the light of the BAG Report and the budget strategy.

OCTOBER   – Preliminary external consultation.

DEC/JAN   – Service Committees review and agree departmental estimates.

FEBRUARY   – Final external consultation.

FEBRUARY   – Budget and Rate Precept agreed by Full Council.

Although there were deviations to the above planned timetable, it was remarkable the extent to which it was adhered to.

Most of the initial work was undertaken by the departments. They responded to the request by BAG to provide details of their 15 per cent margin of activity and prioritisation of that margin within 5 per cent bands. The creation of data, necessarily a deconcentrated activity, is the foundation upon which any budgetary process may be built. It is worth dwelling on the successes and problems of this part of the ZBB exercise.

–   Several departments welcomed the stimulus to an exercise of internal self-appraisal. Teams of officers, who may not have previously been involved in a budget process, undertook and were motivated by a systematic review of their department's activities. In the main the analysis was genuine. There were few obvious examples of the 'sore thumb' and 'fairy gold' bargaining tactics that have undermined other budgetary processes. (Glenester 1981). The required scale of the analysis may have made such tactics difficult.

–   Many ZBB exercises have foundered in a morass of standardised forms. (Cheek 1979). Mid-Glamorgan avoided this pit-fall. In contrast the exercise was, in this first attempt, ill-prepared. The instructions to departments were vague and limited. The responses varied widely in their scope of analysis and style of presentation. The most common error was to perceive the exercise as one of hypothetical 'cuts' rather than as an exercise of evaluating departmental and corporate priorities. When this was the case the margin was defined as X jobs or Y institutions, rather than their associated policies and outcomes.

–   Problems were caused by the traditional incremental process of bargaining through bids of 'committed growth'. It was not clearly pointed out to departments that in a ZBB exercise high priority growth items could and should be based well within the margin of activity, displacing existing policies. The expectation of departments was that existing activity could be prioritised and committed growth then added on.

Once BAG received the Departmental responses they arranged to interview members of the Department. They sought and often received fuller and clearer information. Ultimately, however, BAG members had to decide what to do with the information. The challenge had to be one of deciding whether the marginal activities of one department were of greater value than the marginal activities of another. No matter how little or great the indication of policy output, usually it was little, it was bound to be a matter of applying values and judgement. Once the nature of the challenge was more clearly recognised several BAG members developed fright. Far from seeking to dominate political issues, when these leading officers faced real political choices they drew back. Refuge was sought in Audit Commission comparisons but none was found. Insight was sought from the Expenditure White Paper which hypothecated allocations to local government services throughout Wales. This could not be made clearly relevant to Mid-Glamorgan. In contrast to the English experience, there were no Welsh Office targets for each of the County's services.

In June BAG agreed the first report which was now to go to the General Purposes Committee. The requirement was to report on the character of a 'baseline' budget at 95 per cent of current expenditure. BAG reported that on all the evidence received such a hypothetical budget could only be conceived as a pro-rata 5 per cent cut for all departments. The justification was that the evidence proved that no department could tolerate such a cut without a serious loss of service. The report was a 'cop-out'. At this stage BAG did not collectively have the stomach for comparing major programmes of one department with another. Moreover, given the hypothetical nature of the exercise, was it worth the effort?

By August the second report had to be prepared. This would identify spending patterns for levels of expenditure from 98 per cent to 100.5 per cent of existing expenditure. Now real decisions would have to be made. The exercise became a lot more palatable when the suggestion was made that the 0.5 per cent growth option was discussed first. This option was particularly interesting to discuss because given the 1 per cent drop in the school population the most one could award the education budget even in the growth option was a standstill. The question was which department should benefit. The obvious candidate was Social Services which had argued strongly that with increasing unemployment, deprivation and an ageing population it alone had a claim for growth. Moreover the Expenditure White Paper had prioritised Social Services and hypothecated real increases in expenditure. The counter-argument was that social service expenditure per head in Mid-Glamorgan was already higher than in comparator Authorities, and that the Department did not have the best record in managing growth. BAG accepted the case for social services. The £1 million (0.5 per cent) growth option allocated no change for education, a 1 per cent growth for most departments and a 2.2 per cent growth for social services. In devising the other options BAG decided that its priorities had been determined in the growth option and that therefore one needed to work backwards on a pro-rata basis from the growth option. Thus Social Services maintained a £$\frac{1}{4}$ million growth at a standstill budget and small growth at a budget cut of £1 million. The theory of Zero-Base Budgeting had been reversed. The effective base line had been the allocation for £1 million growth.

In August the Management Team discussed the BAG Report. Crucially, the Treasurer opposed the priority accorded to Social Services. The Director of Education proposes that any cuts should be pro-rata across the Departments. There is substantial support for such a proposition. Ultimately the Chief Officers report to General Purposes that they have "major reservations" and "could not endorse its conclusions".

Table 16.2

THE BUDGET OPTIONS

	[1] 1985/6 Budget	[2] £1m Growth Budget	[3] Less Reduction	[4] Stand-Still Budget	[5] Less Pro-Rata Reduction	[6] £1m Savings Budget
Education	129,575	+ 47	-513	-466	-760	-1,226
Social Services	24,642	+545	-306	+239	-145	+ 94
Highways/ Transport	14,004	+125	-125	-	- 82	- 82
Fire	5,842	+ 6	-	+ 6	-	+ 6
Accommodation	1,763	- 48	-	- 48	-	- 48
Treasurer's	1,731	+ 28	- 28	-	- 10	- 10
Clerk's	1,135	+ 17	- 17	-	-	-
Land/Buildings	1,002	- 11	-	- 11	-	- 11
Planning	815	+ 3	- 3	-	-	-
Consumer Protection	542	+ 10	- 6	+ 4	- 3	+ 1
Supplies	471	+ 2	- 2	-	-	-
Economic Dev.	410	+ 22	-	+ 22	-	+ 22
Superannuation	-	+250	-	+250	-	+ 250
	182,088	+1,000	+1,000	-	-1,000	-1,000

In September the General Purposes Committee receive the BAG Report along with a detailed report of the Treasurer which explains the precept implications of different levels of expenditure. At this stage Labour members have no wish to publicly debate the Reports and there are no opposition members on the General Purposes Committee to initiate a debate. The reports are taken to the Labour Group and there is a deafening public silence for the next three months. Within the Group there is debate on the need for any 'cuts' and the level of external financing. The leadership is firmly committed to maintaining a firm limit on external financing and is willing to tolerate a cut in service provision to ensure this. Ultimately the recommendations of the leadership are accepted by a majority within the Labour Group:

- Total Expenditure of £238 million, 7.8 per cent above the previous year, 8 per cent above 'Threshold',

- £1 million 'cut' in service provision,

- £1 million external financing,

- 10.7 per cent rate increase.

These Group decisions are ratified by meetings of General Purposes and Full Council in November. The extent of the Group divide is illustrated by the unprecedented vote by 11 Labour members against the recommendations. In the nature of Mid-Glamorgan these members have since been disciplined.

In the tradition of local government the heated debate in Group concerned the aggregate figures. BAG and the ZBB exercise was concerned with allocative figures. Having decided on a £1 million 'cut' the Labour Group looked to the BAG Report. They found the summary of analysis and recommendations presented in Table 16.2 above.

Column [2] was the BAG Baseline, its allocation for £1 million growth. Column [3] illustrated the chosen reductions from the growth option to achieve the standstill option – Column [4]. Column [5] illustrates the pro-rata reductions chosen to move from the standstill option to the recommendations for £1 million savings – Column [6].

The Labour Group formally accepted the BAG Report. But when the decision of the Group emerged as a recommendation to the General Purposes Committee the Group had committed itself to Column [5], merely figures inserted for means of illustrating the calculation, i.e. instead of the recommended Column [6]. The Group was now committed to pro-rata reductions instead of the re-ordering of priorities recommended by BAG. Instead of the recommended shift of priorities to social services from education, education was protected and suffered less cuts than that which the Authority had previously agreed was justified by falling rolls. The effect of this substitution of columns was to make the whole of the BAG analysis entirely redundant.

There are two explanations for this mis-use of the report. Some members simply did not understand the presentation of the data by BAG. Given the lack of debate in Committee and the lack of access to officers in the Group, Mid-Glamorgan is an illustration of how closed government can become muddled and misinformed. Some senior members were aware of the way they were manipulating the Report. They were committed to protecting education. They were not persuaded by the case for increasing the priority accorded to social services. These members had every right to over-ride the BAG analysis with their values and experience but not to justify their value judgements by claiming to accept a report they were wholly rejecting.

Conclusions

It is now possible to relate this case study to the criteria for analysis given in the introduction. The ambition of this budgetary process was remarkable. The ZBB process of undertaking such a broad appraisal of priorities put the stress firmly on a 'policy orientation'. The relatively wide margin of analysis, 15 per cent of previous expenditure, made the intention 'strategic' rather than 'incremental'. There was no intention of involving members in the process of analysis. The assumption was, therefore, of a 'rational' rather than 'political' budgetary process.

The ambitions were not achieved despite a great deal of endeavour and valuable analysis within parts of the organisation. By both design and accident, the members rejected the exercise in assessing priorities. They imposed a pro-rata cut across the organisation. Their objective was solely that of a 'control orientation'. The Group was content with incremental change as the easiest way of maintaining a consensus. In Mid-Glamorgan there is a clear separation between the deliberations of officers and members. In the end the rationalist aspiration of the officers was over-ridden by the conservative political values of the members.

The stark contrast between intention and result requires explanation. Haynes (1981) argues that organisational change requires planned innovation in three areas - procedural, structural and cultural. Procedurally the changes were hurried and poorly communicated. There was a mechanistic, top-down assumption that a centralised decision would automatically be implemented. Structurally, new channels of communication and negotiation were needed. The rationalist assumptions were always naive. An exercise of analysing priorities needed the involvement and understanding of members. Because of the structural divide between officers and members, other than that hierarchically achieved through Directors there was no means of creating the necessary understanding and support among members. The greatest obstacle was undoubtedly cultural. The cultural values within the organisation support a closed and centralised policy process. This excludes the wide debate that is required to create any shifts of consensus. Such a culture cannot create, or test through open questionning, the wide understanding that is necessary for innovation. A culture which creates expectations of a severe concentration of authority does not easily accommodate innovation.

It is tempting to regard this as a case-study concerning the failure of innovation but that would be to disregard the many lessons to be learned from the attempts at self-appraisal that did take place within the Authority. Nevertheless, it is appropriate to conclude by reporting that Mid-Glamorgan County Council has now abandoned the process of Zero Base Budgeting.

PART IV
NORTHERN IRELAND

17. Belfast City Council

MICHAEL CONNOLLY AND RAY MCCHESNEY

Introduction

The budgetary process in Belfast City Council is governed by a set of circumstances which are unique to local government in Northern Ireland. Fundamental differences in the political, financial and structural arrangements of the Province's 26 district councils ensure that the task of preparing annual budgets is substantially different from that found elsewhere in the United Kingdom.

In particular, local authorities in Northern Ireland operate with fewer executive responsibilities and in a context of considerable political tension compared with authorities in the rest of the United Kingdom. An examination of the budgetary process in Belfast, the largest of the councils, offers an opportunity to explore the impact of these factors upon local authority budgeting.

Context

Prior to 1973, local government in Northern Ireland operated on a multi-tier system in which Belfast City Council was an all purpose authority providing a full range of those activities traditionally associated with major local govenment providers. Following the passage of the Local Government Act (N.I.) 1972 distinctions between authorities were removed and 26 district councils were set up to provide a limited number of services. (Birrell & Murie, 1980).

This reform of local administration was influenced by a variety of factors including administrative developments elsewhere in the United Kingdom, and a local concern to improve the efficiency of service delivery. However, a major consideration was the criticism that service delivery was not equitable and that there was an alleged political bias built into the structure of the system. As a result, a number of decisions were taken in the late 1960s and early 1970s which removed executive responsibility for housing, personal social services, health, education and planning from local government and transferred them to non-elected area boards, public agencies or government departments. (Birrell & Murie 1980).

Hence, local authorities in the Province were left with few executive functions. These include:

(a) various regulatory services, for example the licensing of cinemas and dance halls, building regulations and health inspection;

(b) provision of a limited range of services including street cleaning, refuse collection and disposal, burial grounds and crematoria, public baths, recreation facilities and tourist amenities.

Additionally the 1972 Act provides that local authorities may grant-aid local organisations concerned with the economic development of the district (Section 107) and spend a very limited amount on non-specific services (Section 115).

As well as these executive functions the Macrory Report (1970) [1], which formed the basis of the 1972 Act, argued that local government had three further functions, namely ceremonial, representative and consultative.

Ceremonial functions refer to the dignities and ceremonial traditionally attached to local government, such as allowing local authorities to become boroughs, with the chairmen of the council being entitled to be called mayor.

By **representative functions** Macrory meant that local councillors should be represented on relevant bodies so as "to express views on the provision and operation of ... public services in their area". [2]

For example, the education and library service is administered through five education and library boards with 40 per cent of the board members being local councillors appointed by the Department of Education (N.I.) following nomination by their respective councils. A similar system exists for the health and personal social services, except that there are only four area boards and the percentage of councillor membership is 30 per cent.

Consultative functions, i.e. the district councils should be consulted on matters of "general national interest". [3] In addition, councils are consulted on matters which are the responsibility of central government but which affect their area, for example planning applications, housing and roads.

This radical reform of local government has greatly affected local authority budgeting. In particular, the removal of high spending activities from local government control has drastically reduced the size of local authority budgets. It could also be hypothesised that the reduction of functions has decreased the degree of complexity in decision-making. We might therefore expect to find in Belfast a budgetary process which involves a high reliance on past experience and a low reliance on techniques such as zero-based budgeting.

The nature and role of local authority politics is substantially different from that found in Great Britain. The national political parties are not represented locally. Instead party politics within the Province largely gravitate around attitudes to the continuance of union with Great Britain with politics characterised by a high degree of pluralism. Unionist parties support the maintenance of the link with Britain. Unionism provides the basis for parties such as the Official Unionist Party (OUP) and the Democratic Unionist Party (DUP). Nationalists who favour unification with the Irish Republic may express their desire by voting for the Social Democratic and Labour Party (SDLP) or Sinn Fein (SF) – the political wing of the Provisional Irish Republican Army. Party competition tends to be **within** unionism or nationalism and not between the two groups.

Thus the main rival of the OUP is the DUP, while Sinn Fein is the main rival of the SDLP. Moderate opinion in the Province is represented by the Alliance Party (AP) whose fortunes tend to fluctuate in direct relation to the stability of the local political scene.

Local government elections are conducted using the Single Transferable Vote system of Proportional Representation – a method which ensures minority representation of councils and, as we shall see, has a bearing on the composition of local authority committees. It also tends to produce councils, including Belfast, where no single party has an outright majority, with the result that bargaining and negotiation between parties is an essential feature. In addition, there appears some evidence that where individual councillors tend to be concerned about their own position, this can involve competition with party colleagues. These issues will be explored later in the paper.

In all there have been four local government elections since 1973, the results of which can be seen in Table 17.1 below.

Table 17.1

COUNCIL SEATS HELD BY POLITICAL PARTIES IN BELFAST

	Official Unionist	DUP	Alliance	SDLP	Rep. Clubs	Sinn Fein	NILP	Others	Total
1973	25	2	8	7	2	–	2	5	51
1977	16	7	13	8	3	–	–	4	51
1981	13	15	7	6	–	–	–	10	51
1985	14	11	8	6	1	7	–	4	51

As the Table indicates, there have been interesting changes in electoral fortune since 1973. One of major significance has been the decline of the Official Unionist Party (OUP) from 25 seats in 1973 to 14 in 1985. In 1977 the decline was caused by a low Unionist turnout following the failed loyalist strike in that year and the OUP lost seats to both the moderate Alliance Party and the more extreme DUP. In 1981, the OUP lost further ground, this time to the DUP but in 1985 the Official Unionists regained ground slightly and the Democratic Unionists fell back, leaving the OUP the largest party on the Council.

On the nationalist side the major change has been the rise of Sinn Fein, largely at the expense of the various independent and minority republican parties. The major province-wide party on the nationalist side, the SDLP, has declined slightly in seats and can no longer be said to be the dominant nationalist party in Belfast.

These changes have meant an increase in tension within the Council, with the combined Unionist parties campaigning against the presence of Sinn Fein in the Council. The Council, following other Unionist councils, (Connolly and Knox, 1986), adopted an adjournment policy but the situation was greatly complicated by the signing of the Anglo-Irish Agreement in November 1985. As a result, Unionist councils, in addition to their adjournment policy, increased their protests, including refusing to set a rate. Some of the consequences of this we discuss later but we have tried to describe the 'normal' process, while not neglecting the impact of the increased political tension.

Internal Organisation

The reduced responsibilities of Belfast City Council as a result of the 1973 reorganisation led to a loss of 50 per cent of its administrative staff, a reduction of eight executive heads of department and a complete overhaul of the Council's committee structure. Currently the administrative structure is comprised of ten departments [4] with the number of standing committees amounting to eight. Three departments (Town Clerk, Town Solicitor, and City Treasurer) are under the major Council committee, i.e. the General Purposes and Finance Committee. All other committees are responsible for a single department, with the exception of the Health, Markets and Meat Plant Committee which has two departments. Further, the Town Planning Committee, because of the nature of its role in which it acts in a consultative capacity, commenting on planning issues as requested by DOE (N.I.), has no serving department.

With regard to committee responsibilities, several points may be noted. The formal organisational structure of Belfast City Council is one of standing committees who are responsible, subject to ratification by the Council, for the discharge of statutory and/or permissive duties and for the control of departments within prescribed limits. Limits to action and decision making are set out by statute and are supplemented by the Council's own Standing Orders.

With the notable exception of financial matters (and therefore some staffing matters) there are few requirements for interdependent action between committees. Each committee has its own budget itemised under sub-headings (previously agreed by the Council) which it can choose to spend or not spend. However, each committee's decisions are largely subject to ratification by the full Council meeting. In effect this means that decisions having major financial implications can only be brought to the Council after the General Purposes and Finance Committee have agreed with that committee's decision. This gives some indication of this committee's power as does its responsibility for such matters as creation of new staffing posts, regrading and approval of revenue and capital estimates prior to full Council ratification.

Although it was pointed out above that there are few requirements for committees to act interdependently, such interdependent action does occur. For example, departments have to use the services of the building and vehicle maintenance facilities provided by Technical Services. The provision of these facilities is accompanied by a levied charge and on occasions, a certain amount of tension.

Belfast City Council has a well developed committee structure. After election, councillors are asked to provide the Town Clerk with three preferences in the knowledge that they will be asked to serve on two committees. Under proportional representation counting is a complex matter lasting over two days but since early election gives a councillor priority in committee choice there are distinct advantages to be gained thereby. Once the preferences are known, the Town Clerk circulates the lists and parties can get down to the task of ensuring adequate representation on committees.

While members' choice is one feature in the composition of committees it is by no means the only consideration:

"In reality each party group meets and, after discussion, the leader forwards names to the Town Clerk."

Alliance Member

"If too many people want to serve on a particular committee, then some many be asked to move."

Official Unionist Member

The current composition of committees within Belfast City Council is shown in Table 17.2.

Each committee then chooses its chairman and deputy chairman, each to serve for two years with the implication, though not the inevitability, that the deputy will become chairman in two years' time. One councillor indicated that the selection of committee chairmen is facilitated by "a degree of horse-trading between the parties", while another (currently chairman of a committee) pointed out that he had been deputy chairman in the last administration but did not make chairman on that occasion because of "pressure from other parties". His present position is a direct result of "the changed composition of the new council following the elections in May 1985". Again, the post of chairman is usually reserved for members with relatively long service on the Council. However, one (Unionist) chairman has attained the position after only 21 months service. He refused to be drawn on this point, stating only:

"The results of the May 1985 elections permitted a number of newer, younger people to take over from the 'older hands'".

This same councillor added another limitation to member choice on committees when he pointed out that entry to the Council via a by-election means that committee membership is already decided.

While it can be argued that changes in committee membership limits the opportunities for members (particularly chairmen) to develop special expertise in the work of a committee, some councillors expressed the view that changing membership allowed the member to build up a better experience in more aspects of the Council's work.

This is turn leads on to consideration of the role of political parties on councils. Again little has been written on this issue, except in relation to sectarian issues and eccentric behaviour of councillors. However, as one officer pointed out:

There is little or no party political influence on policy issues. Indeed an officer when recommending a particular course of action may find a remarkable degree of support (or opposition) from the committee which encompasses all the membership.

Table 17.2

COMMITTEE MEMBERSHIP OF BELFAST CITY COUNCIL (JUNE 1985)

Committee	Party Representation							
	Official Unionist	Democratic Unionist	Other Unionist	Social Democratic & Labour	Alliance	Sinn Fein	Workers Party	Total
General Purposes and Finance	5	4*	2	2	2	–	–	15
Community Services	2	3	2	2	3*	1	–	13
Gas	3*	4	–	1	2	3	–	13
Health, Markets and Meat Plant	4*	3	–	1	2	3	–	13
Leisure Services	3	3	–	2*	2	2	1	13
Parks	4*	3	1	–	2	3	–	13
Technical Services	4	2*	1	2	2	2	–	13
Town Planning	3	2*	2	3	2	–	1	13

* denotes Chairman

Another officer, somewhat more cynically, believed that this may be because of the absence of media representatives from committee meetings. However, more generally, this may be because there is a feeling among officers that the major thrust in developing and managing services comes from them:

> Most suggestions for improving services come from officers. Officers must give the lead but that is not to say that they wouldn't take on Council suggestions.
>
> Council Officer

It is unlikely that this view would find favour with many members. One councillor has stated:

> Officers can only advise. Councillors have to decide and in Belfast this is normally done with the good of the city in mind. In times of crisis decisions of substance need to be made and these require the combined wisdom of the committee.

This councillor did, however, admit that while he did not recall a serious mistake having been made there had been occasions when officers had "pulled them back from the brink".

The introduction of these comments permit consideration of some other aspects of officer-member relationships within Belfast City Council. While relationships between officers and members in local authorities in England and Wales have been the subject of various investigations (e.g. Alexander 1982, Gyford 1984), similar research has not taken place in Northern Ireland. Evidence from this study indicates that there are a number of features of officer/member relations unique to the local government system in Northern Ireland.

First, the role of Leader of the Council does not exist in the same way in Northern Ireland as it does in other parts of the United Kingdom. There is no officially designated office of Leader of the Council. Indeed that office is not one that has ever existed in local government in the Province.

Second, there is evidence from the data on Belfast that the role of chairman of committees is much more limited in local government in Northern Ireland compared to elsewhere in the United Kingdom. Their role seems confined to agreeing the agenda with chief officers and chairing meetings. Officers will on occasions talk to committee chairmen about matters within the responsibility of their committee, but, certainly in Belfast, there is no evidence that the striking of a bargain between a chief officer and his chairman will secure success in committee. Such bargains are not attempted. Instead there is evidence that chairmen who attempt to regard the role as placing them in a special position vis-a-vis their colleagues on the committee tend to receive a hostile reception.

Another insight into officer/member relations may be gained by reference to a view held by many officers and expressed through the comments of one:

> With the loss of services in local government the standard of intelligence of councillors has decreased. The council used to attract businessmen but they are not now interested to the same extent. More laymen are coming in and there is a greater

paramilitary influence.

As is to be expected this does not represent the members' view.
While admitting the presence of more 'laymen' there is no feeling
that this is a bad thing — the advantages of querying that which is
not understood and demanding explanations before arriving at a decision
being emphasised:

> Members may be seen as a nuisance to officers — they don't like
> people who make waves.
>
> Alliance Councillor

Budgetary Considerations

The data presented in Table 17.3 provides a summary of revenue matters
for Belfast City Council between the years 1980 and 1986/7. In most
respects it shows a pattern of modest growth, although after accounting
for the effects of inflation it could be argued that there is a
remarkable stability in the figures.

Several points, however, are in need of classification. First, the
extremely high increase in the rates in the years 1981/2 (16 per cent)
and 1982/3 (18 per cent) coincide with an increase in the recreational
facilities in line with government policy at the time. (Belfast City
Council has some 15 recreation and leisure centres). Second, figures
for the current year show an increase of 10.6 per cent over the
previous year. This increase may be partially explained by the fact
that the normal processes involved in arriving at the rates were
circumvented by a suspension of council business in protest against
the signing of the Anglo-Irish Agreement. The rate was struck by
government appointed commissioners acting in the place of council
members. Whether the outcome would have been different in normal
circumstances remains a matter for conjecture.

It should also be noted that local authorities in the Province are
not subject to GREAs, Guidelines or Targets. Instead, each year
councils are in receipt of a general grant containing two elements:

(a) a resources element designed to permit less well off councils
    to provide a satisfactory level of service; and

(b) a de-rating element which compensates authorities for loss of
    rate income due to the de-rating of property used for manufacturing
    purposes.

In Belfast the General Exchequer Grant is comprised of a de-rating
figure only.

The Process

Compared with other local authorities in Great Britain the budgetary
sequence in Belfast begins in August of each year and culminates when
the estimates are approved by the Council in the following February.

With regard to capital, forms relating to the five year rolling
capital programme are forwarded to chief officers in August and are
completed on the basis of the various projects which have emerged

Table 17.3

REVENUE DATA FOR BELFAST CITY COUNCIL

Year	Expenditure	Miscellaneous Income	Specific Government Grants	Net Cost	General Grant	Rate in £	Est. Product of 1p Rate
1980/1	22,960,525	4,295,565	936,770	17,728,190	2,103,077	40.10	377,528
1981/2	26,369,015	4,619,840	792,720	20,956,455	2,400,289	46.50	390,421
1982/3	30,377,235	5,058,010	859,875	24,459,350	2,740,058	54.90	390,396
1983/4	33,568,500	5,827,010	739,840	27,002,650	3,410,191	60.60	385,211
1984/5	36,299,516	6,368,201	1,115,820	28,815,495	4,274,605	64.85	375,000
1985/6	39,481,857	6,942,392	1,193,460	31,346,005	4,799,825	69.04	372,120
1986/7	n/a	n/a	1,395,050	34,517,139	5,349,190	76.36	368,880

235

throughout the year from their departments and the relevant committees. In October the General Purposes and Finance Committee meet to agree the programme (which in 1985/6 stood at some £106 million, including £6.5 million of new proposals for that year).

This exercise had its origin in the PESC exercise but there is evidence to suggest that local authorities (and to some extent the Department of the Environment) view this as a paper exercise having only a marginal effect on their plans (Connolly, 1986). The point was made many times that the inclusion of a project in the five-year plan gave no guarantee that it would go ahead: "The actual programme will depend on many factors" (Officer). There is a general view that the PESC exercise was fairly meaningless.

Of primary importance to any project is securing the necessary finance. In general, four methods of financing can be employed:

(a) **The procurement of a capital grant.** The size of grant aid is such that local authorities recognise their dependence on central government for support of any major scheme and while requests are made formally to the Department one officer indicated the value of the informal approach, claiming that "discussions on the golf course could smooth the way". (Of the 211 projects detailed in the capital estimates for 1985/6, 102 indicate the attraction of a grant is embodied in the calculations).

(b) **Borrowing funds.** Local authorities wishing to borrow money to finance capital projects are required to obtain loan sanction from the DOE (N.I.) on each capital item for which they intend to borrow money. Current DOE policy on loans is that decisions to grant loan sanctions will depend on three factors:

i.   the purpose for which the expenditure is required;

ii. the amount of the expenditure proposed;

iii. the financial position of the council at that time.

There is a view which was put by some officials within DOE (N.I.) that the first of these factors is the dominant one and that it would be difficult to withhold loan sanctions if the capital project falls within the legal remit of the authority. Contrary opinion from the same source, however, suggests that it is the current financial position of the authority which decides the granting or withholding of the sanction. In fact loan sanction has never been refused for a capital project and usually the authority and DOE (N.I.) engage in negotiations about the project, with the Department persuading the authority that the project was too big or the timing was wrong. Here, inclusion in PESC appears to be a help. As one Finance Officer put it: "If you have a project already in the system through your PESC returns, it speeds up the giving of loan sanction". (Connolly, 1986). In discussing loans one Unionist chairperson advocated restraint in the use of this method of finance. "Even with loans you must exercise care. You must not charge today's ratepayers for tomorrow's services." (Again, in reference to the 1985/6 capital programme, some 190 projects include the obtainment of a loan as, at least, part finance of the project).

The final two methods, **capital receipt** and **revenue contribution** are of limited importance in Belfast City Council's capital programme. Scrutiny of the programme reveals only one project in which capital receipts play a part and 17 where revenue contributions are included in the calculations.

Two other points need to be made in relation to capital budgeting in Belfast City Council. First, each new proposal is accompanied by an estimate showing the net annual revenue expenditure to be expected when the project is completed. Attention to the revenue consequences of capital expenditure was a feature emphasised by several members. One Unionist member was at pains to point out that money provided by a previous minister to build leisure centres had heavy consequences for current revenue budgets. Another referred to a frequent occurrence where the Council were asked to purchase tracts of land at nominal cost and claimed that many such offers were rejected on the grounds of ongoing revenue expense.

Second, there are circumstances when additional expenditure can be forced upon the council by central government.

> Following the tragedy at Maysfield Leisure Centre (in which a fire caused loss of life) the council were forced to review health and safety operation at leisure centres. The result has been "a Rolls Royce of health and safety" as inspectors covered themselves, with little possibility of grant aid to help in the cost.
>
> Committee Chairman

Revenue Budgeting

The preparation of annual revenue estimated for Belfast City Council takes place between **September and November** each year. It is a task co-ordinated by some senior officer(s) in each department with varying degrees of involvement from the chief officer concerned and based on information supplied by each section/cost centre manager. There is no standard procedure operating throughout the Council for collection of this information, each department using its own method. Three methods in particular are identifiable.

(a) The officer(s) in charge visit each section and ascertain (with the section head's help) the number of personnel and other resources required in the coming year.

(b) The officer(s) in charge convene a meeting attended by cost centre managers who are asked to identify changes from the previous year.

(c) The officer(s) in charge issue standard forms to each cost centre manager who submits proposals in respect of his centre.

These methods are employed by various service providing departments and to their own calculations must be added their share of costs of administration from the Town Clerk's and Town Solicitor's departments. (Such costs are apportioned on a 'per capita' basis, thus the larger the department the heavier its central administration burden). Additionally, where one department uses the services of another for (say) maintenance of green space, buildings or vehicles, a recoupment figure (supplied by the providing department) is included in the estimates.

Upon approval by the Chief Officer, the estimates are submitted to the City Treasurer in **November** and a discussion process may ensue prior to preliminary scrutiny of all estimates by the General Purposes and Finance Committee in early **January**. (This committee may request savings to be made in any or all estimates, but does not use its power to alter).

At this point the estimates (with requests for savings) are placed before the relevant committee at its January meeting by the City Treasurer and, following the committee's approval, are returned to the General Purposes and Finance Committee for final consideration. The full Council meets in **February** to approve the estimates and to strike a rate.

It will be apparent from this description that the budgetary process could be said to be 'officer led'. Certainly the methods employed (where a committee only has sight of the estimates **after** scrutiny by the Chief Officer, City Treasurer and the General Purposes and Finance Committee) lend credibility to the officers' belief that the major thrust in developing and managing of services comes from them. One officer claimed:

> Any closer involvement by the committee is not necessary. Their decisions are based upon provision of service – it is our job to calculate the financial side.

Another, less emphatic, pointed out that budgets reflected any proposals that the Committee had agreed to during the year; while a third officer speculated:

> The preliminary approach to General Purposes and Finance permits oversight of the total picture. Any amendments thought necessary can then be considered by the appropriate service committee.

Conversations with members revealed an overall satisfaction with this system. One member stated:

> While each councillor has a duty to scrutinise the estimates and push their own ideas, I see no loss of control. Each director compiles his estimates in the knowledge of what his committee will approve.
>
> Official Unionist Member

He went on to comment that no restriction on decision-making derives from prior examination by the General Purposes and Finance Committee. Not only is each service committee chairman a member of this committee (thereby ensuring that committee views are represented) but within his experience one committee at least had refused to make cuts in line with their recommendations from the senior committee.

Another member pointed out that budgets do sometimes require amendment during the year, when (say) an expected grant did not materialise and revenue expenses need re-ordering. The implication is that such changes cannot be done without committee approval and this is an example of practical decision making.

Member attitudes may, perhaps, be summed up in the words of one councillor who, having reiterated the arguments outlined above, went on to say:

> Members have opportunities to review the current budget during the year. The comparison of actual with budgeted expenditure gives them an experience they can use to judge the adequacy of the estimates placed before them .... Besides, a major portion of each year's estimates is committed to maintaining what already exists and attention will focus (although not exclusively) on changes.

Strategic Considerations

Centre managers are invited to identify the resources they require for **the coming year**, or to indicate changes in their needs from the previous year. There is no deliberate attempt to forecast medium term commitments, except through the compilation of the capital programme (which is regarded as a paper exercise). Neither can the budget process or its operation be regarded as being conducive to corporate planning. Indeed many officers made the point that corporate planning was not a feature of Belfast City Council.

At this stage it is opportune to examine some of the consequences of this approach. First there is some evidence that the departmental structure was devised without reference to compatibility of services. One officer, speaking about Technical Services, described it as a "rag-bag of odds and ends"; the accuracy of the description is indisputable when one considers that its duties include tasks as disparate as architectural services and street cleaning; public conveniences and maintenance of vehicles. Again, within the Council, Parks and Leisure Services are free standing departments each serving a separate committee, although other councils appear to be able to combine them to advantage. While few people are willing to comment upon the separation, one council member stated:

> My visits elsewhere do not indicate any advantage from the combined approach. The expertise of the director plays a large part. Should he be an expert in leisure it may lead to a prominence of this field in any combined department.

Without any further comment on this statement it may be stated that the present structure and attitudes are not conducive to the establishment of a corporate approach.

Second, it is possible to comment upon the extent to which limitations of finance inform the compilation of annual budgets. While it would be wrong to suggest that the council's budgets are constructed without regard to financial constraints, the point has been made elsewhere that councils in Northern Ireland are not 'rate-led' in the completion of annual revenue budgets (Connolly, 1986). The reason for this is tied to the method of rate collection used in the Province. Briefly, councils each year strike a district rate (which is directly related to the expenses incurred in providing services within their area). Beyond this the Department of the Environment strikes a regional rate which purports to cover the expense of providing services to the Province as a whole. Both taxes are based on the rateable value of property and are collected together, ratepayers being presented with a single bill. The outcome is that district rate increases may be masked (to some extent) in the overall rates figure.

This circumstance must not be interpreted as a disregard for rate considerations by any council. In fact, most of those interviewed pointed to a need to protect the ratepayer from excessive demands. Some officers indicated that annual increases had fallen back dramatically in recent years, while others claimed that their department's percentage of total council expenditure was decreasing.

Members' comments on rate increases were fairly predictable. One Unionist member claimed that such a path should only be contemplated when all other avenues had been exhausted and it has been determined that the efficiency of the enterprise cannot be improved. Perhaps the most telling remark came from one councillor who stated:

> Raising the rates is not always feasible since the bulk is paid by commercial people who will only take so much before they close down and go elsewhere.

In further discussion he added that the last two councils had seen a decrease in the number of businessmen offering themselves for election, so this view may not be shared by all.

In one respect, however, the Council appears to be unanimous and that concerns the subject of franchising. In the course of an interview one Chief Officer claimed that if he were permitted to franchise catering and security his department could save approximately £350,000 per year. Unfortunately (from his point of view) the Council were united in their opposition, despite representations from the City Treasurer and the Local Government Auditor. "Despite all this the council are sticking to an unwritten policy of no privatisation." Whether this view represents an all party concern to protect council employment (since some members expressed worry over the increase in unemployment which would follow 'contracting out'), or reflects the variability of electoral fortunes occasioned by use of proportional representation remains a matter for conjecture.

Finally, it is necessary to draw attention to the effects of cutbacks in Belfast City Council. In general terms it may be stated that financial constraint on local authorities is not as severe in the Province as elsewhere in the United Kingdom, nor has it been necessary to introduce any of the measures employed elsewhere. To some extent this may be explained by the restricted nature of services entrusted to local authorities in Northern Ireland. The Province's providers of health, education and environmental services have not been so fortunate, since curtailment of funds available are a feature of their present circumstances.

Within Belfast City Council initial responses from officers indicated that cutbacks were not a major phenomenon that they had to contend with. However, this may not be completely accurate.

From the point of view of capital expenditure there is little doubt that not all proposed projects proceed to completion. Indications are that the withholding of grants and refusal of loan sanction can and does permit central control of such expenditure - one officer illustrating the point by reference to the delay in completion of a smoke control programme caused by failure to obtain the necessary grant from DOE (N.I.). There is also some evidence to suggest that control of grants etc., can influence the priority given to capital projects. One committee chairman drew attention to an occasion when the committee submitted plans to build a community centre at one of two locations, accompanied by a recommendation favouring location A. The controlling government department replied that grant aid would only be made available for such a project if it were sited at the other location.

From a revenue expenditure viewpoint there are many examples to indicate a cutback situation. In the main these apply to situations where the Council acts as the agent of a central department or regional service provider. Thus Parks Committee act in a maintenance capacity for green spaces belonging to the Belfast Education and Library Board, while Environmental Health carry out work on an agency basis for the Department of the Environment, the Northern Ireland Housing Executive and the Department of Agriculture. In such circumstances increased budgetary constraints on these bodies will inevitably affect the work of the Council department involved.

Conclusion

This paper began with the assertion that local differences lead to unique approaches to the budgetary process by local authorities. In the analysis which followed emphasis was given to the differences found in the work of Belfast City Council. Limitations in the range of activities carried out by local government in Northern Ireland, internal organisational arrangements within the Council and methods of procedure all combine to present a picture of a largely officer led authority operation along traditional, incremental lines. The research indicates that none of the people involved found cause for dissatisfaction with these arrangements, nor did they see any need for change.

From a wider perspective the absence of those restrictive measures currently employed by the centre to control local government expenditure in Great Britain may give rise to envy. However, it must be remembered that the avoidance of large scale cutbacks has only been possible because the services subject to such treatment are not part of local authority activity in the Province. In effect the centralised boards and regional authorities responsible for health, housing and education face substantial cuts in their budgets in the year 1986/7. Thus, the transfer of these activities has facilitated a more direct control to be exercised by central government. In local government the power of the centre is adequate to control expenditure on the services which remain within local authority responsibility.

This is most clearly seen by the actions taken by the Department of the Environment (N.I.) following combined Unionist opposition to the Anglo-Irish Agreement. At local level, the Unionist councillors in the City have gone along with the campaign of adjourning Council meetings and refusing to strike a rate. This in turn persuaded Alliance councillors in Belfast to take the Council to the courts in order to force the Unionist majority to resume normal service (Sinclair, 1986). This has not happened – instead the Unionist councillors have continued to resist the pressure, resulting in their being fined.

In addition, the role of the Town Clerk in maintaining Council business was disrupted. Under the adjourment policy, the majority of councillors delegated powers to the Town Clerk. As a result of the High Court decision, he can now only continue to take the decisions he was already taking. As a result, the Town Clerk cannot take decisions in such matters as discretionary payments to voluntary bodies and capital projects. The DOE (N.I.) were forced to send in someone for two days with the legal authority to exercise these functions. DOE (N.I.) were also constrained to set the district rate for those local authorities who had not performed this function. In Belfast this amounted to an increase of 10.6 per cent. Although this was in line with the data presented in the Estimates, the action highlights the ability of central government to control local government affairs when the occasion demands.

NOTES

[1] Review Body on Local Government in Northern Ireland. HMSO, Belfast 1970 (Cmd. 546)

[2] ibid, p.42.

[3] ibid, p.42.

[4] Town Clerk's, City Treasurer's, Town Solicitor's, Technical Services, Parks, Gas, Community Services, Leisure Services, Environmental Health and Meat Plant.

18. Conclusion: dimensions of the budgetary process

HOWARD ELCOCK

Introduction

The authors of the sixteen preceding chapters have presented a series
of studies of how a wide variety of local authorities prepared their
budgets in 1985/6, for the financial year 1986/7. The chapters both
describe varied processes and differ in the emphasis on particular
aspects of local government policy-making. This variation reflects
not merely the differing interests of the authors but also variations
in the dominant influences on the formation of each authority's budget.
It seems, for example, that strong political influence on budget-making
may to some extent reduce the need for strong co-ordination at officer
level. The late Victor Wiseman (1963) drew attention to the importance
of the Labour Group on Leeds City Council as a co-ordinating body.
The Group's Advisory Committee was even more important in this regard.
Since he wrote, corporate management has gained much ground in British
local government but where politicians are dominant in policy-making,
its significance is reduced. In Avon and Liverpool, for example,
politicians determined policy and while officers, notably Chief
Executives and Treasurers, provide them with support and advice, their
influence on decision-making tends to be weaker than in local
authorities whose political and financial situations do not produce
as vigorous partisan controversy or conflict with central government.
Political influence on the budgetary process tends to be maximised
in 'hung' councils or those (like Liverpool and Sheffield) where
politicians are determined to implement their election manifestoes
despite the central government's attempts to constrain them. The varied
emphases of our case-studies thus reflects the different natures of
the local political systems we have studied. Some basic differences

Table 18.1   BASIC FEATURES OF THE AUTHORITIES STUDIED

	Population (1000s)	Area (Hectares) (000)	Rateable Value (£000)	Political Control 1985/6	Total Budget 1986/7 (Exp. as Budgeted) (£000)	GREA/ Guideline 1986/7 (£000)	Rate Levy 1986/7 (p per £)	% Council Houses 1986
Avon CC	935	135	124,761	No Control (Lab Largest)	370,730	341,000	28	20.7
Banff & Buchan DC	83	153	4,881	Ind	5,031	4,855	10.7	36.6
Belfast CC	321	12	41,905	OUP/DUP	35,912	N/A	76.36	30.7
Birmingham CC	1005	26	167,550	Lab	481,826	502,385	197.94	31
Ceredigion DC	62	170	5,164	Ind	4,148	4,411	19	19
Harrow LBC	202	5	34,779	Con	61,944	88,421	178	12
Kingswood DC	87.9	47	8,998	Con	3,344	4,265	16	15
Lancashire CC	1382	306	145,392	No Control (Lab Largest)	569,314	517,097	232	18
Liverpool CC	497	11	70,190	Lab	303,000	262,000	268.97	39.6
Mid-Glamorgan CC	536	101	40,418	Lab	236,000	200,000	204.4	29.47
Oldham BC	220	14	23,600	Lab	105,146	97,800	198.37	20.7
Portsmouth CC	180	3	28,000	Con	20,892	16,483	46	41.4
Redditch DC	732	5	9,977	Lab	4,084	3,852	28	46
Sheffield CC	543	37	56,000	Lab	269,529	224,648	271.77	47
Stirling DC	81	217	52,000	Lab	22,149	26,952	42	46.4
Tayside RC	394	750	211,000	Con	205,000	194,000	29.02	46

are illustrated in Table 18.1.

We can explore these variations further by looking at two sets of influences on budgetary processes. First, there is a range of external influences, including local political cultures, political parties, pressure groups and the central government. Secondly, there are the internal processes of inter-departmental bargaining, executive co-ordination and political decision-making by which the budget is made. A common theme is the impact upon these processes and relationships of fiscal stress. In the first chapter, Grant Jordan discusses a wide range of views about how demands for expenditure reductions might affect policy-making structures and processes, as well as the outcomes for the local authority's staff, customers and electors. The case-studies show that such effects have occurred but that the impact of demands for cutback management on structures and processes has not been great, nor have their consequences for staff and customers been severe. Indeed, actual cuts in budgets or services are rare indeed; almost always, cutback management has produced spending growth reduced below previous plans and expectations - which is often enough to produce 'shroud-waving' by staff and protests from customers - but not actual reductions. The need to reduce planned spending growth has nonetheless brought about changes both in the policies being pursued by local authorities and in their management processes. We can explore these changes first in local authorities' relationships with their external environments and then in their internal decision-making and management processes.

The External Dimension

The external dimension involves not only the consideration of purely local political systems and cultures but also the differences in the environments within which local authorities operate in the four countries which make up the United Kingdom. There is much that demonstrates that the supposed homogeneity of the United Kingdom is a myth, both in terms of the variety of local political systems that exist (Stanyer 1976) and of differences between England, Scotland, Wales and Northern Ireland. We shall look first at the influence of local political systems, then at that of the central government.

The Local Authority and its Locality

As our study has proceeded, it has become increasingly clear that the link between a local authority and the political culture of its area is an important influence on its budgetary process. We can illustrate this in various ways. Liverpool, for example, has a long tradition, common to both main political parties, of there being close links between the council group and the city party organisation, coupled with autocratic leadership of both. (Baxter 1969; 1971) In this sense, Councillors Hatton, Byrne and Mulhearn are the direct political descendents of Alderman Archibald Salvidge and Jack Braddock. A small leadership group is maintained in office by supporters many of whom hold membership or office in both the council Group and the city party organisation, in particular its Executive Committee. (Baxter 1969; Parkinson 1985) The political objectives of the present Labour leaders in Liverpool are very different from those of the Braddocks but their modus operandi is in tune with the Liverpudlian political tradition. Liverpool's low budget base, its severe economic decline and resultant deprivation, combined with the Thatcher Government's determination to reduce local authorities' expenditure to produce a clash with the Government which attracted much publicity and made its leading politicians into national public figures.

Two very different examples of the influence of the locality on a local authority's budgetary process further illustrate the need to consider local political cultures as influences on the balance of power between members and officers. In both Banff and Buchan District Council in Scotland and Ceredigion District Council in Wales, there was a generally held concern in the community, shared by councillors and locally raised officers, to keep rate increases to a minimum, comply with Government grant guidelines to avoid penalty but extract the maximum possible amount of grant from the Government. One councillor's reference to "the thrifty Buchan tradition" reflected a widely shared value in that and other nearby authorities. In consequence Banff and Buchan comes near the bottom of all Scottish local authority expenditure leagues – an achievement it shares with other local authorities in Grampian and neighbouring Regions.

Ceredigion District Council is in many respects similar to Banff and Buchan. Its residents enjoy a reputation for thrift which is reflected both in a determination to restrict spending and to obtain the maximum amount of grant from the Welsh Office. Ceredigion councillors are largely concerned, as are their colleagues in Banff and Buchan, to assist their constituents and promote their wards' interests but they do so within the constraints of resource availability – which in turn is determined by a combination of setting low rates and the maximum Government grant available. Similar behaviour has been reported from other rural authorities.

A third kind of link between a local authority and its locality is that in some cases, the proximity of other authorities influences the environment within which decisions are taken. For instance, Kingswood District Council's area is close to both Bath and Bristol, so that its inhabitants can make extensive use of the local services provided in those two cities. In consequence, Kingswood itself need provide only a relatively limited range of services. This in part made possible one of the most remarkable decisions we discovered during our research; Kingswood's decision to devote virtually all its capital allocations for the next two years to a single project: the conversion of a swimming pool into a sports centre. On the same subject, Belfast City Council has constructed a large number of leisure centres because central government funds were available for them and the Council needed to balance demand for leisure provision in Protestant and Catholic areas of the city. The City Council must now bear the cost of running them. All these examples demonstrate in their different ways the validity of Stanyer's (1976) assertion of the importance of studying local authorities as parts of their local political system.

Local Political Parties

A second major factor with a territorial dimension which influences local authority budgets, is the local political system. There are two aspects to this influence. The first is the party balance on the Council – a factor of increased interest because of the increasing number of councils which are 'hung' or 'balanced'. The second is the power structure of party Groups of councillors, in particular the role played by their leading members and the relationship between the council Group and the outside party organisation. The role of leading politicians assumes particular importance in view of the tendency for crucial stages of the budgetary process to be dominated by small, informal groupings of leading councillors and senior officers. Such groupings commonly play either or both the 'Spanish Inquisition' and 'Sweat Shop' roles (Greenwood 1983) but they may also set budget strategies and determine the authority's overall priorities.

Michael Hill (1972) argued that in non-partisan local authorities, the officers were likely to control decisions, while where a disciplined party Group is firmly in control, collective member influence is maximised. This analysis is inadequate in two ways. First, in councils where no one party has an overall majority, member influence is likely to be considerable because policy decisions cannot be made except by seeking coalitions of councillors willing to support the policy. Also, officers cannot assume that decisions are final until they have been ratified by the full Council, whereas if one party is in control committee decisions are unlikely to be changed at all often at the Council meeting. (See Blowers 1977). Avon County Council's budgetary process, for example, was dominated by the Labour Party for most of the year. The Labour Group behaved as if it was still in control of the Council after the 1985 elections. The other parties did not develop alternative policies to Labour's 'Standstill' budget but when it became apparent that a large rate rise was in prospect, a dispute began which resulted in Labour resigning the committee chairmanships as well as in court actions which attracted national publicity. Above all, the Labour Group prepared detailed budget proposals which would protect service levels and jobs in the authority. The other parties did not or could not follow suit. In consequence, although the final stages of the budget-making process were highly dramatic, the debate was about relatively marginal changes to the rate precept and the amount to be taken out of balances. The policies and priorities enshrined in the budget were not challenged. They had been determined by the Labour Group, in part because the Opposition parties failed to develop alternative policies earlier in the process.

A somewhat similar story can be told about Lancashire County Council, which also became a 'hung' council after the May 1985 elections. The 1986/7 budget was largely generated in the authority's departments, which prepared the Estimates for approval by committees. Then the Finance Committee, at a special meeting, asked committees to confine their requests for resources to the level of their continuation Estimates. As in Avon, the debate in the final stages of the budgetary process concentrated on the rate precept and the amount to be drawn from balances. The established priorities of the authority, set this time by the professional officers in the departments, were not challenged. It seems, therefore, that on 'hung' councils the party which assumes office will tend to determine the priorities and policies to be followed, in collaboration with the authority's officers and that other parties may alter the rate precept or the amount to be drawn from the balances but not policies and priorities. Holding office – even if you are dependent on the support of another party – can therefore still be of great importance, although during the 1970s, the 'hung' state of Liverpool City Council seems to have been a recipe for inertia and the postponement of unpopular decisions. Only when

Labour won overall control in 1983 was decisive action forthcoming and that led to a major conflict with the central government. (Parkinson 1985).

In authorities where one party is firmly in control one of two things may happen. The controlling party may be determined to secure the implementation of its manifesto, as was the case in Liverpool. In Sheffield, the Labour Group has sought to ensure that their election manifesto would be implemented by establishing Programme Committees, which consist of committee chairmen and officers, whose task is to monitor the implementation of the Labour manifesto. They stress obtaining value for money but this did not prevent Sheffield from sailing perilously close to the legal wind in preparing a budget which maintains Labour's commitment not to cut jobs or services.

Alternatively, strong party control can produce a budgetary process largely controlled by the officers. On Mid-Glamorgan County Council, a strong but 83 year old Leader mainly supports recommendations coming from the officers. The main decisions are made by the Budget Advisory Group consisting of second or third tier officers from the authority's departments. It has sought to make departments declare their priorities and increase their efficiency. It prepared the detailed budget but its efforts were misunderstood by councillors. Party control does not necessarily mean political domination of policy-making. Equally, one cannot assume that the absence of party control means that policy-making – including the budget – will be officer dominated. Departments may generate requests for the resources to continue existing services or provide new ones but they may have to modify their plans in the face of shared values of thrift among councillors and in the wider community, as the Banff and Buchan and Ceredigion cases illustrate.

Electorates and Other Outside Influences

The local electorate influences the budgetary process in two ways. First, councillors commonly operate on the assumption that their actions will affect their electoral support. Sometimes they do, although local elections are usually in large part a popular pronouncement on the achievements or otherwise of the national Government. Regional councillors on Tayside were conscious as they prepared their budget, that they would face elections in 1986 and they sought to avoid rate rises or unpopular service cuts. Their concern did not save the Conservative majority on Tayside when the elections came round, however. In Kingswood, the District Council decided to invest almost all its capital programme in a sports centre development because councillors believed that this development would be electorally popular.

More importantly, of course, the electorate influences budget-making by altering the composition of local authorities. In particular, the growing strength of the SDP-Liberal Alliance in recent years has produced an increasing number of 'hung' councils. In consequence, both councillors and officers have had to find ways of continuing to make decisions and administer services while being perpetually uncertain of being able to get the necessary approvals at committee and council meetings. Often, the largest party continues to take committee chairmanships and control decision-making processes, especially where that party was in control before the elections. In Lancashire, adjustments to formal procedures were made to cope with the new party balance. The Annual General Meeting was chaotic, so means had to be found to ensure that the authority's business could be conducted and decisions made. Hence, although Labour took the committee chairmanships, they did not get majorities on the committees and opposition spokesmen as well as chairmen entitled to briefings before committee meetings. Again, Labour controlled the preparation of Estimates and the overall budget, although the Chief Executive was careful to ensure that the other parties were kept informed and involved. Thus the Chief Executive seems to have assumed the role of ensuring that the basis for a cross-party consensus existed and the budget was approved by a combination of Labour and Alliance councillors, without the litigation and public disputes which occurred in Avon. In both cases, Labour effectively controlled the budgetary process until the final stages but consensus management was effective in Lancashire, while apparently almost non-existent in Avon. In general, the electorate's decisions alter the balance of authorities and the voters are the ghost at all councillors' feasts but their influence on budgetary policy is marginal.

Other outside influences are usually even more marginal. Local authorities are now required by law to consult representative organisations on non-domestic ratepayers. Most of the authorities in this study were conscientious about providing representative bodies like the local Chamber of Trade or the local branch of the Confederation of British Industry with information, as well as holding meetings with them. There were no instances of conflict developing during these consultations. In most cases, non-domestic ratepayers got information, sometimes tea but little else. Usually they appeared to be satisfied to be kept informed and be invited to meetings. In any case, often local political cultures ensure that councillors and businessmen promote similar values and interests anyway. The influence of other pressure groups, such as trade unions, was also marginal, although the ambivalence or hostility of local unions towards some of Liverpool City Council's more dramatic tactics, notably the decision to declare all the city's 31,000 employees redundant at the end of 1985, restricted councillors' freedom of action in pursuing their campaign of opposition to the Government's policies.

One last factor we must mention is the voluntary sector. Again, its influence is marginal, although hard-pressed local authorities may find it cheaper to award a grant to a voluntary body to provide a service than to provide the service themselves. This choice is especially available where services are discretionary rather than provided under a statutory obligation. Many areas of the Social Services and most Leisure Services provision (Harrop 1986) are discretionary and it may be possible to meet demands through the voluntary sector at less cost than will be incurred if the local authority provides the service itself. However, there was not much evidence that local authorities were switching services away from their own departments to voluntary agencies. There would be strong professional resistance to such a policy but above all, this confirms the general impression that local authorities have not so far been forced far up the escalating levels of reaction to demands for cuts which ultimately lead to service reductions and compulsory redundancies. (Wolman 1984; see Chapter 1 above) Thus local authorities will first respond by borrowing, shifting spending from the revenue to the capital budget or rescheduling debts if interest rates are falling. Such 'creative accountancy' is in the main a series of means to buy time. If such measures do not suffice, local authorities will seek to made efficiency savings, perhaps using techniques like zero-base budgeting (ZBB) or using performance indicators to identify areas where efficiency might be increased, before beginning to consider service reductions or redundancies. (Wolman 1984) None of these authorities have yet been forced into considering the last options despite the unremitting central government pressure for local authority spending cuts in the last few years.

Central-Local Government Relations

This leads us to the last major external dimension of the budgetary process: the influence of the central government. Not only is Whitehall no monolith; central-local relations in the four countries of the United Kingdom differ markedly, especially because the local government policy communities (Richardson and Jordan 1979) in Scotland, Wales and Northern Ireland are much smaller than that in England. In the first three countries, local authority officers and civil servants can develop frequent, informal contacts which make the conflict of perspectives so apparent in the Liverpool case less likely to occur. Scotland has 65 local authorities, Wales 45 and Northern Ireland 26, whereas England has 447. Clearly, relationships in England will be both more formal and more distant than in the rest of the United Kingdom. Scotland is interesting for a second reason; an expenditure limitation ('rate-capping') law has been in force there since 1981 and it may be possible for England to learn lessons from Scotland's longer experience of this aspect of central-local relations.

Rate limitation in Scotland has produced some famous clashes between individual local authorities and the Secretary of State for Scotland. The Lothian dispute in 1981/2 was resolved only when Labour lost control of Lothian Regional Council in the 1982 elections. A similar conflict occurred when Labour gained control of Edinburgh District Council in 1985 and attempted to raise its expenditure far above its Scottish Office Guideline. However, although the Scottish authorities in our study have sometimes wished to exceed their Guidelines, they have in the main negotiated with the Scottish Office to avoid a direct clash with the Secretary of State. Thus in both 1982 and 1983, Stirling District Council proposed budgets which would have produced major cuts in grant and in consequence large rate increases but compromises were negotiated between the Council and the Secretary of State on both occasions. Since then, relations between Stirling District Council and the Scottish Office have been calmer; the clashes and bargaining between 1981 and 1983 have brought both to accept a modus vivendi whereby a Conservative Secretary of State accepts as reasonable the modified policies of a Labour-controlled district council.

We noted earlier that the other Scottish authorities in the study usually budgeted within their Scottish Office Guidelines but they do negotiate for increased Guideline figures where excessive cuts are needed to stay within the Guideline, so that jobs would be lost and services reduced. Rural local authorities in particular negotiate for higher Guidelines - ofter successfully - on the ground that their sparse populations entail very high unit costs for the provision of many local authority services. In Wales, the Welsh Office has not set Targets for expenditure on individual local authority services because it regards doing this as an undue restriction on local authorities' autonomy. Our two Welsh authorities are very different but both seem to enjoy relatively easy relationships with the Welsh

Office. Ceredigion District Council accepts its Welsh Office Target and does not budget to spend above it, in keeping with the general inclination to thrift in the area but it negotiates for higher Target figures through the Welsh Association of District Councils. Mid-Glamorgan County Council, which is firmly under. Labour control, spends above its target but the Welsh Office recognises the extent of economic and social need in an area greatly damaged by the decline of traditional industries. There is no evidence of real conflict despite occasional criticism of "excessive and unacceptable growth in expenditure" by the Secretary of State for Wales.

Central-local relations are even more anodyne in Northern Ireland – at least in terms of budgeting and the control of public spending. The Northern Ireland Office has no formal powers to control local authorities' expenditure and relies on 'moral suasion' to influence local authorities' financial decisions. In any case, local authorities in Northern Ireland have only a limited range of powers and functions because many former local government services, notably education and housing, are now provided by centrally appointed boards. The poor record of many Northern Ireland local authorities in terms of discrimination against minority communities has led Whitehall considerably to reduce their powers and functions. The focus of conflict in central-local relations in Northern Ireland is now the Anglo-Irish Agreement. Unionist resistance to it, which has included suspending local authority meetings and refusing to set rates, has produced major political and legal conflicts which threaten the destruction of local government in the Province. In this conflict, the budgetary process is irrelevant.

In the main, then, central-local government relationships in Scotland, Wales and Northern Ireland in the context of control over public expenditure and budget-making, are based on negotiation among relatively small numbers of actors who know one another well and can discuss impending conflicts informally. Dramatic conflicts have occurred nonetheless, especially in Scotland. In England, however, the introduction of expenditure limits ('rate-capping') by the Rates Act 1984, has prduced spectacular conflicts, mainly between the Secretary of State for the Environment and a small number of Labour-controlled local authorities - most notably Liverpool City Council and Lambeth London Borough Council. In Liverpool a negotiated settlement of a dispute over the 1984/5 Budget was represented by Liverpool councillors as a triumph over Patrick Jenkin (the then Secretary of State), who therefore refused the following year to make similar concessions. (Parkinson 1985) Rate-capping produced illegal action by the majority Labour Group which may well result in many of its members being surcharged and disqualified from holding office, along with most of the Lambeth Labour Group. Labour councillors in Sheffield may suffer a similar fate.

The Liverpool clash has been more bitter and has been pursued further than any similar conflict elsewhere. In Scotland and Wales, many local authorities are controlled by parties which are in Opposition at Westminster, yet in neither country have any of our authorities been in conflict with the central government to the extent that Liverpool has. The reasons relate mainly to the Government's refusal to recognise the unique severity of Liverpool's social and economic problems but also to the formal, distant relationships that exist in England between the Department of the Environment and local authorities.

Other English authorities have not carried conflict so far but a clash with Sheffield City Council in 1985 was averted only when the Labour Group split at the last minute, producing a majority for setting a legal rate. There are signs too that English local authorities are learning to negotiate with the Department of the Environment when they feel that their Grant Related Expenditure Assessments (GREAs) have been set too low or that expenditure limits are unreasonable. In 1985 the Labour-controlled authorities selected for 'rate-capping' all refused to apply for 'derogation' (effectively for an increase in their expenditure limits) but in 1986 some, like Newcastle-upon-Tyne City Council, did so with some success.

One last point about the central government's role which emerges frequently is the uncertainty created by frequent changes in central policy. This has both destroyed most attempts at financial planning more than one year ahead and made it very difficult for local authorities to determine at the beginning of their budgetary processes what resources are likely to become available to them when their grants are announced towards its end. This uncertainty has especially impeded those authorities which have attempted to establish what resources are likely to be available before departments prepare Estimates, in the hope and expectation that departments will prepare Estimates with an eye to the resources likely to be available to them. An increasing number of authorities are attempting thus to reverse the first two stages (Estimate preparation and resource assessment) of the traditional budgetary process (Greenwood et.al. 1977) but it is hard to give departments reliable guidance when Government policy changes frequently: there have been at least nine major changes in grant distribution system since 1979, plus several changes in the Government's policy on the priority to be allocated to inner cities or low-spending authorities when grants are distributed. Lancashire County Council, for instance, prepared Estimates based on three sets of contingencies only to find that when it received its grant allocation, it was initially less than the Council's worst fears! More generally, the Audit Commission (1984) has estimated that the uncertainty created by frequent changes in grant regimes and other central policies had cost ratepayers £1.2 billion by 1984. Local authorities have felt obliged to maintain higher balances than they would otherwise have done in case a rule or policy change suddenly deprives them of an expected grant - especially since supplementary rates were abolished in 1982, so that a local authority which runs into deficit, for whatever reason, can no longer recoup its losses from ratepayers. The Government is thus itself partly responsible for the heavy burden of local authority rates in the 1980s.

The Internal Dimension

These external factors are of varying importance but they act as environmental constraints on the local authority's internal decision-making processes. Some of the external influences are very important, others are marginal but our studies suggest that the major influences on a local authority's budget are internal. They can be assessed under four headings: structures, processes, strategies and techniques.

Structures

Most local authorities have appointed Leaders of the Council and Chief Executive Officers but their roles vary widely. A major theme of these studies is the emergence of informal groups of leading councillors and senior officers who play either or both Greenwood's 'Spanish Inquisition' or 'Sweat Shop' roles. In particular, the majority of councillors are not involved in the preparation of their authority's budget, often by choice: their main interest is in protecting their ward's interests and helping citizens obtain redress where they feel aggrieved It has been well established (Corina 1973; Newton 1976; Elcock 1982) that only a fairly small minority of councillors are interested mainly in the making of general policy but such policy-oriented councillors are especially likely to become Leaders, committee chairmen or Policy and Resources Committee members. Budget-making is largely controlled by these policy-oriented members - not, usually, because they arrogate power to themselves in a clandestine, dictatorial fashion but because their colleagues are content to leave the complexities of preparing the budget to them, so long as they are consulted and can make amendments or protest before final decisions are made. Tayside's 'Magnificent Seven', Stirling's Budget Strategy Group and Birmingham's 'Sweat Box' are examples of such informal but powerful groups. Mid-Glamorgan is unusual in that much of the task usually undertaken by groups of leading members and officers is undertaken by a Budget Advisory Group consisting of second and third tier officers whose activities are largely accepted (if misunderstood) by members. The more usual 'Spanish Inquisition' or 'Sweat Shop' consists of senior members and officers and the distinction between them can become blurred. Both become distant from back-bench councillors and junior staff. Generally, the importance of these informal groups has increased under the pressure of demands for spending cuts from central government or elsewhere. The few authorities which do not possess them are those, like Belfast, which are under relatively little financial pressure.

Processes

In most local authorities, however, departmentalism and the service orientation (Stewart 1983) are still powerful influences on budgeting. In consequence, those responsible for the central control of the budget, notably the Treasurer's or Finance Department and the central groups of councillors and officers must bargain with or pressure departments in order to obtain even reduced spending growth. Such pressures often produce 'shroud-waving' and special pleading at various levels. Some authorities have sought to reduce the power of departmental interests. Tayside's Finance Department appoints Assistant Directors of Finance to prepare budgets of groups of departments, rather than relying on departmental finance officers who might 'go native' and advance departmental interests rather than securing overall budgetary control. 'Spanish Inquisitions' and 'Sweat Shops' are by definition detached from departmental interests and can therefore impose overall priorities more effectively than can Leaders, Chief Executives and Treasurers who lack the support of such groups of leading colleagues. Avon's 'standstill' budget was built up from departmental demands. The Alliance Group's attempt to control spending through special sub-committees was unsuccessful. In any case, the budget-making process easily becomes one of bilateral bargaining between departments and the central group, reminiscent of the Public Expenditure Survey process in central government as described by Heclo and Wildavsky. (1978, 1981)

The other main processual development is less common. A few authorities have adopted monitoring processes to improve performance or secure the implementation of council policy. Sheffield's Programme Committees are an example of the latter, while Stirling has developed a sophisticated performance review system which generates so much paper that its impact is limited. Leading councillors and senior officers cannot read it all. Such review processes will produce significant benefits only if the managers who write the reports required for them use their own reports to identify how they might improve their performance, rather than relying on overburdened councillors or superior officers to point out their faults to them.

Strategies

Review may be assisted by the establishment of a budget strategy against which achievements and failures can be measured. The provision of realistic Estimates by departments and committees is more likely to occur if they are given some idea beforehand about the level of resources likely to be available in the coming financial year. Our studies confirm Greenwood et. al.'s (1977) suggestion that fiscal pressure may cause local authorities to reverse the first two stages of the budgetary process, so that they try to establish the likely availability of resources before preparing Estimates. Such efforts are rendered difficult by frequent changes in Government policy on the amount and distribution of grants. Nonetheless, a number of our authorities tried to make some estimation of the resources likely to be available to them at an early stage of the budgetary cycle, as well as establishing strategies which reflect their policy preferences.

The most common such strategy was to agree to prepare a 'standstill' budget. In theory, this indicated that if a department or committee wished to undertake a new activity, it must reduce or eliminate an existing one to pay for it but in practice, such reductions are not enough to balance the cost of the new activity, so that some growth in spending still occurs – albeit perhaps at a lower rate than might have been the case without the 'standstill' policy decision. In a few cases – notably Liverpool and Sheffield – a policy objective of protecting employment and service levels was adopted which was likely to lead to a clash with the central government. Other authorities, like Ceredigion, Banff and Buchan and Tayside, accepted Government guidelines or targets as imposing a limit on their spending but would practise 'grantmanship' in order to increase the resources coming to their areas from the Government. Most of our authorities adopted, more or less consciously, one or more of these different kinds of strategy but a few prepared their budgets solely through traditional inter-departmental and inter-committee negotiations.

Techniques

Those authorities which experimented with Zero-Based Budgeting (ZBB) quickly diluted and often abandoned it – partly because of the burdens it imposes on managers, chief officers and councillors. None of them truly sought to scrutinise the entire 'base' anyway. More promising was the use of performance indicators, derived from Audit Commission reports or inter-authority comparisons and feedback techniques within departments or management units, to identify areas where greater efficiency could be secured. Again, however, care must be taken not to swamp members and officers with masses of indigestible statistics and lengthy review reports.

The Last Word

Five conclusions emerge from all this. First, budgeting is usually controlled by small numbers of leading politicians and senior officers. Secondly, they often make the main decisions and conduct most of the negotiations required in small, informal groups rather than through formal committee and council meetings, whose role is usually confined to legitimating decisions taken elsewhere. Even in 'hung' councils the influence of the general body of members is usually marginal and exercised only in the closing stages of budget-making. Thirdly, service orientations and departmental power persist; overall strategies and corporate management can be achieved only after more or less tough bargaining and resistance to 'shroud-waving'. Fourthly, techniques have been of limited but not negligible usefulness in assisting local authorities to cope with fiscal stress.

Lastly and perhaps most revealing of all, is the Thatcher Government's failure, even after seven years of imposing increasing financial rigour, to procure reductions in local authority spending. Planned schemes have been abandoned or postponed, recruitment reduced and services have deteriorated but although the growth in spending has been less than it would have been under a different Government, it has nonetheless continued, despite the Prime Minister's often expressed determination to reduce the role of the State in British society and secure reduced national and local taxation.

Bibliography

Adams, David, (1986), "Tale of the Three Treasurers", LOCAL GOVERNMENT
CHRONICLE, 31 January 1986.

Alexander, A., (1982), LOCAL GOVERNMENT IN BRITAIN SINCE
REORGANISATION, G.Allen and Unwin.

Anthony, R.N., (1977), "Zero-Base Budgeting is a Fraud" WALL STREET
JOURNAL, 27 April.

Audit Commission, (1984), THE IMPACT ON LOCAL AUTHORITIES' ECONOMY,
EFFICIENCY AND EFFECTIVENESS OF THE BLOCK GRANT DISTRIBUTION SYSTEM.

Bailey, J. and O'Conner, R.J., (1975), "Operationalising Incrementalism:
Measuring the Muddle", PUBLIC ADMINISTRATION REVIEW, Volume 35.

Bardach, E., (1974), "Subinformal Warning Systems in the Species HOMO
POLITICUS", POLICY SCIENCES, Volume 5.

Baxter, R., (1969), THE STRUCTURE AND ORGANISATION OF THE LIVERPOOL
LABOUR PARTY 1918-1963, D.Phil. Thesis, University of Oxford.

Baxter, R., (1972), "The Working Class and Labour Politics", POLITICAL
STUDIES, Volume 20.

Bealey, F. and Sewel, J., (1981), THE POLITICS OF INDEPENDENCE,
Aberdeen.

Birrell, D. and Murie, A., (1980), POLICY AND GOVERNMENT IN NORTHERN
IRELAND, Gill and Macmillan.

Blowers, A., (1977), "Checks and Balances: The Politics of Minority
Government", PUBLIC ADMINISTRATION, Volume 55.

Brittan, S., (1983), THE ROLE AND LIMITS OF GOVERNMENT: ESSAYS IN
POLITICAL ECONOMY, Temple Smith.

Chartered Institute of Public Finance and Accountancy, (1984), GUIDE TO
LOCAL AUTHORITY FINANCE

Chartered Institute of Public Finance and Accountancy, (1986),
Financial Information Service, Volume 4, BUDGETARY PROCESSES.

Cheek, L.M., (1979), ZERO BASED BUDGETING COMES OF AGE, Amacom,
Appendix B.

Connolly, M., (1986), "Controlling Local Government Expenditure: The
Case of Northern Ireland", PUBLIC ADMINISTRATION, Volume 64.

Connolly, M. and Knox, C., (1985), "A Review of the 1986 Local
Government Elections in Northern Ireland", LOCAL GOVERNMENT STUDIES.

Corina, L., (1974), "Elected Representatives in a Party System:
A Typology", POLICY AND POLITICS, Volume 3.

Dahl, R. and Lindblom, C., (1953), POLITICS, ECONOMICS AND WELFARE,
Harper.

Dempster, M.A.H. and Wildavsky, A.V., (1979), "On Change: Or, There is
No Magic Size for an Increment", POLITICAL STUDIES, Volume 27.

Diesing, Paul, (1962), REASON IN SOCIETY, Greenwood Press.

Downs, A., (1967), INSIDE BUREAUCRACY, Little, Brown and Co.

Dunsire, A., Hood, C. and Huby, M., (1985), "Whitehall in Retrenchment: Who Got Less, When, How 1976–83", Paper presented to the Public Administration Conference, University of York.

Dyer, Michael, (1973), THE POLITICS OF KINCARDINESHIRE, Ph.D. thesis, University of Aberdeen.

Dyer, Michael, (1979), "'Leadership' in a Rural Scottish County" in Jones, G.W. and Norton, A., (eds), POLITICAL LEADERSHIP IN LOCAL AUTHORITIES, Institute of Local Government Studies, University of Birmingham.

Elcock, Howard, (1982), Second Edition (1986), LOCAL GOVERNMENT: POLITICIANS, PROFESSIONALS AND THE PUBLIC IN LOCAL AUTHORITIES, Methuen and Co.

Elcock, Howard, (1986), "Learning from Local Authority Budgeting", PUBLIC POLICY AND ADMINISTRATION, Volume 1, No.2.

Game, C., (1984), "Models of Local Authority Budgetary Processes under the Block Grant System", paper prepared for the Public Administration Committee Research Sub-Committee Workshop on Local Authority Budgetary Processes, York.

Gibson, J. and Travers, T., (1985), "Block Grant: The Story of a Failure", PUBLIC MONEY, September.

Glennester, H., (1981), "Social Service Spending in a Hostile Environment", in Hood, C. and Wright, M., (eds), BIG GOVERNMENT IN HARD TIMES, Martin Robertson.

Goodin, R. and Waldner, (1979), "Thinking Big, Thinking Small and Not Thinking At All", PUBLIC POLICY, Volume 27.

Greenwood, R., (1980), "The Local Authority Budgetary Process", in Booth, T., (ed), PLANNING FOR WELFARE, Martin Robertson.

Greenwood et al., (1977), Greenwood, R., Hinings, C.R., Ranson, S. and Walsh, K., "The Politics of the Budgetary Process in English Local Government", POLITICAL STUDIES, Volume 61.

Greenwood, R., Hinings, C.R., Ranson, S. and Walsh, K., (1980), "Incremental Budgeting and the Assumpton of Growth", in Wright (1980) op. cit.

Greenwood, R., (1981), "Fiscal Pressure and Local Government in England and Wales", in Hood, C. and Wright, M., op. cit.

Greenwood, R., (1983), "Changing Patterns of Budgeting in English Local Government", PUBLIC ADMINISTRATION, Volume 61.

Greenwood, R., (1984), "Incremental Budgeting: Antecedents of Change", JOURNAL OF PUBLIC POLICY, Volume 4.

Gyford, J., (1984), LOCAL POLITICS IN BRITAIN, Second Edition, Croom Helm.

Harrop, K., (1986), "Leisure Services" in Elcock, Howard, LOCAL GOVERNMENT, Second Edition, op. cit., Methuen and Co., pp. 151–153.

Haynes, R.J., (1980), ORGANISATION THEORY AND LOCAL GOVERNMENT, G.Allen and Unwin.

Hepworth, Noel, (1984), THE FINANCE OF LOCAL GOVERNMENT, Seventh Edition, G.Allen and Unwin.

Heclo, H. and Wildavsky, A.V., (1978) and Second Edition (1981), THE PRIVATE GOVERNMENT OF PUBLIC MONEY, Macmillan.

Hood, C. and Wright, M., (eds), (1981), BIG GOVERNMENT IN HARD TIMES, Martin Robertson.

Jackson, P.M. and Meadowes, W.J., (1985), "Central-Local Fiscal Relationships", PUBLIC ADMINISTRATION BULLETIN, December.

Jorgensen, T., (1984), BUDGET-MAKING AND EXPENDITURE CONTROL, Danish School of Public Administration.

Le Loup, L., (1978), "The Myth of Incrementalism", POLITY, Volume 10.

Levine, C.H., Rubin, I.S. and Wolohijian, (1981), THE POLITICS OF RETRENCHMENT, Sage.

MacKenzie, W.J.M., (1967), POLITICS AND SOCIAL SCIENCE, Penguin Books.

Madgwick, P., (1973), THE POLITICS OF RURAL WALES: A STUDY OF CARDIGANSHIRE, Hutchinson.

Marshall, A.H., (1974), FINANCIAL MANAGEMENT IN LOCAL GOVERNMENT, G.Allen and Unwin.

Midwinter, A., (1984), "Reforming the Budgetary Process in Local Government", PUBLIC ADMINISTRATION, Volume 62.

Olsen, J.P., (1982), "Public Policy-Making and Theories of Organisational Choice", SCANDINAVIAN POLITICAL STUDIES, Volume 4.

Parkinson, M., (1985), LIVERPOOL ON THE BRINK, Policy Journals.

Richardson, J.J. and Jordan, A.G., (1979), GOVERNING UNDER PRESSURE, Martin Robertson.

Schick, A., (1966), "The Road to PBB: The Stages of Budget Reform", PUBLIC ADMINISTRATION REVIEW, December 1966.

Schick, A., (1983), "Incremental Budgeting in a Decremental Age", POLICY SCIENCES, Volume 16.

Scholey, J.S., (1978), ZERO-BASE BUDGETING AND PROGRAMME EVALUATION, Lexington Books.

Singleton, D.W., Smith, B. and Cleaveland, J.R., (1976), "Zero-Base Budgeting in Wilmington, Delaware", GOVERNMENTAL FINANCE, Volume 5.

Smiles, S., (1986), SELF-HELP, Penguin Business Library.

Stanyer, J., (1976), UNDERSTANDING LOCAL GOVERNMENT, Fontana/Collins.

Stewart, J.D., (1971), MANAGEMENT IN LOCAL GOVERNMENT: A VIEWPOINT, Charles Knight.

Stewart, J.D.S., (1983), LOCAL GOVERNMENT: THE CONDITIONS OF LOCAL CHOICE, G.Allen and Unwin.

Sutcliffe, A. and Smith, R., (1974), BIRMINGHAM 1939-1970, Oxford University Press.

Tarschys, D., (1985), "Good Cuts, Bad Cuts", SCANDINAVIAN POLITICAL STUDIES, Volume 7.

Widdicombe Committee, (1986), REPORT OF THE COMMITTEE OF ENQUIRY INTO THE CONDUCT OF LOCAL AUTHORITY BUSINESS, Cmnd. 9798, HMSO.

Wildavsky, A.V., (1966), "The Political Economy of Efficiency, Cost Benefit Analysis, Systems Analysis and Programme Budgeting", PUBLIC ADMINISTRATION REVIEW, December.

Wildavsky, A.V., (1975), BUDGETING: A COMPARATIVE THEORY OF BUDGETARY PROCESS, Little, Brown and Co.

Wildavsky, A.V., (1978), "A Budget for All Seasons", PUBLIC ADMINISTRATION REVIEW, November-December.

Wildavsky, A., (1984), THE POLITICS OF THE BUDGETARY PROCESS, Fourth Edition, Little, Brown and Co.

Wiseman, H.V., (1963), "The Working of Local Government in Leeds", PUBLIC ADMINISTRATION, Volume 41.

Wolman, H., (1984), "Understanding Local Government Responses to Fiscal Pressure: A Cross-National Analysis", JOURNAL OF PUBLIC POLICY, Volume 3.

Wright, M., (ed), (1980), PUBLIC SPENDING DECISIONS: GROWTH AND RESTRAINT IN THE 1970s, G.Allen and Unwin.